James Whitham

What a good do!

James
Whitham
What a good do!

James Whitham with Mac McDiarmid Foreword by Carl Fogarty

Haynes Publishing

First published in hardback in August 2008
Reprinted in October 2008
This paperback edition published in May 2009

A catalogue record for this book is available from the British Library

ISBN 978 1 84425 711 9

Library of Congress catalog card no 2009924794

Published by Haynes Publishing,
Sparkford, Yeovil, Somerset BA22 7JJ, UK
Tel: 01963 442030 Fax: 01963 440001
Int. tel: +44 1963 442030 Int. fax: +44 1963 440001
E-mail: sales@haynes.co.uk
Website: www.haynes.co.uk

Haynes North America Inc., 861 Lawrence Drive, Newbury Park, California 91320, USA

Designed and typeset by James Robertson

Jacket portrait by Paul O'Connor, www.paulandpaul.co.uk

Printed and bound in the UK

CONTENTS

FOREWORD

by Carl Fogarty
Four-times World Superbike Champion

The first time I bumped into James Whitham – almost literally – was at the Manx Grand Prix of 1985. We were both trying to figure out which way the TT Mountain course went and how we survived that lap I will never know. I would catch and pass him, glance over as if to say 'Take that, Tyke,' and then he would do exactly the same to me a bit further on. We introduced ourselves afterwards and I remember thinking: 'I'm going to have to watch out for this lad – he's pretty fast and fearless.'

At the end of the race – which I won, of course! – I asked where that Whitham guy had finished, only to learn that he had crashed going over the Mountain section during the final qualifying session and broken his collarbone. And that pretty much sums James Whitham up!

James was a racer who never gave anything less than 110 per cent, who always rode on the edge. That style made him a big crowd favourite but also probably prevented him from winning more than he did. But it wasn't just his style that made him so popular. James always had a friendly word, a smile and a joke for everyone, especially the fans. He lived for racing and enjoyed the whole scene much more than I did, because I only ever enjoyed winning. For that reason, unlike James, I didn't make many friends in the paddock but he is the one true friend that I have made through racing and our families remain very close.

I have learnt a lot from him as nothing ever seems to get him down, not even the cancer that he battled successfully. His attitude was: this has happened for a reason, so let's just get on with it.

During his chemotherapy treatment we went out for a Chinese meal one night and he threw up before we even entered the restaurant, although he was determined to carry on and not to let it spoil his chow mein. He is also one of the most intelligent people that I know – you certainly don't want to get into an argument with him, because you will never win! That intelligence also comes across in his non-stop humour, although I sometimes think that people don't take him as seriously as they should.

But it's only fitting that any book by James should focus on the fun of racing – and that's exactly what this one does. Enjoy!

Carl Fogarty
Blackburn, Lancashire
2008

INTRODUCTION

This isn't a definitive story of my life, at least in so far as other people will have different recollections and interpretations of many of the episodes I describe. Mechanics and team managers will have their own perspective on me as a racer and team-mate; Jim Moodie, and many others I'm sure, will have their own views of some of our tussles on the track. My mum will always regard me as barely fit to look after myself, let alone a family; and dad, bless him, if he were alive, would still be wondering if I was ever going to grow up and get a proper job. To my sisters I'm probably still the gobby kid that got under their feet as they were growing up.

Many of the events described are decades old, so if my memory of them is faulty I apologise now for any offence caused or credit overlooked. While in repentant mode, maybe I should also say sorry to the owners of all the bikes I've crashed, blown up or otherwise trashed, all the mechanics who had to follow me round picking up the debris, and any riders I may have knocked off their bikes at any time. It wasn't on purpose.

But, as well as I can make it, this is a candid and honest account of the first 42 years of my life. You, the reader, may already have your own impressions of me, as racer, commentator, or prat-around-the-tracks. Whatever that impression is, I hope it includes the notion that I had a lot of fun doing it, and still do. I hope you have half as much fun reading about it.

This is also my chance to say thanks to the many people who helped me through my life and racing career. At the top of that list is my wife, Andrea, a constant ally for over 20 years. To my family – every one of them – I'm equally grateful for all their support, and for knocking me down a peg or two whenever I might have needed it. To my own family I'd add Andrea's, especially her late mother, Barbara.

In the world of racing, I have cause to thank people almost beyond number, but several of them deserve special mention. Dave Leach first inspired me to begin racing and showed that even a callow Yorkshire kid could aspire to hacking around race tracks. Pete Moore was a priceless source of information, encouragement and amusement in my early racing days. Without his input I very much doubt I'd have had any professional racing career at all.

Mick Grant spotted whatever potential I had, drove himself half-batty trying to harness it, and remains a valued friend to this day. Later in my career Rob McElnea played a similar role and was the person I instinctively turned to for advice. The entire Belgarda Yamaha team, for whom I raced for the last three years of my career, made racing an absolute pleasure and showed that even at the top level you can be competitive and still have fun. I'd also like to thank all the mates I've made within racing, especially the ones I may have had a bit of a go at in the following pages – and especially Carl Fogarty, for his friendship over the past 20-odd years and, not least, his generous foreword to this book.

From my extensive medical history I have to thank Tony Milling, orthopaedic surgeon, without whom I would definitely not be walking straight; Dr Smith, the pelvis man, without whom I might not be walking at all; and Dr Carter, who treated me for Hodgkin's disease, without whom I'd be dead.

For the book itself, I have to thank the staff at Haynes Publishing, particularly editorial director Mark Hughes whose idea it was that I should write it, copy editor Ian Heath, senior editor Flora Myer for her usual calm efficiency and support, and James Robertson for his design and page-build work. And finally, I'm especially grateful to ⁊ McDiarmid for helping me write the book and for drinking ⁊h.

James Whitham
Huddersfield, Yorkshire
Summer 2008

CHAPTER 1

GEOFF HURST GOT A HAT-TRICK, MUM GOT ME

It wasn't a bad year all round, 1966. England won the football World Cup, egged on by my mum, sporting the rapidly growing bump that would become me. Pictures from *Surveyor 1* finally proved that the Moon wasn't really made from green cheese. An American B52 bomber with four live nuclear bombs crashed into the sea near Spain (but luckily my flying career was some way ahead, so I didn't get the blame). And Walt Disney died, survived by Mickey and Minnie.

Meanwhile, in a windswept moor-top house near Halifax in Yorkshire's West Riding, in the small hours of Tuesday, 6 September, the 8½lb bundle that would become me bawled its way into the world. James Michael Whitham was its name.

As was the custom in those pre-birthing class days, dad – David – would have been out, probably at least as preoccupied by Mike Hailwood's win in the strike-delayed Senior TT four days before as my first foray into the West Riding. Mum – Patricia – had already produced two daughters, Sue and Mary, so dad had seen it all before, although I like to think the arrival of a son had a special meaning for him; not that he was the sort to let on. Another daughter, Jane, came later.

Yorkshire folk have a reputation for being down-to-earth, blunt-spoken and careful with money, and dad was all of these thi[ ] He was into blokes' stuff, quite old-fashioned, typical of [ ] men of the time and particularly in the North of Engla[ ] out and earned the money and his missus staye[ ] made the home. He was an immensely hardwor[ ] bloke, always grafting at something. He had [ ] morning and ran a garage in the afternoon[ ]

The milk round lasted for 20 years, and at various points he also ran a couple of buses, rented some cars, and had one or two other business interests. A lot of his time was taken up grafting, but apart from that he was into bikes and he was into flying.

Our home was a big five-bedroom stone house that he built pretty much himself before we kids began to arrive. He'd had builders working for him but managed the project between everything else he was doing. Dad had always lived on farms, and while this wasn't even a smallholding, there was a bit of land on which he'd parked the caravan he and mum lived in whilst building the house. The place was close to where dad was brought up as a kid, near the village of Wainstalls just west of Halifax. His family had lived thereabouts for a generation or two; his brother ran a farm nearby, so he always had a soft spot for the area.

Those early days are now blurred by time, but I remember it as being a big, brand-new house – but then anything would have seemed big to me at that age. It seemed a right long way from the village, although it was probably no more than a mile and a half. But my most vivid early memories are of aeroplanes.

Dad had got his pilot's licence in the late '50s, so he was an experienced flier, although not immune to incidents. Just a year before I arrived, he'd crashed a Jodel only a few weeks after buying it, when he'd tried to take off with the brakes on. After hitting a wall top, the plane flipped and broke its back. Dad was OK, and able to drag his passenger, Ron Oldham, out of the plane to safety. After being treated for shock, bruises and friction burns, Ron was none the worse for wear, but the Jodel was a write-off.

By the time I arrived dad had come by another aeroplane, an Auster, a high-winged ex-military contraption with a welded steel fuselage and wooden wings with fabric stretched over, almost like a Piper Cub. He kept it in a farmer's field at Northowram just outside Halifax. My first encounter with this device was being taken in the car by dad and plonked inside its hard and unnerving cockpit. Dad clipped me into a four-point harness with a big central turnbuckle, which seemed as big as me. He fiddled with the switches before climbing out and leaving me alone in this big dark monster. I was scared stiff, absolutely petrified. I thought I was expected to fly the damn thing, but all he was doing was wandering round the front to swing the propeller. All the time I was thinking 'Well I can't fly this. I don't know how to fly this.'

Fortunately nothing bad happened that time, although I have dim memories of once visiting dad in hospital after he'd crashed that very aeroplane into some trees while flying from that same field with a bunch of mates. He looked to be straight out of a *Carry On* film, legs all over the place, with just his face peeking out of the bandages.

He wasn't a modern man, but was typical of fathers of the day – not aloof, exactly, but not touchy-feely either, although I can distinctly remember being joggled on his knee. He was quite traditional, very disciplined in that you knew by the age of five or six what you should be doing and what you shouldn't, and what you should tell him and what you'd best keep to yourself, because you'd learned what he'd approve of and what he wouldn't. So if you got into trouble at school the very last thing you did was tell your parents, especially dad, because you'd probably get another bashing on top of the caning you got from the teacher. But he wasn't a Victorian kind of disciplinarian, with rules for everything, and I can see now that in some ways he wasn't at all stereotypical. But he had boundaries, and you soon learned what they were. So long as you didn't upset him, he was all right. And I think a lot of him rubbed off onto me.

Dad's father, Arthur, was even more of a throwback. He'd been born when dinosaurs roamed Yorkshire, way back in 1892, and served in the artillery for the whole of Word War One. He died when I was aged about five, and my few memories of him are of an old-fashioned farmhouse where he lived with Granny Whitham, which always reeked of smoky coal fires. He had a huge, waxed handlebar moustache, like General Haig, and always wore a waistcoat from which he'd magically produce a watch on a chain or a tin of snuff.

Mum was an only child, so naturally we all saw a lot of her parents, Jack and Phyllis. Jack used to ply me with tales from when he'd been a radio operator in World War Two, which fascinated me. At 15 he'd left school to work in a Halifax spinning mill, at 16 he left to go to war, and after the war he returned to the same mill, from which decades later he retired with the customary gold watch. He never swore, always wore a suit and tie.

He and Phyllis were steady, reliable, working people who never said as much but must have sometimes regarded my dad as some sort of lunatic. As kids we went everywhere with Jack and Phyllis. If, say, my sister Sue was off horse-riding with mum, they'd be lumbered with the rest of us, but seemed to relish it. They took us everywhere…camping, seaside illuminations, zoos, all manner of magical days out. Jack died of lung cancer in summer 1987. Phyllis lived on until her late eighties, latterly in a granny-flat at mum's, and died in 2000.

We moved from Wainstalls at Easter '72, to Huddersfield, where most of my childhood was spent. I wasn't even six at the time, so that's where I grew up and ran about and got up to mischief. That's where I'd say I was brought up.

The place was an airfield on Crosland Moor, originally built in 1947 by David Brown of Aston Martin car fame – the 'DB' in DB6. The somewhat less raunchy David Brown Tractors factory was just down the road. There was a paved landing strip, acres and acres of grass, plus a working stone quarry in one corner. For a kid like me, it was brilliant. I can't imagine a more interesting, better place to be brought up, as a lad or as a lass. We soon had some sort of stables rigged up. Anybody who, like us, couldn't afford proper ones would buy old railway cattle trucks with the running gear taken off. You'd bolt a stable door on, and that was it – sorted.

That's where I became aware of the practical side of dad's nature, peering over his shoulder as he dived into some project or other, and he usually had at least one on the go. He seemed to believe he could tackle anything, which led to a few disasters but at the time seemed normal enough to me. In fact I honestly believed, and continued to believe until my teens, that he could do absolutely anything and get anything done. My mates at school mainly thought he was slightly scary, and I suppose he was definitely a bit odd.

He wasn't a big fellow, being about my size, 5ft 8in or 5ft 9in. But he could do magic – get welding done, get metal turned on a lathe. If you stripped a thread he'd Helicoil it, which was wizardry, obviously. No practical task was beyond him, nothing was a massive problem.To a wide-eyed kid in short pants, he could make anything, fix any machine.

Above all, he wouldn't trust anybody who suggested they could make money without working. He thought the only way you made money was by grafting. If you grafted harder you earned more, and it was as simple as that. That was his whole life theory. Like lots of other working people at the time, he didn't believe in stocks, shares, buying anything before you could pay for it, or any kind of hire purchase. And, although as a youngster you're obviously not conscious of it at the time, he instilled a lot of that in me.

Credit may have been beyond him, but it seemed as though nothing else was, for he took on some monstrous projects with almost nothing. Early in our time at the airfield he'd built a cavernous blister hangar, although in itself that was no extravagant thing. Blisters were old wartime constructions, very modular, designed to be put up quickly by a gang of squaddies with nothing more than a block and tackle and an A-frame, so to get a bigger one you just made them longer. Normally they wouldn't have foundations, but dad put down a concrete base, roped in a bunch of mates and threw one up in no time at all. Then we had some big snow in early '81 and the whole thing came crashing down under the weight.

He didn't even seem bothered, just said, 'Well, I'll build another, but stronger.' Even the concept was on the cheap, because he designed it on an A4 envelope that had dropped through the letterbox holding some circular or other. He found a source of tons of enormous castellated beams and trusses going cheap from a railway shed British Rail were demolishing, bought acres of cladding sheets from a bunch of prefabs being pulled down at Illingworth, near Halifax, which we also had to go and fetch. Then he hired a crane, press-ganged the usual buddies, and set to. To almost anyone else it would have been a huge undertaking, but to dad it simply needed building – and no one else was going to do it, so he did. True, it's not pretty, but it's still standing.

He didn't think anything of hard work, in fact he thrived on it. Every summer holiday from when I was seven or eight onwards, all me and my sisters seemed to do was just work. There was haymaking to be done, other little jobs about the place – like building a house or rebuilding another hangar. There were no proper holidays, and no hanging around in town, just mowers and wooflers and balers, hammers and nails and sheets of plywood and other practical stuff.

I'm not trying to make it sound like a Hovis advert, but there genuinely was always something to do. And you got to find out who your mates were, 'cos Dad wouldn't think twice about putting them to work too. So some pals you wouldn't see all summer, whilst others used to enjoy getting stuck in. It maybe doesn't sound like fun, but it was a good upbringing.

The other side of the coin was that I had stuff most of my friends didn't. Dad was into motorbikes, so I'd usually have an old nail to tinker with and whiz around the airfield. And he had a plane, and how many kids get to go flying? This caused a lot of people at school to think we were spoilt, and with hindsight we were, but probably not in the sense they imagined. My sisters had horses, I had motorbikes and tractors and cars to play with. But we earned those toys and came to value time and prize honest effort. That was the culture at home, all we really knew. So, emphatically yes, it was a good upbringing. Some of my mates at school were in the same boat. One lad, David Boothroyd, used to turn up at school stinking of bottlewash because he'd had two hours milking cows and washing bottles before he even got there. And you just thought, 'Good on you.' It certainly teaches you a good work ethic – which you might think a strange thing for me to say, but, despite appearances, I didn't actually set out with the ambition never to hold down a proper job.

Dad was the same. As a youth he did an apprenticeship in sheet metalwork, then, once his time was served, he never did a day's work for anybody else. By trade he was a welder and boilermaker at a place in Halifax. After army National Service, which didn't last long because his father fell ill and he was discharged early to help run the farm, he got into the motor trade. From then until the day he died he was always somewhere between self-employed and unemployed – and unemployable. A bit like me.

He was also always a one-man band, except when he was a kid helping his dad with the milk round. He'd describe the day Neville Chamberlain announced that World War Two had been declared – 3 September 1939, his eighth birthday. The milk business was just him and his dad with a horse and cart and a couple of milk churns on the back. Customers would come out with a pan or whatever they happened to have and they just ladled it out. I think grandad thought milk bottles were a bit high-tech. Along with his elder brother, Ralph, Dad's contribution to Hitler's downfall was to barricade the house with home-made sandbags which were so heavy that, for a time, it was a struggle for anyone to get in or out.

So, with farm work, horses and engines, the lot of us were always outside. We were an outside family, as many were at the time. We'd be out to all hours, always up to something, in a way that's much rarer now. These days it's obviously different, partly because parents feel they daren't leave their kids unprotected, partly because kids are happy to be glued to PlayStations and X-Boxes and all the rest of it. I'm probably remembering life through rose-tinted glasses, but even the seasons seemed more real back then. There were sunny summers full of haymaking, cold winters with a bit of snow, and crap in between. You seemed to know what to expect.

Mind you, one thing we knew not to expect was a summer holiday. We just weren't a holiday family. The only one I can recall was a trip to Butlins in Skegness in 1976, and I mainly remember that because there was a plague of ladybirds at the time. It was a glorious summer, red-hot for weeks on end, and we came home to a water shortage. Everyone except us was using standpipes, but the water board couldn't turn off our water because the airfield was too far from anywhere else. I felt quite smug still being able to turn a tap when everyone else was running around with jugs and buckets.

I'd have been ten at the time and loved Butlins, which seemed like fantasy land – a bit like the airfield, really, but with Captain Blood in place of my dad. The whole place was centred around kids and there was loads of stuff to do, so every day you'd be chasing round with a plastic sword, going swimming, or model-making. I'm not sure what my parents made of it. As a kid, you don't look at mum and dad and think, 'Are they having a good time?'

Even getting there seemed an adventure. Skeggie's only on the Lincolnshire coast, but the journey there seemed an epic trip. We all piled into an Austin 1800, with me lying across the parcel shelf at the back, mainly because I thought it was different. I spent most of the journey crawling about in the car, throwing stuff, poking my dad in the ear when he was trying to drive, and asking daft questions. Looking back, my dad probably didn't enjoy it. He wasn't a sitting-on-the-beach-making-sandcastles kind of bloke. He'd probably have preferred to be building Skeggie a new pier.

So there was dad earning the money and entertaining me with his omnipotence, and mum and three sisters. We always got on well. You might think three sisters could be a pain, but we wanted different things, had different interests, so there was rarely much bitching between us.

And I definitely wasn't interested in horses, as they were, because they took too much looking after and didn't have engines. And my sisters weren't interested in bikes 'cos you couldn't groom and coo to them. Consequently we didn't seem to fall out very often. At least, that's how I remember it, although if you ask them they'd probably tell you I was a right pain. But there always seemed to be all kinds of mopeds and motorbikes lying about. Being in the motor trade and the kind of bloke he was, if dad was offered anything – even if it was seized up or had a wheel missing or something – he'd just bring it home. 'Here,' he'd say, 'see if you can make it go.' Sometimes we could and sometimes we couldn't, but we'd always have a go, and there was usually something I could thrash around the airfield. There were guns, too, a lot of guns. And aeroplanes, of course, although we were supposed to keep our distance from those. Naturally my mates loved it all, and would even tolerate being put to work by dad just to be in on the act.

One inevitable consequence of all this was that mum became used to kids getting hurt. It never seemed to bother her, but she was forever taking someone to get stitches in their arms, pouring Optrex in their eyes where they'd had something blow up in their face, putting Germolene on grazes or cutting singed bits out of fringes and telling us not to fret because our eyebrows would soon grow back. As well as cooking and all the domestic stuff, that seemed to be what she did. She became so used to it, even blasé, that she sometimes used to do her shopping on the way to casualty to save time. Meanwhile, as she's passing the time of day with the butcher, someone like my mate Steven Dean, who tore a big chunk out of his backside sliding down a roof on the wrong line, is in the car convinced he's going to bleed to death or at least lose a buttock.

Maybe it was living with as cussed and idiosyncratic an article as my dad that gave her a tolerant slant on life. She seemed to view her world with a mixture of wry amusement and serene competence. She was just as cool whenever the police called round to say they'd caught me riding motorbikes out on the road again. 'Righto, officer,' she'd say, before getting back to peeling spuds, or whatever other more important business they'd interrupted. Nothing ever seemed to faze her. If dad spent half his life whirling around like a tornado, mum was our ocean of calm. In her way she was just as self-reliant, but there was rarely any drama with mum.

She had been a teacher, but after we kids came along never really went back to work. I suppose looking after us lot was a full-time job. Naturally, she was academically adept, and would help and encourage us with schoolwork and give us extra stuff to do. Sometimes she'd have so many of us gluing and making things, home would look like the *Blue Peter* studio. She'd get enormous satisfaction if you went to school and read better than another pupil because she'd spent a couple of hours with you the night before. From today's perspective it probably wasn't very politically correct, but she was exactly the type of missus that my dad needed to have, because she did everything he didn't do and he did everything she didn't. He worked, earned the money; she ran the home perfectly, cooked, looked after us. Mum was down to earth but had all sorts of interests, which she passed on to us, especially music. She played the piano and got us all into every kind of music thing – clarinet lessons, piano lessons, all sorts of betterment. Susan played clarinet, Mary the flute, whilst I did a bit of cornet, violin and saxophone. Jane was the best of us, eventually playing the oboe with the National Children's Orchestra and even at the Royal Variety Performance. Overall Whitham-land may have seemed a slightly whacky arrangement to everyone else, but to us it was a reassuringly comfortable place to grow up.

It's only now that I have a daughter that I fully understand mum's biggest gift to us, which was her time. Since Ruby arrived I've realised that it's bloody hard work to do the whole kiddie thing properly. You don't get a lot of sleep, and suddenly the focus of your entire life isn't you any more, but this demanding miniature person. After not having kids and doing pretty much what we pleased for 15 years, that was a bloody great shock to my wife Andrea and me. A good shock, yes, but still we found it hard work, much to mum's amusement. 'What the bloody hell, what's wrong with you?' she'd say. 'One kid? I had one five-year-old, one three-year-old, one two-year-old and one babe in arms. And your dad…it wasn't his job, it was my job. And I did the shopping, and I looked after the house and I didn't crack up. And neither did anyone else. That's just what you did.'

But, back at the airfield, I still had a few decades left of doing my own thing.

CHAPTER 2

LIFE WITH A BANG

You'll have heard the expression 'There but for the grace of God go I'? That could have been coined for us, me and my mates and even my sisters and their mates, because dad had us doing some truly daft stuff, usually associated with one mad project or another. At the time, of course, most of us thought it was totally normal. Today we'd probably be taken into care or at least supervised by a Health and Safety inspector from the moment we got out of bed.

So the lot of us grew up with a healthy disregard for any kind of safety, if that's not a contradiction in terms. Most of the time my sisters were into different things, especially after they discovered horses, which to me were just things that went poo while you followed them around with a brush and shovel. I was more into machinery, things that did things other than bite and kick and be a full-time job to look after. If you left a motorbike alone for a week, it was still a motorbike when you got back to it – unless someone nicked it, but that didn't happen for years. Leave a horse alone for a week, and all you've got is a dead horse.

So from the age of ten or so I'd often be left to make my own entertainment. Even for someone less skilled than me at getting into scrapes, that wasn't necessarily a wise thing on several acres of semi-wilderness surrounded by tractors, motorcycles, aeroplanes and even our own quarry. For a daft ten-year-old, the airfield was one big adventure playground. The fact that I'm still here to write about it must say something about my luck, that it didn't go more pear-shaped more often.

It probably didn't help that dad thought that teaching me more mature skills – like learning to drive – would give me a more mature approach to life. I was dangerous enough standing still, so giving me the means to use an engine and wheels was like giving a psychopath a Gatling gun.

My first driving lesson was in our Mini pickup, one of the early ones with bits of string instead of door handles. I can't have been very big at the time, because dad shoved a huge cushion under my arse, moved the seat right forward and asked if I could reach the pedals. It was a stretch, but I could, just about. So, sat on my cushion, I learned to drive by trundling up and down the runway. When I became a skilled driver – or so it seemed to me – I was entrusted with collecting milk on my own from the local farm. This entailed a half-mile drive down a bumpy, stony farm track to their bottling shed, all on private land. Naturally, I thought this was brilliant, particularly if I could take some mates along, since they thought it was brilliant too. So on any given day, the best possible thing that could happen was for the family to run out of milk, as that meant I'd be told to take the pickup for a spin. For a while my entire conversational repertoire was little more than, 'Dad, do we need any milk?' In fact I still like milk, which I suspect is probably a bit Pavlovian.

Inevitably, things evolved to the point where the principal purpose of the exercise was anything but milk. My strategy was to wait until dad was out flying, because while he was whizzing around up there he wouldn't have much idea what I was getting up to on the ground. OK, maybe if he'd done a low strafe across the airfield he'd have seen me hurtling about, doing handbrake turns on the runway and sliding the car around. But generally I thought I was safe, particularly since, like all young boys, I thought most grown-ups, especially the neighbours, were stupid if not actually blind.

Equally inevitably, it ended in tears. It was a Sunday, and I'd been requisitioned to get some milk – about five full-fat pints for all the Yorkshire puddings and custard we'd get through at Sunday dinner, not to mention some for the dogs. Our runabout at the time was an Austin pickup, a lot higher at the back than the old Mini so that it was hard for a little fellow like me to see behind. I jumped in the front and a couple of mates, Paul Massey and Russell Penrose, jumped in the back, and off we went. The Austin was parked in the hangar, and as we'd gone in to get it there was nothing outside, so I yelled 'Here we go' and roared out full chat in reverse – and ran smack through the wing of an aeroplane that had just landed. The first I knew about it was a big bang and the prop smashing the rear window of the pickup, a few inches from the back of my head, with bits of wing and splintered wood flying through the air. The lads in the back had had a grandstand view. One had hurled himself to the ground, the other had thrown himself flat in the bed of the pickup. Luckily no one was hurt.

We'd gone right under the wing. I sat there sort of leering up at it, thinking 'Oops, this isn't good, this isn't good at all.' Dad seemed to agree, especially since it would be down to him to fix the plane, and I got a bit of a leathering for that one. On the whole I didn't mind that, because it got it over and done with, and dad was always fair about it – although I soon learned that the sooner I hammed it up and screamed a bit, the sooner he'd stop. Unfortunately this particular battering was on a sunny day with lots of witnesses, one of whom – we never found out who – shopped dad for child-beating. He got a letter from the NSPCC telling him he was being investigated, although no one ever visited and nothing more was heard about it.

Then there were the guns. Looking back, this was really mad. Dad was into his guns. He kept them, as he was supposed to, in a secure cabinet – but never bothered to lock it. There were also strict police rules about the safe and secure storage of ammunition, but I'm fairly sure they didn't include the airing cupboard, which is where dad stored his. I'm not sure what planet dad was on when he decided all this, but he seemed to think it was all his little secret and no one could possibly know how to reunite guns and ammo. I just knew that three towels down there was an arsenal of 12-bore cartridges. And I knew what was in the shed.

So when no one was around, and especially when a few mates with a similar sense of fun dropped by, we'd blast off the shotguns. We took some care. For instance we never – well, hardly ever – fired them out of the front of the house, or even carried them out of the front door, because that might have been spotted by anyone turning up or a pilot coming in to land. So we'd climb out of the back window and sneak over the fields and just blast off rounds 'til our shoulders ached from the recoil and we were half deaf.

Other times we'd shortcut the whole process and just bang away out of my bedroom window.

It's only looking back that I realise I must have been a bit of a fetishist, because that became my other secret obsession – along with milk. I absolutely loved the smell of cordite, that wonderful acrid aroma left after a gun's fired. You could keep your Chanel No5. To me, cordite was a beautiful, warm kind of firework fragrance, but more concentrated. Yes, I know it probably sounds kinky, and even to this day I love it, despite not being at all into guns. I've no interest in killing things or poncing about like a butch country squire, although guns interest me as pieces of precision engineering, not to mention their place in history. After all, I'm a bloke and I don't think you can be a bloke without having some kind of interest in all that banging stuff. True, the history of pyrotechnics was less on my mind when I was growing up at the airfield than the smoke and the smell and the blowing things to bits. Yet nobody ever got killed, which was strange considering some of the things we got up to.

As if that weren't enough, about half a mile from the airfield was the Standard Fireworks factory. One day me, Russ and Smithy were up to no good skulking around the area where they disposed of duff fireworks, hoping to pick up for nothing something with a few bangs left in it. On this particular day we discovered a huge cardboard box – it must have been four feet square – full of strange industrial-sized fireworks. The three of us just about managed to lug the box back to the airfield, where we set off three or four of these devices at the bottom of the runway.

It wasn't quite Shock and Awe in Baghdad, but it was a Bloody Big Bang in Huddersfield. Despite being broad daylight, the entire sky lit up and the ground shook. We knew instantly we were in bother, so just waited for someone in a uniform to turn up and tell us off. Within ten minutes two police cars and a couple of blokes from Standard arrived. They were actually OK. They realised that three ten-year-olds probably hadn't broken into the factory, but that someone on the inside had planted the box for an accomplice to take away. When we showed them where we'd found these big bangers, they presented us with a box of fireworks apiece.

Mind you, if gunpowder hadn't done for us, the farm machinery was at least as likely to. Thinking of it still scares me to death. Haymaking was always a busy time at the airfield. Three thousand bales of hay is an awful lot for a family with one tractor and one woofling machine. Even when I was quite small, dad would rig up the woofler – which turns over the cut hay so it dries better in the sun – and I'd sit on the wing of the tractor, just to be involved. Our antique Ferguson 35 had no cab, no roll-cage, nothing, but I was as oblivious of the safety implications as dad seemed to be. I'd happily sit there for hours, watching and asking questions, for I wanted to be able to drive it myself one day. I was naturally inquisitive anyway, and always preferred to muck in rather than simply observe. I soon learned that there's more to cutting hay than you'd imagine. Dad showed me how to mow and how to follow lines, how to cut and what to cut and what not to cut – and above all, never to stall the tractor, because it never had a battery. Sometimes you had to cut in different directions because of the way the wind had blown the grass, or it would eventually clog up the machinery.

One year we were in the middle of this rigmarole when dad announced that he was going to get another finger-mower so that I could actually do some mowing the following year. Now, with our version of industrial safety standards, we needed another of these evil monsters like dad needed a posh frock. A finger-mower's essentially what it says, two sets of interlocking blades which thrash about like horizontal guillotines and can easily mow off your fingers. Naturally ours had no guards, and it wasn't at all likely that the new one would either – because it wouldn't be new at all, just something dad picked up cheap.

The only other certainty was that sooner or later it would clog up with grass, because they always do. That's when I'd be expected to employ dad's patent timesaving technique for unclogging it. 'You'll have to clear it,' he used to say, 'but it's easy. Don't knock off the power take-off, just leave it out of drive gear in neutral, so it's still running and the blades are still moving. Then you'll see exactly where it's clogged because the grass that's been dragged along with it will be standing up.'

'Now,' he'd announce, coming to the grand finale, 'stand behind the blade and grab hold of that grass, about six inches above where the blades are clattering about. Then pull it back and you'll be able to use the grass you've pulled off to sweep the blade and clear it.' There was obviously nothing to it. It was as simple as kissing a cobra.

It was a typical dad solution: it was quick, it worked, and usually you got to keep all your fingers. At the time I used to accept it as casually as dad did, thinking, 'Yeah, all right, no problem.' Now I think he must have been crackers. I wouldn't let my kids within 50 feet of one of those things, let alone tell them to stick their hands in it. Besides, although at the time I'd no idea what my future would hold, I doubt there would have been many openings for a bike racer without any fingers.

Despite all that, haymaking time was always a big thing for the Whitham family. Dad would bang into my bedroom at six o'clock one morning, yell 'Right, we're cutting,' and everyone would be expected to jump to it. From a family point of view it was one of the highlights of the year, everyone mucking in to the common cause.

Naturally the timing and success of the operation depended on the weather. Luckily, as well as being up there with Brunel as a mechanical engineer dad was also a skilled meteorologist. He always saw himself as a bit of a weather guru. Like a ruddy-faced old farmer, he'd look up at the sky for the omens, sniff the breeze and announce, 'Oh yes, I think its gonna stay fine, we'll do some hay, we're gonna drop top field,' then he'd bawl us all out of bed. Two hours later it would be pouring down.

Me and him would get kitted up, oil our blades and off we'd go in our tractor and cut the field. If it was a weekday, which it usually was, I'd go straight from haymaking to school. As I got older and could make a useful contribution, it used to give me a bit of a glow. Before that, I'd tended to have the feeling that I was sort of helping, but was really more of a hindrance, because dad would have to spend so much time checking what I'd done that he'd have been better off getting stuck in on his own. It felt good when I knew I'd played a useful part, almost a rite of passage of being in a genuine partnership with dad.

Not that there was ever any question of a partnership of equals. One of dad's pet expressions – and he had a lot – was, 'My house, my rules.' That fell under the general umbrella most blokes had at the time – most probably still do – that he who pays the mortgage makes the decisions. There was a sister expression, 'Not under my roof, lad,' usually followed by the advice that only when you have a place of your own can you do what you want. That was a long way away and in the meantime dad was the boss.

Often these pearls of practical philosophy would be delivered whilst he was sitting in his special chair. Even the most exhaustive forensic analysis would have shown that this chair was actually no different from three or four others, but there must have been something different about it because this one was his personal domain. I certainly knew better than to use it, but if a visiting mate ever sat in it he wouldn't say anything, he'd just stand there sipping on a cuppa until I found a polite way of getting his seat vacated. Then he'd settle down to savour his PG Tips and dispense wisdom, secure in the knowledge that the earth was still on its proper axis. If the conversation turned to something he didn't really approve of, he'd put in his two penn'orth before dismissing himself with something like, 'Not that my opinion matters' – which meant that it ought to matter, if only the country hadn't gone to the dogs and was too screwed up to recognise the immense contribution he could make to world affairs – and get back to his tea.

In fact he remained the gaffer for a long, long time. I must have been in my mid-20s before we reached the watershed, which was preceded by the usual shouting match. Our Sue had a problem with a decrepit old horsebox which she needed to use the next morning. A fuel pipe had torn off over a bump, so there I was, in the middle of winter, lying in the muck underneath the engine, diesel dripping all over me, while dad waved a torch and muttered encouragement. I'd had enough. It was the last straw.

'Look,' I told him. 'You're a fairly successful businessman, I'm a sportsman of some stature. What am I doing pissing about under a clapped-out old horsebox getting cold and filthy?'

He was incensed. Nothing like this had happened before. Then he thought over what I'd said for a moment. 'You know what, lad,' he eventually said, 'you're right.' After that I was never afraid to contradict him, tell him he was talking bollocks.

Although he always seemed to have a few bob tucked away, he was also what he liked to call 'careful' with money, which was just another word for 'tight'. He'd think nothing of clearing out dead relatives' wardrobes and somehow making everything fit. It was a special bonus when Uncle Cyril died, because they were the same size – and since Cyril had been a pretty dapper bloke, for a while dad wasn't his normal scruffy self.

More often, his 'carefulness' gave him all sorts of mad ideas which usually involved lots of effort for very little tangible reward. I think he must have watched *The Good Life* too many times. He always seemed to be on some big self-sufficiency drive or other.

Some of his schemes concerned food. As a kid I knew that shops sold brown bread, white bread and wholemeal bread, but I also thought that you could buy loaves entirely made up of crusts, because for years that's what dad would bring home. It turned out that these came from a Greek Cypriot café in Halifax. Dad was a regular there and noticed that whenever he had his lunch he was never served a crust, since the owner simply threw them out. This was anathema to any true Yorkshireman, so he had the café owner save them and every week for years he brought home about three loaves of crusts. We actually preferred them – and what we didn't eat, the horses did. He later developed a similar plan for turning the Cypriot café's offcuts of fish into fishcakes. In fact he must have tried everything over the years, but his main thing was energy.

We weren't on mains gas at the airfield, so any heating was with fuel oil. Once this had been quite a cheap way of heating your house, but after the Middle East war in 1973 the price soared threefold. Dad never liked to fritter away money on anything frivolous, like staying alive, so by then he didn't like having the heating on at all. The house was freezing. He didn't seem to feel the cold and if we complained he'd just tell us to put on more clothes or jump up and down.

From time to time he tried different wood-burning stoves until he heard of one made in Belgium, the Rolls-Royce of stoves, which would burn any sort of solid fuel. The attraction, of course, wasn't that recycling was good for the planet so much as gentle on his pocket. To begin with he'd chuck scrap wood in it, but we only had so much of that. That's when he decided that if they could burn cow manure in India, there was no reason we couldn't burn horse muck in Huddersfield – and by then we had a few horses so were already self-sufficient in shit. I think the creators of *Wallace and Gromit* must have had spies at our house, because dad was the original. He constructed an elaborate crap-compressing machine working off a hydraulic ram pinched off a JCB. You shovelled the horse muck into a tapered metal tube, and this device forced what I can only describe as a machine-forged turd out of the other end. These broke off into varying lengths which you stacked up to dry.

It burned quite slowly, although with a lot more pong than heat. The turd-forming process was also a right balls-ache to do. To make enough horse muck briquettes to keep your fire going for a day would involve an entire day's hard labour. In fact the best thing about it was that you'd be so knackered making them that when you'd finished you wouldn't actually need a fire – you'd just collapse into bed. We tried adding shreds of old newspaper and other bits and pieces to the mix, but eventually dad submitted to the obvious and gave it up as a bad job. The house was colder, but at least it smelled better.

One day another bloody machine arrived for turning waste into warmth, in this case old newspapers and cardboard boxes. Me and my sisters would spend hours tearing up mountains of paper and putting them into buckets of water to soak for a few days. The resulting soggy mush went into another compressor which was miraculously supposed to turn this into something that would burn. The trouble was that a metre-tall pile of newspaper disappeared into making a pathetic half-brick, and even if you made a full one it took about three good summers before it was dry enough to burn. When we weren't messing around making pulp we'd be touting around the neighbourhood like a bunch of tinkers, scrounging unwanted paper. That brainwave didn't last long either.

Salvation finally came in the shape of Malcolm Hill, who had a plane at the airfield and owned a furniture-making company. All their waste chipboard was just thrown away, a concept dad found even more irresistible than horse muck. This scheme worked. For years all our heating was supplied by the offcuts from other people's fitted kitchens and bedrooms.

Dad also had a thing about strange foods. He was of a generation that ate things like pig's trotters, sweetbreads and tripe. He was eight when the war started, and since the family had a smallholding they probably ate better than most working people, growing vegetables, keeping chickens and the odd pig. But his definition of 'edible' was pretty broad.

In 1988 he had a heart attack. He was very ill for a while but recovered, despite not taking a blind bit of notice of instructions to change his diet. A couple of years later I got a call from my sister, Mary, very upset. 'It's dad,' she blubbed, 'he's had another one…it's bad…we're losing him.'

So off we toddled to hospital, to the same coronary care unit as before.

'Our name's Whitham. Have you got us dad?'

'No. We've no record of a Mr Whitham.'

Well, he had to be somewhere, so we wandered round to Casualty.

'Have you got a David Whitham in here?'

'Well, he was here, but he's been admitted. He's on ward seven.'

When we eventually found him, he was sat up in bed and didn't seem too bad apart from complaining about huge stomach cramps. A few days later his test results came back. He hadn't had a heart attack at all, but some sort of botulism food poisoning.

'Ah,' he said, 'that'll be that black pudding.'

'That what?'

It turned out that a butcher mate had given him some rancid black pudding, for the dog. 'It was way out of date,' dad said ruefully, 'but it looked soooo nice…'

Another of his money-saving eccentricities was the phone. Our house didn't have a normal telephone like other families. Instead, we had a payphone behind the front door, and I don't mean one of those neat little things you find on the bar in pubs: this one was bolted to the wall above a big metal box, into the top of which you fed cash. There was a slot for 5p coins, another for 10p, and when you made a call this device would go *toot, toot* to tell you to give it money. It was exactly like being in a public phone box, except that ours wasn't full of cards offering exotic massages and didn't stink of piss.

As well as being an eccentric in his own right, dad rubbed shoulders with a few others from similar moulds. One, Ron

Oldham, who you last encountered upside-down in an aeroplane, was an actual inventor, of the type you imagine but hardly seems to exist, also right out of *Wallace and Gromit*. Starting off from a tatty caravan he'd invented a machine that vacuum-packed food in plastic, later setting up a successful company in Ripon called something like Ryburn Plastics. Unlike Wallace, he made good, earned pots of cash and would sometimes visit us in a flash car or even his helicopter.

He would often bring his son, Richard, who I'd be expected to entertain whilst Ron and dad chewed the fat and set the world to rights. He was a couple of years younger than me but a good lad so I didn't mind looking after him, even if he did go to boarding school and talk posh. One day tolerance turned to outright admiration, for Richard turned up with a brand new Puch Magnum, a genuine little motocross bike. At the time I didn't know any living soul with a proper motorbike. The nearest you'd see would be cut-down BSA Bantams or C90s – anything you could get hold of to stick knobbly tyres on. All I'd had until then was the odd knackered C50 Honda and similar pieces of junk.

I almost swooned when I saw this Magnum. Suddenly, milk runs and cordite didn't seem to matter. I could barely move for cooing, 'Oh man, that's a proper thing, a proper, proper thing.' That Magnum was the first proper thing I ever rode, and it was a revelation. I decided there and then that I was going to get myself one, whatever it took and whether dad helped out or not.

A shiny new Puch Magnum never did arrive, but shortly afterwards dad turned up with a stolen-recovered Honda CG125. It had been on fire and completely written off. It cost him a fiver, but underneath all the rust and charring and odd bits of melted plastic there was nothing wrong with it. It hadn't even done many miles, so the engine was mint. We put some tyres on it, a pair of cowhorn handlebars, got it running – and that was me, tearing about the airfield for as long as I could scrounge enough petrol.

After a while I became quite good at wheeling the thing. One Sunday afternoon dad was chatting to his flying mates while I was showing off to mine, and he said, 'When you can wheelie it the length of the runway' – which was half a mile of uphill tarmac – 'I'll give you £10 out of my own pocket.' Ten pounds? To me that was a king's ransom, an unbelievable amount of money. So I practised and practised, but never did manage it. The closest I'd get would be three-quarters of the way up, stood on the foot pegs, before I'd flip it and land on my arse. So I never got my tenner, although I'll never know whether dad would have stumped up anyway.

But dad was a bike enthusiast. He'd had bikes for as long as he could remember, but described himself as the last of the 'had to have a bike' generation. He remembered blokes he'd worked with during his apprenticeship who thought they'd made it when they had a nice outfit, a Panther or something lashed to a Busmar double-adult sidecar. Dad's first bike was a Calthorpe he bought when he was 16, but it wasn't necessarily a hobby. In those days it was just your transport and, although your mates had bikes for exactly the same reasons, they were just your wheels, whether you liked them or not. By the '60s working men were better off and cheap cars like the Moggie 1000 and Mini made motoring affordable to many more people. Biking wasn't there yet, not by a long way, but it was on its way to becoming a leisure activity rather than just a means of getting from A to B.

Dad used to go on about Geoff Duke and other racing stars. In the mid-'70s he turned up with a Manx Norton he'd just bought. Apparently it had sat for years in a little one-man engineering shop owned by a guy named Craven in Halifax. Dad had coveted it since first laying eyes on it, but the owner would never sell. I think it became a bit of a game that dad would make an offer every time he visited the shop and every time be told to get lost. Then, when the owner died, he left a covenant in his will insisting that the Norton had first to be offered to David Whitham for market value, which was touching. So, for once, dad stumped up some proper money for a motorbike.

That bike was special to him. The instant he got it home, he fired it up and ran it up and down the runway, savouring the heady smell of Castrol 'R'. Although you only had to look at it to see that it was obviously several centuries old, even I thought it was brilliant. Having spent so much time drooling over it, dad had known its history long before he bought it and had papers which proved its provenance. Apparently it was a full factory machine, with girder forks and a plunger rear end, built for the 1937 TT but taken there as a spare bike and never used. At the end of the season it was sold to Denis Parkinson, who became something of a Manx Grand Prix legend, winning five times – at least once on this very bike. It was unrestored and completely original. Dad used to compare it to someone of my generation having a factory Honda in their garage, which seemed a bit much but I sort of knew what he meant.

Once the Manx had a flat tyre, so we set to fixing it. Dad pulled off the wheel, levered off the tyre, then just stopped, looking close to tears. I thought something must be badly wrong – a cracked hub or something equally terminal. But no, it was just a poignant little memento. In the era in which the bike was raced it was the normal practice to fix inner tubes with a patch which was vulcanised in situ with a hot stamp. The posher teams had their own custom stamps and there, embossed on the tube, was the legend 'Denis Parkinson Racing, Wakefield,' and a four-figure telephone number. 'Look at that,' croaked dad, 'that's 40 years old. A bit of history, is that.'

He was always a Norton man, and obviously the Isle of Man was always the place most closely associated with the Manx, so that was a regular pilgrimage in the years before he was married. He'd tell us about buying a TT day ticket at a local travel agent. Him and his mates would get on a train at Halifax, go to Liverpool, get on the Steam Packet ferry, go over, watch the racing and come back, all in one day. He'd do this every year, sometimes twice a year if they took in the Manx Grand Prix as well. At the time, Geoff Duke was a national celebrity and the TT was big news, reported on the BBC.

Dad's factory Norton is still in the family, still lives up at the airfield. Even though it's a million miles from the sort of bikes I raced, I wouldn't mind going for a run round on it, and I'm sure dad would want me to do a parade on it, but it would need proper sorting first. It's special to me, too, because he was so passionate about it.

Although my dad was obviously interested in bikes and even the TT races, he knew nothing at all about the contemporary short-circuit racing scene. It just didn't seem to interest him, and for a while it didn't interest me. All that changed on 3 June 1978.

Every year dad would tell me he was going to take me to watch the TT races, and 1978 was the year he finally did, although it took a serious overdose of nostalgia before he finally got round to it. Sometime around February, he picked up *Motorcycle News* and damn-near exploded with joy. 'Hailwood's making a comeback,' he shrieked, 'it's confirmed…riding Yamahas and a Formula One Ducati.' Then he went into a eulogy about Mike the Bike, the greatest rider who ever lived, blah, blah, blah. Meanwhile I'm thinking, 'What's an old has-been like that doing racing again?' I'd have been 11 at the time.

But the prospect of seeing Hailwood was all dad needed. 'That's it, son,' he announced. 'We're going.' Minutes later he was on the payphone booking ferry tickets, arranging permission for me to be absent from school and telling his mates what a brilliant do we were going to have.

Dad decided to team up with one of them, Clifford Leach, Dave Leach's dad. Clifford was a TT regular who never missed a year on the Isle of Man. He also bought a new bike every year and, being a mate of my dad's, would ride across to the airfield to show it off. It became a regular thing – beep, beep, and there's Clifford with his new toy. The first one I remember was a disc-braked GT750 Suzuki 'Water Kettle'. It seemed so exotic, I wouldn't have been more impressed if he'd turned up on the space shuttle.

Clifford's 1978 toy was a Yamaha XS750 Triple, silver and black. Dad had just bought a Honda 400-four. We met up – dad, me, Clifford with Dave on the pillion, and a couple of Clifford's pals with their lads on the back – late at night at a transport caff in Ripponden. Over the bacon butties and mugs of tea, the main topic of conversation was about which ferry we were actually booked on, whether they still craned the bikes onto the boats – Isle of Man ferries being notoriously primitive at the time – and if they damaged them there'd be hell to pay. Some of the guys were anxious about missing the ferry, but the café owner solved that one by kicking us out and sending us on our way to Liverpool.

Most of the other blokes seemed to be TT regulars and knew where they were headed, but dad didn't have much of a clue where he was going, and ours was the slowest bike. On a good day it would barely do 100mph, and with me, dad and half a campsite on the back this wasn't a good day. So Clifford told the rest of them to bat on ahead while he rode shotgun for us. 'I'll stick with David and see you at the ferry,' was Clifford's parting shot.

With dad announcing that we'd cruise at a steady 80mph, off we went across the Pennines on the M62. Ahead of us is Clifford, although you couldn't actually see him for an enormous rucksack on Dave's back, packed with most of their gear for a week. In those days bikes weren't as stable as they are now, especially if you put a lot of weight high up at the back – for which Dave's pack certainly qualified. So the Yamaha was weaving a bit. Then the rucksack itself seemed to start moving of its own accord. Apparently the shoulder strap had broken. Dave tried grimly to cling on to it, then… whoosh…it tore back his arm and landed in the middle of the fast lane at 80mph.

I expected it to bounce more than it did, but it hit the tarmac and disintegrated. Suddenly three lanes of motorway are littered with flying underpants and shirts and toothbrushes going in all directions. Clifford, oblivious to this growing trail of debris, just carries on. So now dad's on a mission. He cogs down a gear, gives the Honda full wellie, and – well, the exhaust note maybe hardened a little, but we certainly didn't go noticeably quicker. It took us ten miles to catch Clifford, by which time his week's wardrobe is but a distant dirty memory. I don't know what Dave was thinking of, although he was always a really quiet, reserved lad, but in all those miles he never indicated anything was amiss. Eventually we made it to Liverpool for the midnight ferry and – yes – they did crane the bikes aboard, lashed to lengths of manky string. When we arrived in Douglas Clifford had to shell out for a week's new clothes for himself and his lad.

After that, everything went well and you can't imagine there ever having been a better first TT than 1978. In the course of it I went from thinking that Hailwood was a dozy old gimp, to practically worshipping the bloke. In the '60s he'd won everything – nine world titles, 76 grands prix and 12 Isle of Man TTs. But he hadn't raced for 11 years, had a damaged ankle and a bad limp from a car racing accident, and a lot of pundits were convinced he'd either wobble round making a prat of himself or get badly hurt. I arrived on the Island definitely in the 'prat' camp. But not the dads. From the first moment they got together, Clifford and dad and their mates couldn't stop going on about how bleeding Mike the Bike would show those hot-shot kids, make all the doubters eat their words and win every race. I had to sit through all this for days, thinking the silly old sod will probably cripple himself and hoping a young bloke would win. Despite that, it was obvious from the moment we got off the boat that there was a special air of excitement and expectation about the races that year.

We all watched the opening race, the Formula One, from Glen Helen, a beautiful wooded valley where the bikes dive around a low stone wall before powering up the hill to Sarah's Cottage. I have a vivid picture even now of beautiful weather, huge crowds crammed onto the grassy banks, men with their shirts off, of sunburned faces and ginger beers being passed round to us kids.

Although Hailwood struggled with machine problems on his Yamahas later in race week, Saturday was the day he and the little Ducati beat Phil Read, himself eight-times World Champion, and mighty Honda. This cynical little scrote from Huddersfield spent the day utterly transfixed, craning to hear the commentary on Radio TT, to the extent of resenting any other rider who dared come past and drown out the commentator. Hailwood seemed to be in charge right from the start, news greeted by a huge cheer from the Glen Helen gallery. Later he had a slow pit stop, allowing Read to claw back some of the lost ground, while we all sat in silence in the sun, everyone mutely willing the Ducati to fire up. When it did, more cheers rattled through the trees. 'Go on, Mike. You can do it.' Finally, on the fifth lap, the Honda came past us bellowing smoke and everyone cheered again. If the Ducati would only keep going for one more lap, just 38 more miles, the race was Hailwood's. When he crossed the finishing line victorious I could barely speak. It was that emotional. Even now I tingle reliving it, and it was clear at the time that you were witnessing something very special, something practically unique in racing history, something on a par with Muhammad Ali's comeback.

There were astonishing emotional scenes. You still read in accounts of that day of grown men crying, which sounds like a cliché, but they literally were. Total strangers were hugging each other. There was an air almost of reverence. As we clambered down from the banking nobody spoke, everyone just walked away with their private thoughts and tears in their eyes. They seemed genuinely to love Mike Hailwood, who to most of them was a total stranger, which seemed very odd but also very powerful.

So in no time at all Hailwood went in my estimation from zero to total hero. Obviously I was impressed then, but I'm even more impressed now. I've been packed in from racing for a mere five years and would barely know which end of a bike to get on, yet he came back after 11 years and beat everyone fair and square in one of the toughest races in the world. I truly have no idea how he did what he did. It's just incredible.

And not just Hailwood, but the TT itself was a revelation. The entire Island was packed. Every single road would be four bikes deep, and if you wanted some entertainment you just walked down Douglas Prom, which was absolutely awash with bikes of every make and type. The dads would amble past this hardware taking note of the tiniest thing: 'Look at this, Dave,' Clifford would say, 'look at what this bloke's done here. He's got a swing-arm off a bloody so-and-so, and he's altered that, and done this and the other…fantastic.' Everything was brilliant, everything was good. You couldn't help but be upbeat about everything.

It was, though, a wretched week for accidents, although at the time dad steered me well clear of that sort of bad news so my sense of the week remained untarnished. Snuffy Davies had already died during practice, and three men – Mac Hobson, his passenger Kenny Birch and Ernst Trachsel – were killed on Bray Hill in Monday's sidecar race. Then, in the final race of the week, Friday's Classic TT, New Zealander Mike Adler died almost at the spot where we'd watched Hailwood's triumph six days earlier. I was privy to none of it and spent the entire week in a state of motorcycle euphoria.

As well as bikes, guns, cars and life-threatening agricultural machinery, aeroplanes obviously loomed large in daily life at the airfield. As the one young boy always on the scene, I became something of a mascot to the pilots using the place. On a weekend there might be six or eight blokes prattling with aeroplanes, doping them, painting them, flying them, testing them, going places. I got to know most of the regulars, and would hang around at the caravan they used as a tearoom until my mate Roughy demolished it with an out-of-control Citroën Dyane. They'd inquire what I'd been up to, how I was doing at school, and then – the real reason I was hanging about and on my best behaviour – say something like, 'I'm just going over to Breighton. Do you want to go flying?' There's only one answer to that, so me and my mates seemed to spend half the time flying about all over the place.

Dad had a plane too, a four-seat 1050 Jodel, the same plane that I have now, which is how we got to see the 1979 TT. He piled Susan, Mary and me into this little thing and flew us across to Ronaldsway. Jane couldn't join us because she was playing with the National Children's Orchestra, who had some sort of gig at the time.

Meanwhile, we had a flipping great time. For one thing, it felt special because we'd arrived by plane when everybody else had been crammed into a bouncing ferry for five hours. And it was Mike Hailwood's last year racing on the Isle of Man, when he won the Senior and had that amazing dice with Alex George in the Schweppes Classic TT. We borrowed a car, and were ferried out to watch at Creg-ny-Baa, Quarter Bridge, the usual places, with dad thoroughly enjoying himself explaining what was going on and giving a running commentary of the action. I'd been hooked on the TT since being taken on the back of dad's bike the previous year, but even the girls seemed to enjoy it. Dad was in his element, and me in mine.

CHAPTER 3

BACKWARD AT SCHOOL

I was backward at school, although I didn't start that way. I enrolled at Wainstalls Infants School near Halifax in January 1972, aged five. Four months later we moved to the airfield, and I transferred to Crosland Moor Juniors, initially carrying on where I left off. Then for some reason they changed the qualifying date which decided which year you were in – a bit like the way they decide the age of a racehorse – so when most of my classmates moved up a year in September '72, I stayed behind to do the same year over again. It seemed daft.

At 11 I moved 100 yards up the road to Moor End Secondary Modern. Although Halifax still had the grammar school system and the eleven-plus exam, Kirklees – the Huddersfield area – had gone comprehensive, so strictly speaking it was Moor End Comprehensive. But everyone still called it the secondary modern – especially dad, who'd passed his eleven-plus and always wanted me to. In fact he never really got his head around the difference. He'd often tell me I'd soon be doing my eleven-plus exam, and it didn't seem to matter how many times I told him they'd done away with all that, that was still the way he saw it.

Moor End wasn't a bad school. It was conspicuously multi-racial even then, which had to be a good thing. It wasn't something you even thought about, but seemed naturally to get on with, as did almost everyone else: the Asians did the same, the West Indians did the same, and by the time you got to 16 you had mates who were black, brown and any number of different shades in between. In no time you took this ethnic hodgepodge for granted, which contrasted with the sort of old-fashioned view many of the generation above me seemed to have;

not necessarily racist, exactly, certainly not cruel, but definitely a bit them-and-us.

It was very diverse in other ways, with a fair share of farmers from the outlying areas, and a chunk of people from Beaumont Park, which was Huddersfield's answer to Mayfair – well-heeled dads with big cars and cigars and all the rest of it. At the opposite end of the spectrum were kids from the local council estate.

Not surprisingly, given my interests at home, metalwork – what they call 'technology' now but don't allow you to do very much, because that would obviously be too dangerous – was always one of my favourite classes. Mr Lenton, my old metalwork teacher, would let you do almost anything you wanted. You might mention to him that your go-kart had a busted axle, and he'd dive into the metal store, emerging with exactly what you needed, then show you how to turn it into a new one.

Nothing was too much trouble and his enthusiasm was infectious. He could stand there, drooling like a complete anorak over, say, some bearings, and you'd find yourself thinking how wonderful they were too. Once I turned up with a box of original Victorian moulds for lead soldiers, and that became a major after-hours project for half the class – sooting up the moulds over a candle flame so the molten metal didn't stick, melting lead on Bunsen burners, pouring, the whole nine yards. We made hundreds of the things.

Moor End's still there. I even went back recently. The local pub for the teachers is the Sands House, which is also my local now, so I still bump into them now and again. One of them, Mr Gill – a big, stern fellow who used to frighten me a bit – suggested I give a talk at the school. Apparently every year they get back an old boy or old girl to give a talk. They don't pick people who've been big in sport or otherwise famous so much as those who've been successful in whatever walk of life they've tackled. For all I know the old boy before me might have worked at Barclay's Bank or Tesco, or joined the forces. The theme, if there is one, is motivation rather than getting your name up in lights.

After a couple of near misses due to other commitments, I finally got to speak for about an hour a couple of years ago, trying to entertain and motivate the pupils. Now, I've done lots of after-dinner talks at bike clubs and the like, which is fairly easy because everyone in the audience knows who you are and what you've done – and they're interested, otherwise they wouldn't be there in the first place. I always try to make an effort, but suspect you could get away with any old shit just because to them you're a name.

The Moor End talk was different. Most of the pupils wouldn't have known a motorbike from a boil on their own backside. But it turned out to be easy. I didn't have to dress it up in pink ribbons and bullshit, because I loved school. I have only good memories about the place. What's not to like about it? I had some good mates, and some good clever mates too. Perhaps I was lucky that I got on with the lot who thought they were dead cool, always scrapping with people and going out drinking when they were 15, and with lads at the other extreme too; lads like Roughy – Andrew Rough – who was very funny but a bit of a swot and a bit scared of doing anything wrong. To this day I can still hear him saying, 'Are you sure we should be doing this?' when I was egging him on in some mischief. Of course, my answer was always 'Yes.'

I'd get up to daft stuff often enough, but at school I was more mischievous than an out-and-out wrong 'un. Most of my closest mates – Roughy, Stephen Dean, Russ Penrose – were quite bright, so the peer pressure on me was generally to put in a bit of effort in class. In our group only Sedge – Neil Sedgewick – was from the opposite extreme. He wasn't a wrong 'un at school either, although that was partly because he never went.

When Grandad Whitham had died, his wife came to live with us at the airfield for the last 18 months of her life. By this time she was suffering from Alzheimer's disease, which is always sad, but there were sometimes funny moments too. Having brought up four boys, of whom dad was the youngest, she had a fair idea of what lads got up to. Or thought she had. In one moment of apparent lucidity she demanded to know if I'd been to school.

'Yes, granny.'

'What you been doing?'

'Just schoolwork.'

This seemed to surprise her. 'You mean you weren't fighting? Why not?'

The truth was that I was never much of a scrapper. I suppose the best description of me at school would have been 'gobby'. I wasn't very big, didn't think of myself as tough and certainly wasn't much of a fighter. If I couldn't run away fast enough, I'd prefer to deflect any aggression by being funny. This was the way I managed to talk my way out of most scrapes – preferably without making myself look an idiot, but if I had to appear that way I would. Anything, even a degree of humiliation, was better than pain.

So I became the class joker – which was fine, except that it meant you were rarely taken seriously. On the other hand, because of where I lived and who my dad was, I was usually consulted if anything mechanical went wrong. They'd know that if I couldn't fix something, dad probably could. Sometimes he'd have a stream of kids up at the house, wanting bits welded or riveted or whatever. It might be an old toy, a bicycle, or even a car. Someone might bring a car to the airfield long before they'd reached driving age, and expect dad to fix a leaking radiator. He could have done without the hassle, because I expect he rarely got paid, but I sort of became his agent. At school I still wasn't part of the 'in' crowd, never 'cool', but I was useful. I could get things done.

When it came to sports, it couldn't have been more different. If they were selecting teams for any sport I'd be last to be picked, left standing on my own until someone finally condescended to say, 'Go on then, we'll have you.' The first to be picked were always Julian Bartholet, a shit-hot goalkeeper who had trials with Leeds United in later years; Gary McCallister, another talented player who's now my postman; and so on down the talent and coolness pyramid. It would be, 'Right, we'll have Snooky…OK, then we'll have Pecker…Woody, you're with us,' until they got down to the dregs, which always included me.

There was another lad, name of Akram, who turned up at school one day having just arrived from India with his family. He couldn't speak a word of English, and although he was a sinewy, athletic little fellow, had never kicked a football in his life. He probably didn't know the offside rule from a bacon sarnie, not that I was any more clued-up. Yet I knew, even before it happened, who'd be last to be picked. They were bound to prefer this scrawny little chap to me. And they did.

I never really liked team games – partly because I was rubbish

41

at them, partly because I always felt I was somehow letting the side down. But even so, this sort of thing was always a bit of a kick in the teeth, although I'd put on a brave face and joke about it. The only 'clubby' activity that did appeal was the Cubs, and later the Boy Scouts. I loved all that Baden-Powell stuff – mainly, I think, because every individual seemed to matter. You were given what felt like real responsibility and were usually taken seriously when you opened your mouth to speak. Maybe I was just lucky in getting a good scoutmaster, Dave Calverly.

Whatever the reason, I used to enjoy the orienteering and hiking they had us doing, and even the troop sports day, which was mainly individual sports. Above all, I'd get enormous satisfaction from being given a task and being left to get on with it. I'd tell myself, 'Right, I can do better than they think with this,' and really give it everything. It probably helped that they knew where I lived, for once our Akela, Mrs Oldfield, asked if they could bring the troop up to the airfield and have dad show the Cub Scouts round some of the aeroplanes. Dad, naturally, was happy to show off his aviation pedigree, although he seemed to spend most of the time in intimate conversation with Mrs Brierly, Akela's number two. 'Oh yes,' he'd brag, Biggles reincarnate, 'this is my aeroplane...'

'Bloody 'ell,' I thought, 'my dad's tapping Baloo up.'

CHAPTER 4

TODAY CARNABY, TOMORROW...ELVINGTON

From the time of my Epiphany at the '78 TT races, I was utterly hooked on bikes. Anywhere that I knew there were bikes to be seen, that's where I'd want to be. I'd get a bus or walk down the mile or so from Crosland Moor to Earnshaws bike shop in Huddersfield just to hang about and, just maybe, actually get to do something that involved their shiny new bikes. I already knew of the 'Earnshaw' sons, the Lodge brothers, who were already racing by the time I was about 14. There was Jason, Jeremy, Martin and Jamie, all of whom raced Honda 125s, although their racing careers were staggered so all four were only on the same grid once or twice. Nonetheless, this seemed the closest I was likely to get to actual racing in Huddersfield.

I was like a bad smell. The Earnshaws staff must have hated me. 'Do you want some help, mister?' I'd say, imploringly.

'Sod off.'

'Do you need a hand with that?'

'Sod off!'

'Can I have a look at your motorbike?'

'Sod off, you little scrote!'

I must have been pretty thick-skinned, or determined, because I'd still hang around if they didn't physically throw me off the site.

Finally, a genuine reason to bother them arrived when I heard from Dave Leach, who by then was 17, that he was going to be picking up a new bike at Earnshaws later that day, so why didn't I pop down to check it out? So down the hill I went and loitered around for hours. Eventually Dave arrived and took custody of a huge box with 'Yamaha' printed in big letters on the side. Inside was a brand new 350LC. Apparently Dave and a mate, Curly Crowther –

43

so-called because of his lank, straight hair – had each bought one of these specifically to go racing. At the time Dave worked at Cable Motorcycles in Halifax, which didn't sell Yamahas, but Earnshaws' manager, Steven Bradbury, had offered him a trade deal.

Suddenly Dave, someone I actually knew, was a superstar – in my eyes, at least. I actually knew a real racer, and never mind that he hadn't actually started yet! Leachy joined the Auto 66 club, to race at Carnaby, Elvington, occasionally at Cadwell Park and Scarborough, all of which sounded exotic far-off places to me. Then one day, out of the blue, dad said that if I wanted to join Dave at Carnaby races, he'd drop me round at his house early on Saturday morning. Did I? I couldn't wait. So, come Saturday morning, there's me at Leachy's back door with a box of sandwiches and flask of tea, packed by mum. And off we went to Carnaby. I'd have been 14 at the time.

Being there amongst all the bikes and riders was exciting, but also noisy and smoky, with bikes being bump-started and tearing around the paddock and off to practise. There was obviously some sort of method and organisation, but it all seemed hugely confused and chaotic. My main emotion was of nerves: I was so anxious about getting in the way, nervous for Dave, terrified of something going wrong. But eventually I got into the swing of it, gradually getting more involved. Soon I wanted to be with Dave at every race meeting. It became a regular thing.

I wasn't Leachy's mechanic, not by any stretch of the imagination. Tinkering with wrecked old bikes at the airfield scarcely qualified me for that. Instead, Dave always had a mate with him who'd attend to the technical stuff. I was more like his gofer, cleaning bikes, making tea and running errands – anything to be useful to what was, in its very modest way, a real race team. Sometimes I'd be allowed to do something real, like put petrol in the bike. And Dave himself seemed to have changed. He still hardly said a word, but wasn't altogether the same quiet, shy lad I'd known before. There was an edge to him now, a hardness, and he obviously had some talent for racing and did well right from the start. If he got hurt, he'd just shrug it off and get ready for the next race, because going out there and winning was all that mattered to him. I was awe-struck. Dave was my hero.

Mind you, travelling to meetings with Dave could be bloody hard work. Unlike me, he was never a chatterbox. I distinctly remember one trip to Carnaby where I'd tried to start a conversation but got just the odd grunt in reply, so I shut up. I think my only meaningful contribution on the entire journey was saying 'Clear left' a couple of times as we were waiting to drive out of junctions. It was hard work to know whether Dave liked you or he didn't, he gave so little away.

Despite such stunted moments, Dave Leach, without any doubt, was the catalyst for my starting racing. It wasn't a case of immediately thinking I had to have a go at this, but it did cross my mind that when we'd been messing about at the airfield I was probably as good as Dave on a bike, and he was doing well, so why not? I know now that simply being able to ride a bike well, even being able to pull all sorts of stunts, has nothing at all to do with how you'll do on a racetrack. But at the back of my head I thought that if he could do it, so could I. On the other hand, Dave was obviously a hero who thus existed on a far loftier plane then me. And, frankly, I was still scared stiff of the whole noisy enterprise.

For the best part of two years I played ping-pong like this in my head. Then, as I turned 16, I found my mouth telling dad that I'd love to go racing. I was a bit shocked. I heard the words, and dad obviously did, but I wasn't entirely sure they were mine. He was typically matter-of-fact. 'Right,' he said. 'If you want to go racing, we'll have to see if we can get you a bike.' 'Blimey,' I thought, 'I've done it now.'

A while later dad arrived back at the house announcing that he had found me a bike: 'It's a little 125, will that do you?' It sounds ungrateful, but my heart dropped. Dad's idea of a 125 racer was bound to be some totally unsuitable scrapper, because he just didn't understand the game. 'Oh, yeah,' I replied, 'fantastic... that'll be perfect,' thinking he'd just condemned me to being the laughing stock of the grid.

Dads, even mine, aren't always as daft as you sometimes think. Amazingly, the bike was perfect – a Honda Cup MT125 bought from Mal Carter, who owned the same Pharaoh Racing which once sponsored Ron Haslam. True, it was four years old, but had seen very little use and looked brand new, and I hadn't expected a new one anyway. It still had the original fairing, undamaged, original tyres, and a racing spares kit which, on any Honda, is a work of art in itself: blister-packed onto thick cardboard there were three sets of piston rings, con-rods, other bits and bobs. All that had been used was one piston and ring set, so that lot had to be good for a season or two.

So I was a racer, even though I couldn't even drive. On race days dad would drive me and the bike up to Leachy's and the pair of us would go to meetings in his van. Whichever meetings Dave entered, I'd enter the same, usually with the Auto 66 Club.

Before my first race meeting all I'd done was run the bike up and down the runway a couple of times when I heard that two of the Lodge brothers, Jamie and Jeremy, were going to Oulton Park in Cheshire for a practice day. In contrast to the likes of Carnaby, Oulton was a big-league circuit which you saw on TV, so I was buzzing when I tagged along with them. You didn't even need a race licence to take your bike for a run. You just queued up at a little booth, signed a form saying you were a maniac and everything that could possibly happen was your fault, and handed over your £11.

Oulton is magical, a proper race circuit. As if to prove the point, as I was finding my way round in my very first session there was a howl and a blast of air and Wayne Gardner, the future world 500cc champion, hurtled past on a three-cylinder Honda. I doubt he was impressed by my riding. I seemed to have trouble using all the road. After being used to ordinary roads, I couldn't believe you could use the full width and swoop through corners from one side right to the other, kerb to kerb to kerb. Instead, I tended to follow the edges a bit, although I don't think I was actually worried about something coming the other way. After a couple of sessions I seemed to get into the swing of things, but the whole exercise seemed slightly unreal.

My first meeting as an actual racer – although I could still scarcely believe I was such a thing – was in June 1983 at Carnaby in Yorkshire. I can still remember sending off my entry form and postal orders for that first outing with the Auto 66 Club, a good club for a beginner, especially one as young and skint as me. It didn't cost much to join, the races were cheap to enter, you got

46

plenty of them in a day's racing and the standard of racing was pretty good. There must have been 25 Auto 66 guys who went on to make some sort of name for themselves. As well as Northern riders, because Carnaby was so far north a lot of the Scottish hotshots would also make the trip down. Niall McKenzie often travelled down to race with Auto 66, as did Eric McFarlane and Howard Selby. Donny McCloud had been a regular in the recent past and even old Bill Simpson, Ian's dad, was still campaigning in the proddy class. Then there was the younger generation of future Scottish stars, like Brian Morrison and Iain Duffus.

Selby and McFarlane were scary – not for being dangerous, but just for being so damn good. They'd always give the local lads a run for their money. Then there were guys like Mark Westmoreland, who's always been bloody fast, other quick guys from the Midlands, plus the local lads – the Askin brothers, Gord Allott, Kurt Langan – all proper hard riders, hard men. Even Nigel Bosworth would pop up from the Midlands now and again. All in all, it was quite intimidating. So it was easy enough to approach that first meeting with the same mind-set I would adopt in my later career: I crapped myself.

Before actually arriving at Carnaby in Leachy's van I hadn't been so bad. I was wildly excited, a bit giddy, and couldn't stop thinking to myself, 'I'm a bike racer, a frigging bike racer…I race bikes…that's what I do.' And I had a real racing bike, even though all I'd done so far, apart from that day at Oulton Park, was sit on it, tinker a bit and paint the bodywork with a couple of aerosols of Halfords auto paint. I was determined to be super-organised, so my race numbers were already on the bike before I set off. My gear had been packed days in advance, I knew the routine like the back of my hand thanks to all those meetings with Leachy, so I was bound to breeze through scrutineering, then I could relax and put my race-face on.

Well, that was the plan. The reality was that I could hardly speak for nerves. It didn't help that I'd been blabbing off about the big racing debut to my old school-mates, so they turned up via a weekend in Bridlington, which only added to the pressure. And, since the one drawback with Auto 66 was that there was so much racing crammed into the day that you only got about three laps of practice, I actually knew my way round Oulton Park better than the place I was to do my first race.

Auto 66 also had an odd system which dictated that anyone wearing a novice jacket, like me, had to start from the back of the grid regardless of their past performances – which didn't bother me since I had none. Everybody else picked a numbered clothes peg which they clipped to their screen and then made their way to that grid position. Actually, this suited me just fine. I was literally quivering with nerves, actually telling myself not to get a good start because the last place I wanted to be on that first corner was in the middle of the pack. I'd watched enough races following Leachy around to know that looked a hairy place to be. Besides, I imagined it would feel a lot safer if I could start near the back and pick off one rider at a time, depending how it all went, rather than have a posse of nutters chasing me.

Trouble was, I might not have been great shakes on the corners, but I was already pretty good at bump-starting the bike. That's one of the benefits of having your own airfield. I'd practised starts a lot and could just push away with one foot, drop the clutch, the engine would fire into life and I'd be away.

The flag dropped, I pushed and – ring-a-ding – my Honda was the first engine to fire. You might imagine that was the moment my doubts dissolved and the racer's instinct cut in, but they didn't. Rather then risk that first corner mêlée I actually waited until a few others riders had got away. Other than that I can't say that I had any sort of strategy, but from then on it went to plan – better, in fact, than my wildest dreams. There were about 30 starters and I finished seventh, so I must have passed quite a few, although the race passed in a blur and I can't actually remember much about it. But was I giddy, or what? 'Fucking hell,' I thought, 'I can do this, I'm all right, I'm a racer.' It was the wildest mixture of satisfaction and relief.

An hour or so later a total stranger sat on my 125 Honda at the back of another grid for his second-ever race. The wimp who'd lucked out in the first race must have gone to Bridlington for an ice cream or something, because this guy's thinking, 'You thought race one was impressive, just watch this. Am I going to kick some ass.' This time the bike fired up just as quickly as before, but this time I *went*…cannoned into a few people, ran over a foot or two, ricocheted to the front barely in control, rode like a demon – and still finished seventh. I couldn't understand it. It didn't seem to make any difference how aggressive I was, I still ended up in the same place. I placed sixth in my third and last race of the day and came away very relieved, and very happy with two sevenths and a sixth, although increasingly respectful of the likes of Tony Flinton, a lovely old boy who'd won all three. Stuffed in a box somewhere I've still got my racing licence and programme from that first Carnaby meeting. How sad is that?

After my triumphant debut at Carnaby I went to Elvington in the Vale of York, racing against much the same guys as before, and this time picking up something like a fifth and a sixth. Other than finishing as high as possible, the most important goal that year was never, ever, to let another orange novice jacket beat you, and I usually managed that. Then it was back to Carnaby again, followed by my first meeting at Cadwell Park.

Cadwell was a revelation. Carnaby and Elvington are flat, featureless airfield circuits, but Cadwell, nestling in the Lincolnshire Wolds, is all hills and whoops and swoops. The meeting was on the Club rather than the full circuit, so left out the 'Mountain' section, but I still adored it. I spent most of the meeting dicing for the usual fifths and sixths then, in my final outing of the day, placed third. Even though there wasn't actually a rostrum, since they didn't do that in club racing, in my mind I was a rostrum finisher…me!

More than that, it meant that for the first time James Whitham, 125 Honda, Huddersfield, would actually appear in the results. Most clubs publish results down to sixth place, so I'd have been in there already, but Auto 66 had so many races they only printed the first three. The following Wednesday I was straight down to the newsagents to buy *Motorcycle News*, and there in black and white in the world's biggest motorcycle weekly was Mrs Whitham's lad.

Although there were only three or four months of racing from when I started until the season closed at the end of October, I managed ten meetings, enough to get rid of my novice jacket. That first half-season was brilliant in every way. I didn't even fall off, not once. But most of all I'd found something I was good at and enjoyed more than I could describe. I was totally taken over, utterly obsessed by racing. Life was sweet.

CHAPTER 5

'LOOK, MATE, YOU NEED TO BE STEADYING UP'

Over time, Dave Leach became increasingly serious about his racing at a time when it was still just a good craic to me, and we began to drift apart. He'd go off doing the Marlboro Clubman's series, which was a step up from the Auto 66 Club scene, whilst I was still firmly rooted with club meetings. By now he was campaigning a pair of Yamahas, a 350LC for the proddy class, and a proper TZ250 racing machine. This meant there wasn't much room in the van for me and my 125, although he was always generous about it. If I told him I'd like to do a particular club meeting, we'd go, but it was becoming increasingly inconvenient. Until I got rid of my novice jacket, Dave was competing in meetings I wasn't even eligible for.

Luckily there were plenty of other local club riders, most of them doing Auto 66 meetings. Even at little meetings like those, the race programmes would list not only the names of riders and their machines, but their hometown. I'd scan down the list to see who was there – Tim Salveson, Gary Buckle from Sleaford riding an MBA, Dave Leach, Halifax, 250/350 Yamahas – and look for riders living near me. Usually there would be the Swallow brothers, Bill and Richard, Dean and Lewis Askin, and a few more. Then one day in the paddock I got chatting to a rider who turned out to be from Brockholes, which was almost next door to Crosland Moor. His name was Pete Moore and, although I didn't know it at the time, he as much as anyone would become a major influence in my racing. In fact, without him I would probably never have had any sort of racing career at all.

Pete told me about a regular racers' gathering at a pub at Thurstonland, near Huddersfield: 'We go to the Clothiers' Arms every Thursday, mainly the Earnshaws lot. Why don't you come?' This was the same Earnshaws bike shop at which I'd made myself such a pest just a few years before, for several of the Lodge brothers were still racing. From then on Thursday nights at the Clothiers', sometimes other nights at the White Hart in New Mill, became regular events. All we'd do is talk about bikes....blah, blah, blah...more bikes...petrol, cams, wheels, tyres, scrutineering, all the usual bollocks that bikers obsess about when they're together. It was ace. For the first time in my life I felt like I truly fitted in. I was home.

Of course, it helped that I started winning, starting with my second meeting of the '84 season at Mallory Park. Although I spent most of the season racing with the Retford Club, I was still competing against much the same people as before, on exactly the same bike, but for some inexplicable reason felt faster than I ever had in my novice year. Somewhat to my surprise, I actually sat on the grid believing that I could win. Pete, naturally, reckoned he understood. 'The only thing that's been stopping you from winning before,' he commented sagely, 'was you thinking you couldn't. It's all in the mind.'

Pete may have had a grip on what was in my mind, but I'm pretty sure I didn't. But what I did seem to know, even as I started the race, was that I could win. I think I even half expected to. When the flag dropped I led for most of the race and took the win fairly comfortably, so much so that it was almost an anticlimax. I was chuffed, of course, but in some ways winning was as much a relief as a victory. More wins followed and I finished the season as the Retford Club's 125cc champion.

It wasn't the biggest deal in racing, but it felt as if my whole life changed. Before that I hadn't been an insignificant person, exactly. I'd always had something to say for myself, sometimes too much, and got a kicking as a result. But almost overnight I went from being directionless – fairly happy, but not sure what I was going to do with my life – to the point where racing was absolutely everything. In fact I couldn't imagine what life was like before bike racing. I used to love going to the pub with all the lads, putting in my two penn'orth and actually being taken seriously, which had been a rarity before. The conversation might be about the best way through Coppice Bend, and they'd ask if I did this or that, go down one gear on the way in or just drive it through, or whatever. And they really wanted to know what I thought. Christ, they're taking me seriously! That's a new one. Bloody 'ell.

Getting to know the Clothiers' crowd also offered a solution to my transport problems. So if Leachy wasn't planning on riding in the same meeting as me, I'd ask the likes of Pete, one or two of the other Huddersfield lads, and later Butch Cartwright, if I could travel with them. Sometimes the local lads would be going somewhere I wasn't, Thruxton or somewhere equally exotic and way down south, but they'd usually put me on to someone else, like Simpy, who had a van and could give me a lift. His real name was Simon Sykes, which obviously became Simple Simon – although he wasn't – then Simpy. For a while I scrounged my way to meetings like that, but it wasn't very convenient, so when I reached 17 I saved up and bought my own van, which became part of the Huddersfield racing 'pool'.

At the time Pete Moore would have been 33 to my 16, so there was a huge difference in our ages, yet we gelled right away. He'd already raced for a few years, on all sorts of kit: TZ Yamahas, Formula Two bikes, LC Yamahas and a Suzuki X7 before that. To me, he'd seen it all, done it all, whilst everything was still novel and mysterious to me. Pete's idea of a good race meeting was to enter every single race, although he usually ended up only doing half of them because he couldn't be arsed. But between, say, 350 open, Formula 2 and 1300 open he might have eight or ten rides in a day. He was actually a pretty good club rider, usually a top-five finisher and now and again winning the odd trophy. But he always seemed to bite off more than he could chew, so as often as not by mid-afternoon he'd stomp around his van, cursing and kicking his bike for some imagined wrong it had done before announcing that he'd had enough and was packing in.

Naturally, because he was a mate and sort of my mentor, I'd try to say something consoling, when really what was in my mind was grabbing the opportunity for my own ends. Eventually I'd broach the subject: 'Er, Pete, have you entered the unlimited race at end of the day?'

'Yeah,' he'd bark.

'Well, if you're not riding can I borrow your bike?'

52

He'd always say yes, so I'd trot down to race office with a fiver, change the designated rider from him to me and change the bike's race number to mine. Well, usually. Sometimes I didn't have time – or a fiver – and just thought, 'What the hell,' and went out and raced on Pete's number. The trick was to arrive on the bike at the holding area at the very last minute, just as everyone was leaving for the grid, keep your visor down, and just go. It was always noisy and chaotic, engines revving and the air full of two-stroke smoke, so usually the marshals didn't have a clue who was who anyway. Everybody took the same shortcuts with the rules, but I sometimes used to dread what might happen if someone spannered themselves riding on the wrong number. I could imagine the conversation with Pete's next of kin:

'There's been a horrible accident with your Pete at Cadwell Park.'

'Will he live?'

'Yes, but it's bad. Even with plastic surgery he's going to spend the rest of his life looking like James Whitham.'

But Pete gave me more than just the odd buckshee ride. Although I did reasonably well right from the start of my racing, it was a while before I did any winning, and things often went pretty pear-shaped trying. Pete was the guy who'd sit me down when I'd done something particularly silly in a race and say, 'Look, mate, you need to be steadying up.' Whenever things weren't going well, it would be Pete who'd keep me going. Over the years he was hugely instrumental in my continuing to enjoy my racing, and without him I suspect there were times when I'd have been tempted to pack it in. Whenever I felt like spitting my dummy with the bike, I'd ring him. Invariably he'd say something comical, but to the point, and whatever was bugging me wouldn't seem to matter any more.

He was a tough lad, too. His dad had worked in Yugoslavia after the war, where he married a displaced person, a Yugoslavian woman. She was a lovely lass but hard as nails – a big, leathery farmer's daughter. You wouldn't have fought her. Pete had sort of inherited that hard-as-nails Slavic look from her. And as well as looking the part, he was also a bit of a fighter and liked a drink.

One evening the pair of us went to a sports dinner in Bradford, intended to raise money for some benevolent fund or other. The main speaker was the British Lions' rugby team captain, Bill Beaumont, a big gnarly bloke with a smashed-up face and ears. His talk was all right, pretty funny in places, and got a good round of applause.

Afterwards, Beaumont's in the bar having a craic with the guests and drinking, at which he also seemed quite talented. Pete, who'd had a few drinks too, strolled up to this big, ugly rugger-bugger, gets right in his face and, out of nowhere, goes, 'You're not that big are you?'

There was a sudden intake of breath from everyone else in the room, then it went deathly quiet. Beaumont never even looked up from his pint before growling, 'I fucking am if I take you outside, lad.'

That was Pete: a great bloke who got me into – and out of – a lot of trouble.

Pete was also the nearest I had to a technical guru. He was a spot-on engineer, a time-served maintenance engineer, rather than just a fitter. Where my dad was more inclined to just bash things until they had no choice but to fit together, Pete knew what tolerances were about, interference fits, all that. Although I was always fairly practical and hands-on, and later picked up a fair bit of relevant experience in a toolmaking apprenticeship, I simply didn't have his level of technical understanding. Many a time we'd have some problem with the bike and I'd be convinced the game was up, but he'd come up with a solution. 'No, no we can sort this,' he'd say as I was ready to pack up the van, 'I'll have a word with so-and-so and see if I can get hold of this or that. There's bound to be some way round this.'

Pete was also the first to put me in the picture about oils. At the time, vegetable oils were on their way out and synthetic two-stroke oils were just arriving. I just followed what everyone else did and slung Castrol R30 in the Honda, mixing it 40:1, 20:1 with the fuel – as much as you could cram in without it fouling spark plugs. The smell was gorgeous. Even old boys who hated two-strokes would go bleary-eyed with nostalgia on the exhaust fumes, because they smelled just like Geoff Duke's factory Nortons had 30 years before.

The trouble with 'R' was that it gummed up everything inside your engine, as well as covering everything behind the carburettor with this horrible slimy goo. You'd have to strip the engine after every other meeting to clean off all the deposits. During the 1983–4 winter Pete used to pop up to the airfield to check up on me. 'Bloody hell, forget that,' he said one day when he noticed the results of the Castrol 'R'. 'Strip the whole thing, clean that shit off everything – bearings, the whole bloody lot. Throw away that petrol.' I didn't know what he was on about, but it sounded serious. For a moment I thought my engine had got some sort of disease. Was it infectious? Could I die of it? Would they have to quarantine us all?

'This is what you want to be running on,' announced Pete, brandishing a bottle of Castrol 747 he'd just brought from his van. I poured a bit of this magical potion into a jam jar lid. It looked like water, brown water. It was runny, nothing at all like 'R'. How could it possibly stop bits of metal wrecking each other at 10,000rpm? But it worked – made the engine run much cleaner and more sweetly. Great stuff.

The last big meeting of the '84 season was the Marlboro Clubman's Final on Silverstone's long circuit which, in those days, was a seriously fast track. The Honda wouldn't have had a chance. It just wasn't quick enough. My best Marlboro results on the MT125 had been a couple of third places in the dry, and a second in the wet at Cadwell against Robin Milton, Jamie Lodge and the rest, all of whom were running MBAs.

The MBA had transformed and revitalised the 125cc class to the point where nothing else was in with a shout. The Honda was giving away around 10hp, a huge amount when you're only playing with around 30hp. So most of the time it didn't matter how hard you rode, you just couldn't compete.

To buy one, let alone run it, I needed £4,500 that I simply didn't have. I'd managed to save £500, but a load of letters to potential sponsors had drawn a blank except for a bit of help with oil and tyres from good old Earnshaws. It was obviously time to tap up dad again. 'Look,' I told him, 'this Honda is getting a bit long in the tooth. I can't win on it, and I'm never going to be able to afford anything better.'

At the time I knew of a rider, Doug Flather, who'd been pretty good but was about to retire. This didn't necessarily mean very much, because he retired every year and then started again the following spring, discovered he still couldn't handle it and packed in again. I'd raced against him a few times and knew him as a decent bloke and a steady rider who always seemed to have good bikes. Sometimes he'd beaten me, sometimes the other way round. Midway through '84 he'd bought a new MBA, with spares kit, spare wheels, the whole shooting match. He'd only raced it twice, but it seemed to be sorted. It might be for sale.

So I told dad that this was the bike I needed. I was twitching a bit and half-expected him to just laugh, but he was as serious as I was.

'Do you need it?' he asked, very matter-of-fact.

'Yeah. Really.'

'Can you win on it?'

'Yes, I think I can.'

'Right then, we'll go and have a look at it.'

It was as simple as that. So off we went to Liversedge, on the way to Leeds, where Doug showed dad around his MBA. I think dad knew it was a motorbike, but otherwise Doug might have been speaking Cantonese.

Dad took it all in, or pretended to, and said, 'Right, we'll have it.'

'Right,' echoes Doug, '£4,500 with the spare wheels and the stands and all that.'

'We don't need any spare wheels,' replied dad, not having much of a clue. 'There's nowt wrong with the ones on it.' I had to explain the extra wheels weren't in case they were damaged, but so I could have a set with dry weather tyres and another set for wets, since even in Yorkshire the sun doesn't always shine on racing.

'Oh, do we need them?'

'Yeah we need everything.'

'Oh, right, we'll have them then an' all,' said dad. He handed over the cash and we drove home with my new MBA. What a good bike it would prove to be. The first race bike dad had bought – the one which I'd been so convinced was a lemon – had seen me through the last part of my first season and almost the whole of '84. It had been a good little thing and, although I didn't know it at the time, would be the only Honda race bike I ever got on with. But as my first race bike, it obviously has a special place in my affections.

It hasn't done a lot since and is still in Huddersfield – so, if you're reading this, Marcus Lodge, I'd still like to buy it back.

Meanwhile I'd barely sat on the MBA before we arrived at Silverstone for the Marlboro finals, but we were in business. It handled beautifully, had all the power the Honda didn't and brought me third place, just narrowly, in a close, hard-fought race. The main contenders, all on MBAs, were Jamie Lodge, Gary Buckle, Robin Milton, Robin Appleyard – and Dave Lowe, who, if I remember correctly, pipped Lodge for the win.

But third, first time out? 'That'll do me,' I thought. 'That'll do for the end of the season.'

A week later it got even better. Almost as an afterthought I managed to grab a late entry for the final British Championship round at Oulton Park. Inevitably, it was Pete's idea. All season he'd been on his guru trip, telling me the only thing stopping me being successful were my own doubts. He seemed to have none, convinced I could easily manage a top-ten place even at national level.

As usual, Pete was right. After practice I realised I was running well enough to maybe finish in the top five. Conditions for the race were tricky – half wet, half dry – but we took a gamble to run intermediate tyres where most were running full wets. From the start, Alex Bedford cleared off into the distance, but after three or four laps I saw a shower of sparks ahead of me going into Lodge Corner. That was Alex, on his chuff, and I was leading. As the track dried I took 1.7 seconds off the lap record and took the win ahead of Neil Robinson on another MBA. I'd not only beaten the best in Britain, fair and square, but took home £250 for the win. It was the first time it ever occurred to me that maybe you could make a living at this racing lark.

Things would be different for the following year, in ways I couldn't have anticipated. Now that I had a truly competitive machine, I had my sights on doing all the national championships and maybe even a few international meetings too. The Marlboro series would still be running, for what I think was its final year. But some of the gloss had gone off it and it wasn't quite the 'must do' championship it had been, so I would only do a few rounds. But there were two other major series I could do. The 125 class always seemed to be lurching from one crisis to another, but the resurgence in interest generated by the MBAs, in particular, meant that the British 125 Championship had been exhumed and dusted off yet again. There was also to be a 125cc class in the ACU UK Star series, although by and large the same lads would fill the grid in both competitions.

Being the youngest of our crowd, I always seemed to be slightly out of sync with the rest. Guys like Pete, Butch and Jamie Lodge had already done plenty of Marlboro Clubman's rounds and were in the process of slimming down their racing efforts at exactly the time I was getting more serious, wanting to do more and bigger meetings. Their idea of a perfect season was maybe a handful of the bigger club meetings, rounded off in late August with the Manx Grand Prix. I was exactly the opposite. Especially now that I had the MBA I was keen to do more and bigger stuff.

Far from being a problem, this turned out wonderfully well. It perhaps sounds an egotistical thing to say, and just seemed to occur spontaneously at the time, but their main focus seemed to move from their own racing to mine. 'Right,' they said, 'we'll come with you.' It got to the stage where, say, Pete had entered a meeting at Carnaby, then learned I was doing the Snetterton Marlboro round on the same weekend. 'Sod it,' he'd say, 'who's bothered about poxy Carnaby?' So he'd enter the Marlboro and drive down to Norfolk with me. Lots of the Huddersfield lads would come to meetings now and again, but mainly it was Pete and Simpy. Simpy wasn't as knowledgeable as Pete – at the time I didn't know anyone who was – but he was a clever lad, a good bloke, interested in racing, really keen and great to have around. They'd help me drive to meetings and back, get the bikes ready for racing and practice. Just having them around was a huge help, especially when things were going wrong.

From that point of view it worked out well. But, like most people new to racing, I simply couldn't understand why anyone would want to do less of it rather than more. If I had a weekend off racing I was bored, aimless. If I wasn't actually at the track, all I wanted was to be in my workshop working on the bike. If I wasn't there, I'd be thinking about racing or, if there was anyone to talk to, talking about it. I was fully bitten by the bug. Later in my career, as racing became more routine, more of a job, and especially if things weren't going well, I might occasionally think I'd be bloody glad when it's all over. But by then I'd have other things to maintain my momentum: the fact that it was my livelihood, that I was being paid for it, that a whole crew of people depended on what I did. When you get to that stage, you simply can't just chuck in the towel. But the majority of club riders seem to go through what Pete and the rest were going through: you spend two, three, four years getting this crazy racing bug out of your system, and then move on. But for the present, the only way that I wanted to move on was on the MBA.

Along with the spare wheels and lots of other bits and pieces, Doug Flather had handed me a list of MBA do's and don'ts. As with all two-strokes, you had to keep on top of the MBA's engine to keep it running sweetly, otherwise it would simply get slower and slower with every race until eventually it blew up, so I observed this religiously. It had to have new piston rings every two meetings. You had to measure your piston clearances, and when the piston skirt got below the prescribed figure you'd replace the pistons too. The pistons were forged – they'd been cast on the MT125 – so they weren't cheap. I was fastidious in keeping a log of racing distance, because Doug's list insisted that the crankshaft had to be replaced every thousand miles. Crank kits were a frightening price but dirt cheap compared to the cost of one going pop during a race and wrecking the engine.

This was a whole new world of race preparation. I was worried, too, partly by the knowledge that this was a very finely-tuned and finicky bit of kit, but equally with the thought of paying for all the goodies for which it seemed to have an endless appetite. Since mileage was so expensive, it was easy to decide that club meetings were going to be an expensive waste of time, except for maybe the odd one early in the season as a glorified practice day. Other than that, all I did was the Championships and the UK Star series. On paper both series were wide open. Several of the top 125cc runners from 1984, like Mez Mellor and Smutty Robinson, weren't around, and I started winning regularly almost from the first round. If I stayed on – which I'd done in every race but one since beginning racing – I had to be a serious contender. But boy, did I fall off a lot.

The first get-off was in my second or third meeting of the year – nothing special, but that was just the start. Inevitably, it all started off with Pete Moore.

Pete was still racing on a neat Yamaha TZ350G, which he'd entered in a meeting at Carnaby. When he heard that I'd be riding the MBA at the same meeting he decided it might be more fun to watch me race it instead. Despite being a non-championship meeting, it was at national level, which meant there would be a fairly high class turn-out – 350cc was *the* class at the time. The field would include Niall McKenzie and Donnie McCloud on Silverstone Armstrongs, Mark Westmoreland, Nigel 'Bozzy' Bosworth, Pete Hubbard, Kevin Mitchell and other big-hitters. Without doubt the 350 race was the most competitive of the day. The TZ350 Yamahas were affordable, runnable and reliable, and the racing was intense.

At the time the 250cc class was different, since the bikes were still under active development, whereas the 350cc grand prix class was on its way out. You needed a new 250 every season, either a right good Armstrong, a new Yamaha – or a Honda, whose new 250cc V-twin had just been released. In other words, although guys like Bozzy, Carl Fogarty and Mitchell were riding 250s, you needed to spend a lot of money to be competitive in the class.

Naturally, since most racers are skint, the 350cc class was where most of them gravitated. With a bit of tweaking you could keep a 350 Yamaha competitive for three years; bolt on a set of Swarbrick pipes, a pair of Powerjet carbs, a better ignition, and even an old 350G could be kept competitive. Pete certainly knew enough to keep his on the boil, so handed it over to me for the day, telling me that with me riding it'd be good enough for a top-ten finish, no bother.

And I was quite competitive, at least for a while. To be truthful McKenzie, McCloud and Westmoreland disappeared into the middle distance, but by then I knew my way around the circuit pretty well, and was running fairly comfortably in about sixth when the engine did a piston on the back straight. With nothing better to do, I pulled in at the hairpin and sat on a straw bale to watch the rest of the race. You get a different perspective watching than you do riding, and I was impressed. 'Friggin' 'ell,' I thought, 'these lads can ride bikes.' McKenzie, especially, was just incredible...speed in, lean angle, speed out. The way he threw the Armstrong on its side you wondered how he ever stayed on board.

Despite the wrecked piston, Pete was keen for me to do more meetings on his TZ. The last one, another non-championship national, called something like the Yellowbelly Tropy, was also at Cadwell Park. It was a disaster. I fell off three frigging times – off my MBA at the Hairpin, then at Park Corner when the bloody thing seized, and finally off Pete's 350 coming out of the Hairpin – and all of them in the morning. It wasn't even lunchtime and I was on my way home with a van-full of scrap bikes.

In addition to trashing the MBA and Pete's 350, part-way through the '85 season I was asked to ride an 80cc racer for a nearby bike business, Lee Brothers Motorcycles, owned by Rodney Lee. Essentially his was a motocross shop, a big one, at a time when motocross was pretty big, especially in our area. But Rod was a bike fan in general. He went to the Isle of Man every year, a load of other road race meetings, and I sometimes bumped into him at Carnaby. I'd bought a few bits and pieces from him, and we knew each other slightly.

One day Rod decided to build an 80cc racer. There was a bit of interest in this new class at the time, since Ian McConnachie was doing well in grands prix. It had a lattice frame built, I think, by Derby Racing Services of Spondon, based on a Kreidler grand prix bike. Rod had bolted into this an engine from a schoolboy motocrosser, a Kawasaki KX80. It had Marzocchi forks and all the usual other kit. It looked a neat little machine.

Unfortunately, in six or seven meetings it never ran properly and we never managed to get it sorted. You might think that an 80, especially a slow one, can't do you much damage, but you wouldn't want to step off one down a straight. It seized up going into Coppice at Cadwell Park's UK Star meeting and pitched me off – just oiked me right over the top. Maybe I should have reacted more quickly, got the clutch in and caught it, but it was the first lap, I was head down right in the middle of the pack, so I couldn't hear the engine and in that situation you're too busy racing to keep an eye on the rev counter. Inevitably, mum and my sisters were there to watch.

I was all right, but my collarbone had snapped. Amazingly, this was the first time I'd broken anything in nearly two years' racing. I was given a once-over in the circuit's medical centre before going down to Louth General Hospital, where all they could do apart from X-raying it and telling me what I already knew was put me in a sling and a figure of eight bandage.

The following week was the British Championship meeting at Mallory Park. At that point I was leading the British 125 Championship and decided that I had to go, to at least see if I'd be able to ride. Even if I wasn't in top shape, and I wasn't, I might be able to get a fifth or sixth and salvage some points, which might become critical by the end of the season. After all, I reasoned, it's only a 125, and after a few days' rest I didn't feel too bad.

At the time Mallory Park still had its original layout. There was no bus-stop chicane after the Hairpin, let alone the ones that have since ruined Gerrard's and The Esses. You just nailed it out of the Hairpin and right through Devil's Elbow onto the start/finish straight. I'd been hoping to get away with just sneaking out for practice and seeing how I went. Unfortunately for me the organisers knew all about my little escapade at Coppice, so before long the tannoy's shouting for James Whitham to report to the race office.

'Look,' says the medical officer, 'we know you've got a broken collarbone and you're probably going to tell us that you're fine to race...'

So far I was in full agreement.

'...so we'd like you to prove it by doing some press-ups for us. Five should do.'

Even at the time, I thought, 'I'm never going to be able to do one, never mind five.' But I got down on the floor and started. Christ, it hurt, and I could hear bone grating next to my ear, but I did them, all five. I must have been ashen and lathered in sweat by the time I stood up again.

'Right. Well done. You can race.'

After that, qualifying was a breeze. I qualified for the front row of the grid. At the time Robin Milton lay second in the championship, so was the man with most to gain if I'd missed out. It might sound a horrible thing to say, but we all do it – and after all, a collarbone isn't exactly life-threatening – but he must have been rubbing his hands in glee, assuming I wouldn't be able to race. I remember looking at him on the grid, thinking what a bastard he was for just thinking, in my imagination, precisely what I'd have been thinking in his position. He had a quizzical look on his face, probably thinking the same about me – thinking I can't be right, I must be slow.

When the flag dropped and the race settled down, it was me and Milton for the lead. I actually felt all right and managed to see him off, breaking the lap record and pulling a couple of seconds' lead. Suddenly, after all the hurly-burly of the opening laps, I had time to think, which for me was generally fatal. I started rushing and pushing instead of riding smart, hit the bump where the drain goes under the track going into the Esses, lost the front – and broke my other collarbone, as well as separating the one I'd broken the previous week.

My, did I feel sorry for myself. No points, a mangled bike, and I couldn't even wipe my own arse properly. Simpy and Pete threw the bike in the back of the van and off we set for home, me feeling pale and wretched. Collarbones heal fast, but for the first couple of days they hurt like hell. Even at home I felt bad: couldn't get comfy, couldn't cough, couldn't fart.

Over the next few days most of my upper torso turned interesting shades of purple and yellow. I got a bit of tut-tutting – not from my mum, who always seemed OK so long as I was happy, if a bit worried when I knocked myself about. My sisters were less tolerant. Mary insisted I was ruining what body I'd got, which was a pretty skinny thing anyway. Dad was at the opposite extreme. Other than me taking up so much room lying about groaning, he seemed totally unbothered about the state I was in. He didn't want anything to happen to me, obviously, but reckoned that there's some sort of price to be paid or risk involved for everything you do in life, whether it was his flying, my sisters' horses, or me spitting myself off bikes. Put it this way: mum knew her way to casualty. It seemed like she was there half the time. For dad, it all seemed grist to the mill. He'd hurt himself a lot, crashing aeroplanes, motorbikes, sticking his hands in moving machinery – pretty much what you'd expect from the least safety-conscious

63

person on the planet. If it came to a choice between a safety guard and making the job go two seconds quicker, off it came. But mostly I think he was kind of proud of me. It's only now, since my daughter's started growing up, that I fully realise how hard it is to watch your kids doing something that's possibly going to hurt them and what a loose rein we were allowed.

Some injury issues, though, were new to all of them. After a couple of days of sitting around feeling sorry for myself as mum ladled sweet tea and soup into me, I couldn't wait any longer.

'It's no good,' I announced to mum, 'I'm going to have to go to the toilet.'

'Sure you can manage?'

'Yeah, I think I can.'

Well, I managed most of it. Got to the toilet, pyjama bottoms down, business done. But the final clean-up was beyond me. I simply couldn't get my arm round to the right place. I tried everything: laying toilet paper on the seat and sort of squirming around on it, limbo-dancing under the roll, you name it. After 20 minutes I'd got 15 yards of toilet paper stuck to my arse and nothing else to show for it. This was embarrassing. I wasn't a toddler any more.

'Mu-u-um,' I yelled down he hallway, 'I can't wipe my bum.' She had to come in and clean me up.

That wasn't the only clean-up operation. In our haste to leave Mallory, we'd forgotten our tent. I don't know how we managed this, because we had to have done a nine-point turn just to reverse the van around the damn thing without running over it. But we managed it. We could manage most things like that, even when I wasn't off my head. I guess Simpy had a knack.

The tent was our home at the circuits. At night the bike and tools lived in the van. Pete, Simpy and me lived in the tent. It was a sturdy little thing, a four-man frame tent, but the trouble with Mallory was that the ground was mostly hard gravel. You could just about get pegs into it, but it was no fun for sleeping on. Since no luxury was too much for Team Whitham, I'd scrounged some offcuts of carpet – good stuff, proper Axminster – which I'd cut to the shape of the floor.

For one reason or another it took us ten days to get the 100 miles to Mallory for the tent, by which time I was feeling a bit less sorry for myself. It was a lovely day, so rather than take the van Simpy thought we could go on his bike, a lovely GPZ600 of which you'll learn more later. He worked nights, so arranged to pick me up one morning after he'd finished his shift. Simpy said for me to take my rucksack, which he reckoned would easily swallow the tent.

Mallory was locked up, but I found a bloke in the office.

'We're here to pick a tent up, we left it at the British Championship meeting a couple of weeks ago.'

'Oh yes, I've seen that tent. Fucking posh tent, is that.'

'What do you mean?'

'Fitted fucking carpets!'

Anyway, it didn't have any after that. Simpy's space-time calculations had failed to take account of the Axminster and it wouldn't fit in the rucksack.

On the way back from Mallory, Simpy and I managed to blag our way into Donington Park for a televised World of Sport Challenge race meeting. Although by this time I was accustomed to being at fairly big meetings, the upper echelons of the sport still seemed miles above. Whilst pimping around the paddock we bumped into Trevor Nation. I didn't know Trev, but I knew of him. He was getting over a huge crash at the North-West 200, where he'd smashed up the back of his hand. He was a big, imposing chap with farmer's hands, like five great Cumberland sausages on a shovel. But they weren't much good to him, because he'd ripped up all the tendons in one of them. He couldn't pull his fingers back.

I have to say that his solution was ingenious, if frightening. As we were introduced to him he was in his leathers waiting to go out on the track. 'Oh,' I said, 'I didn't think you'd be riding. I thought you'd damaged your hand.'

Trev looked over his shoulder a couple of times to make sure nobody official was watching. 'Yes, it's bad,' he said, conspiratorially, 'so I've done this...'

On his glove he'd crimped on a press-stud here, a press-stud there, with some lengths of strong elastic between them.

'Look,' he said, pulling on his glove, 'when I pull like that my fingers move and grip the handlebar.' Then he went *ping, ping* again on the elastic to make his fingers twitch and grinned that big daft grin of his.

It was gruesome. I wanted to run away and hide because this bloody great racing gorilla frightened me so much. There he was just about to jump on a RG500 Suzuki and dice at 160mph with Mick Grant and the boys, and he's operated by fucking elastic. It scared me for him, and it scared me even more for me – because I asked myself what I was getting involved in, if professional racing meant backyard Boris Karloff jobs like this. 'They're mad,' I thought, 'totally bloody mental,' little knowing that soon I'd be just as bonkers as them.

Maybe I already was. For the whole of '85 I was seriously competitive, rarely finishing outside the first two, but chucking away good positions far too often. As a result Robin Milton, a more experienced and canny competitor, pipped me to the 125cc UK Star championship. I also ended the season as runner-up in the 125cc Marlboro Clubman's series, and fourth in the ACU Star 80cc championship. But when I'd stayed on I'd been a winner. It was a feeling I liked.

CHAPTER 6

ME? HELP MICK GRANT? DON'T BE DAFT

As well as being the season I moved up to British championship events, 1985 had also been a momentous year in that it was the time I first got to know Mick Grant. Granty was also a racer from Huddersfield, but in a different league from the rest of us. Although he was coming towards the end of his career, he'd done everything we dreamed of doing. He'd won grand prix and TT races and ridden for most of the major factories – a huge name in racing. I'd actually seen him win on the Isle of Man, and knew he was the big racing celebrity round Huddersfield way. Whenever we drove past his house in Lepton we'd goggle and tell each other, 'That's where that Mick Grant lives,' not that anyone ever needed reminding. He was a legend, a proper local hero.

I'd first encountered him a couple of years earlier, around the time I was going to race meetings as Dave Leach's gofer. At the time Mick had just lost his contract to ride Honda's NR500 grand prix bike and was running his own team from his home, about four miles away on the other side of town. One day the payphone behind the front door rang. No one else was around so I picked it up.

'Hello.'

'It's Mick Grant speaking.'

'Mick Grant, the bike racer?' I quivered.

'Yes, that's right. I'd like to speak to your dad.'

'He's not in.'

'OK, maybe you can help?'

Me? Help Mick Grant? Don't be daft.

Mick explained what he was after. Apparently he'd got some new gearboxes he wanted to test, and since all he needed was a decent strip of tarmac rather than a full race circuit he wondered if he could use our runway. Dad was only too happy to help, so later that day Mick turned up with a truck, got out his bike, and spent an hour or so tearing up and down the airstrip whilst I watched him in near-disbelief. OK, it wasn't Mike Hailwood, but to a bike-obsessed 14-year-old, it was pretty damn close. I was star-struck. From being a kid who never stopped talking I was suddenly struck dumb.

Later Mick rang dad to thank him for use of the strip, in the process asking if he thought I'd be interested in going to Scarborough to watch him race the following weekend. Evidently he'd got the impression I was a 'nice, polite lad'.

So off we went to Scarborough for the Cock o' the North meeting. This was a step up from tagging along as Leachy's gofer. At night I kipped in Mick's team caravan, and by day was right in the centre of the action. It was brilliant, although I was still too nervous and overwhelmed to utter anything but the odd 'Ta, Mick.' It may even have still been 'Ta, Mr Grant.'

On Saturday evening Mick and his wife, Carol, took me out for a meal. At the time I'd never actually been in a restaurant, unless you count Harry Ramsdens or Old Mother Hubbards, both of which were just glorified fish and chip shops, so it was a different world to me. I was still totally tongue-tied, so Mick asked if he should order for me.

'Whitby crab,' he said, perusing the menu. 'Do you like crab?'

He may as well have asked if I liked grilled unicorn, but I said 'Yes' just to go along. When it arrived, the crab looked like nothing I'd ever eaten before, more like a big version of something you'd find under a stone, but I was determined not to upset anyone and choked it down. Mick rounded off the meal by paying with a credit card, something else I'd never laid eyes on in my life.

Mick's racing, though, went totally to pot. At the time Mick was a privateer, between his Honda NR500 contract and riding for Suzuki. He was running a big Formula One bike, basically a fettled GSX1000 engine in a race chassis. In practice his F1 bike blew a seal or something, spewed out all its coolant, boiled and seized up. As luck would have it – or not, as it transpired – two local blokes Mick knew, Dougie Ibbotson and Simon Beaumont, were also at the meeting. Simon was running a TZ750 Yamaha whilst Dougie, who was a good club rider who also did the odd national meeting, had bought Mick's old RG500 Suzuki off him the winter before. They were parked next to us in the paddock.

Now Mick had a major problem. There was no way his bike could be fixed before the race, and if he didn't ride he didn't get paid. He would have been on start money of perhaps a couple of grand, plus whatever prize money he could earn. Dougie wouldn't have been on any such deal. He wasn't running anywhere near the top half-dozen, and wouldn't have been on start money – effectively just a racing punter, filling out the grid. So Mick took him aside, and after a bit of to-and-fro arranged to slip him some money to borrow his bike.

It was all a bit rushed and frantic, but not as much as after Mick took the RG out for his first race and seized that as well. He stomped back to the paddock, spitting feathers and blaming Dougie, whilst Dougie was deeply pissed-off with Mick for wrecking his bike, not to mention his weekend. 'It's all right tootling round at 20mph,' ranted Mick, 'if you'd ever gone any quicker you might have had the right gearing and jets in the bloody thing, you useless sod.' It was scary, really serious and intense. But they calmed down after a while. Since Mick had begun the race he got his start money, after all, and later he fixed the bike for Dougie.

I'd see Mick just now and again after that, mainly at the airfield. It got to the point where he knew he was welcome to use the runway, so if he'd any testing to do he just turned up. Sometimes I'd arrive home from school and he'd be screaming up and down on his race bike. So by the time I started racing, about two years after that ill-fated Scarborough meeting, I sort of knew him, but not well. I was still in awe of the man.

One of the obstacles to me going racing was the lack of any leathers. I certainly couldn't afford any, and I'd already tapped up dad enough. As usual, dad had a simple solution: 'Why don't you go up and see Mick Grant? He'll know where to get them from, be able to get you a deal.' Dad liked the idea of that. He was always looking for a deal. It must have got to the stage where Mick regretted ever asking to use the airfield, but off I went on my pushbike to Mick's place.

It was a big, square, intimidating building. I knocked on the door, a bit out of breath because Lepton's at the top of a huge hill, and wishing I was somewhere else. Mick opened the door and smiled: 'Hello, young James. What can we do for you?'

It all came out in a torrent. 'It's my dad's idea, not mine… thought you might be able to help… I'm going to need some leathers because I've no leathers and need some leathers but I'm skint and I'm starting racing and need some leathers and…'

'Oh,' said Mick, 'you starting racing, lad?'

He actually seemed quite flattered. He wouldn't have known that I'd spent the previous year or so going racing with Leachy, and I suspect thought that maybe he'd inspired me a bit – although even I had never thought of kicking bits of bike around the Scarborough paddock as especially inspirational. But, yes, he was a kind of role model to anyone interested in bikes in the Huddersfield area.

Mick asked what bike I'd be racing, and was very positive when I told him about the Honda. 'Great. Good little bike, good thing to start on. If I can be of any use, just let me know. You never know, one day we might even be doing the same meetings.'

I was still digesting this rather fantastic concept when he ushered me out to a container in the yard – a full-sized lorry container, as big as an articulated truck. He opened the door and it was just full of leathers. It looked to me like 300 sets, but was probably nearer 25: Kawasaki leathers, Honda leathers, Suzuki leathers. It was like an Aladdin's cave of dead cows.

'How big are you?' he said, standing back and looking me over like a bloke in Burtons. Having sized me up he produced a set of Granby Motors leathers, which I think he'd raced in only the previous year. They were black with red and yellow arrows, Shell badges, lots of sponsors' lettering, the real McCoy.

'Here, they look as though they'll fit. Try them on.'

Luckily I'm about the same height as Mick, although he was a bit beamier, so they were a bit baggy but fitted well enough. The arms and legs were in the right places, but the arse was a bit droopy. I could live with that.

'Will them do you?' he said.

For me, the penny still hadn't dropped. 'What, *have* them? Like, they're mine?'

'Yes.'

And they said 'Grant' on the back in big letters. Bugger me, I thought, I'm the man. I rode back to the airfield still wearing them and slept in them that night. Mick also gave me a pair of racing gloves, and arranged for one of his sponsors, Kiwi, to send me a free helmet, which is what I began racing in.

If Pete Moore was the most positive influence on my early career – when he wasn't picking fights with rugby players – then Mick Grant was the man who would most guide me after I took the step up to bigger bikes. I'd first become aware of his interest in my racing late in '84, when I'd won in my first British championship meeting at Oulton Park. Since it was a championship meeting, Granty was there riding with the British Suzuki squad, and when I won he began to show a bit of interest.

Early the following year I entered the ACU Star championship meeting on the Woodland Circuit at Cadwell Park. This is the shortest option at Cadwell, taking in The Mountain and Hall Bends, then a right-hand hairpin back to the jump over Mountain. Although it wasn't often used, I'd ridden it a couple of times before, liked it, and fancied my chances. It was a tight, scratchy track, right up my street.

The big-hitters at the meeting were Roger Burnett, Reg Marshall and Granty, who was riding a Formula One and a Superstock Suzuki in Skoal Bandit colours. I was quickest in practice in the 125cc class, so a bit full of myself, and wandered along to the Bandit truck to see him.

At the time I still didn't know Mick well, but he was interested, asking me about the MBA and how it was going. I pointed out my van where Pete and Simpy were fiddling with the 125, and he said he might wander down to watch my race.

A couple of hours later, Mick was stood in the holding area at the top of The Mountain waiting for me to strut my stuff. Now, even more than the MT125, the MBA was always a brilliant starter. It was the first bike I'd used with total-loss ignition, which meant that a battery, rather than a magneto or generator, supplied the sparks. Once that sensor went past the magic eye…bang…you got a huge spark. It'd practically fire up if you just shouted at it. When the start flag dropped, I just gave it a desultory shove with one foot, and it crackled into life – a cracking start, from the front of the grid.

On the warm-up lap I'd seen Granty standing in the holding area in his leathers, ready to watch my race. All I could think was that I had to impress this man. It felt like waiting for an interview – but one that really mattered, rather than standing in a badly fitting suit outside a smelly factory in Huddersfield. But so far, so good. It was a chilly spring day, long before the arrival of tyre warmers, so when I tipped it into the hairpin a bit too eagerly on cold tyres, the front let go and I low-sided onto my arse. Luckily I'd been near the front, so although there was a bit of a mêlée behind me – bikes going in all directions, ramming into each other, scraping noises where other riders were sliding off – I hadn't lost many places by the time I picked the bike up and got going again.

I'd been fairly wound-up at the start, but naturally all this kerfuffle had given me an extra dose of the old red mist. What racing nous I possessed, which was little enough to begin with, had been washed away on a torrent of adrenalin. I managed to career past a few people, one of them into Old Hall, totally panicked, out of shape and out of control…then into second place with another death-or-glory move at Hall Bends, before drawing a bead on the leader. At the Hairpin I scuttled inside on the brakes to take the lead. As the bike finished fish-tailing past and I gathered it into the corner, I had my first coherent thought since the flag dropped. 'Right,' I told myself, 'we're all right, in the lead and in control…let's be steady.' Then I grabbed a handful of clutch to keep the engine in the power band coming out of the Hairpin and flicked myself over the top of the tyre wall.

As I picked myself up again, the MBA was still spinning round like a mad thing in the middle of the track. I wasn't hurt and might have been able to carry on, but a couple of other bikes hit mine, breaking off a lever and a few other bits. So, in one and a half laps I'd led twice, fallen off twice, and was now out of the race and the meeting. With Mick watching. With hindsight I suppose if I'd wanted to give him an honest impression of James Whitham, Racer, I couldn't have done much better. But that definitely wasn't how it felt at the time.

From his vantage point at the top of The Mountain, Mick had

enjoyed a grandstand view of both my crashes and at least two overtaking manoeuvres committed by a man who was obviously without all his marbles. Pete and Simpy had been standing nearby. Apparently he'd done a lot of tut-tutting and head-shaking before walking off, presumably in disgust. So, if it was an interview, I'd failed. Emphatically.

As the season went on my riding settled down. I was still a bit wild, but subsequently did a lot more winning than crashing on the MBA and, although I wasn't aware of it at the time, Mick was taking notice of my results.

Now and again he'd take me aside. 'Look mate,' he'd say, 'I'm not being funny, but if you want my advice…' at which point he'd carry on whether you wanted his advice or not. 'If you want to make a living out of this job,' he'd continue, 'you're going to have to stop pissing around with those 125s. Mark my words, this lark is going to be all about big four-strokes, big road-based diesels. The British racing mentality has always been about 350s and above, and that's the way this job's going. You're not going anywhere with those little bikes – I'm not being funny, you're just not.'

I was still digesting the notion of racing bikes as a job – maybe it had been to Granty, but at this stage it certainly wasn't to me – when he added that I was also going to have to race on the Isle of Man, which had never entered my head as a career move either. 'If you ever get into a factory team, they'll expect you to do the TT. You'd be better learning your way round the Island now whilst nobody gives a shit how you get on, than you'll ever be weighed down by a contract.'

Mmm. The Isle of Man. And I'd been there and had great memories of the place. Since I'd started racing I'd sort of thought that I probably would race there one day. I was never 'will I, won't I' about the TT. As a northern rider, in particular, it was just something you eventually did. But I definitely didn't see it as part of some sort of Mick Grant master plan, just as the same sort of fun as hacking around Cadwell, only longer. I was really thrown when he rounded off his monologue by telling me I might actually make a living out of racing. 'You've got something,' he said. 'You could go a long way.'

Mick's comments carried a lot of weight, because of who he was, yet they seemed slightly unreal to me. As far as I was concerned I already had a job as an apprentice toolmaker at Taylor and Jones. I didn't particularly like it, but that was what I did. Racing might be my be-all and end-all, but it was for the weekends, a hobby. Nobody had ever suggested before that I could actually make a living out of racing motorbikes. That was something that only people you read about in the bike papers did. It was nothing to do with me. The whole idea seemed surreal.

On the other hand, it seemed a pretty attractive concept. At the time I was earning crap wages, something like £25 a week on a Youth Opportunity programme, yet even in a period when there wasn't a lot of money in domestic racing, you'd get something like £250 in prize money for winning a British championship round – and I'd already had a few pay-days like that. Even UK Stars paid £180 for a win. In other words, they paid you up to ten weeks wages just for going round a racetrack and enjoying yourself. Even with all the costs involved, it was a very agreeable equation, particularly as turning up at Taylor and Jones on a regular basis was becoming increasingly inconvenient.

In fact it sounded like such a good idea that I promptly put it to the back of my mind and got on with my racing. But I did go to the Isle of Man.

CHAPTER 7

'SHOULDN'T SIMPY BE BACK BY NOW?'

Even without Mick Grant's urging, in the mid-'80s, especially if you were from the North of England, it was always expected that you'd race on the Isle of Man. Looking back now, although it certainly didn't seem so at the time, it's clear that we were on the cusp of two eras – where for the first time you had the choice of doing the short circuits and ignoring the TT. The first person I actually heard say outright that he wasn't going to do it was Terry Rymer in '87, at a time when we were both promising up-and-comers. He felt he didn't need to do anything but the shorts, and that was that. It had never occurred to me that I had a choice.

From around '84 onwards, my second season in racing, I'd been surrounded by Isle of Man talk, mainly from Pete Moore and Butch Cartwright. The TT was still something that mattered, the place where all the top stars strutted their stuff. Pete had done the Newcomers Manx Grand Prix in '84, and was going back for a full go in '85. I decided that'd do me, too, but in those days there were classes for neither 125cc nor production bikes. So I didn't have a bike and couldn't borrow one, but Rod Lee, for whom I was racing an 80cc Kawasaki now and again, managed to arrange a bike through Bob van de Graf, his Dutch contact. It was basically a Kawasaki KR250S, a 250cc tandem twin road bike with a bit of tuning. It was a model not well known in Britain – the broadly similar KR1S came later – but they did well on the Continent. It wasn't the most reliable thing, didn't carburate too well, but had good top-end speed.

Team Huddersfield set off for the Isle of Man ferry in Pete's Transit with his Yamaha TZ250G and Kawasaki GPZ900, Simpy's GPZ600, my dad's cherished Honda 400-four for running errands, and my 250 Kawasaki. Squashed in front of the van were me, Pete, Simpy and Carl Toffolo, who wasn't really into bikes but knew us from going to the same pub and thought it'd be an entertaining trip. And was it.

The ferry docked in Douglas early on Saturday morning, and we drove down to our digs at the Grosvenor, a typical Douglas guesthouse where Pete had arranged a bit of a discount deal. We even had the run of a garage round the back. Despite mounting evidence to the contrary, we actually thought we were quite organised, and I was personally convinced I was the most together racer in the world. Inevitably, and almost immediately, it started going very badly wrong.

We'd been up all night getting to the Island, and while the rest of us got our heads down, Simpy, who worked nights in Stork Brothers' Mill as a carder and finisher so was still wide awake, decided to go for an early morning lap. We waved him off on the 400-four, thinking he couldn't do much damage with that old slug, and went to bed. At about 11 o'clock we got up and went for breakfast in the Ranch Café on Broadway, then off to the garage to unload the van.

Sooner or later someone asked, 'Shouldn't Simpy be back by now?' By then he'd been gone about five hours, so we thought he probably should, but imagined he was up at the grandstand, enjoying the unaccustomed daylight. But no, he wasn't, and didn't even turn up for dinner. Next, the police station. No news of him there either.

Nobles Hospital was looking like a better bet with every moment, but the story was the same: no Simpy. But apparently there were a couple of cottage hospitals I might try. I rang the one in Ramsey.

'You wouldn't happen to have a Simon Sykes in there, would you?'

'Yes, Mr Sykes – he's just left.'

'Has he come off a bike?'

'Yes, I believe so.'

Well, at least he wasn't dead. We couldn't get in touch with him – no mobile phones then – so headed off to Ramsey in the van. We knew we were looking for something, we just didn't know what – until we reached Milntown Cottage and saw a huge fresh scrape mark in the road. 'Mmm,' we thought, 'this'll be it.' We got out to investigate and there, behind the cottage wall was dad's beloved 400-four, which a few hours earlier had been mint but was now bent, scraped and twisted, with a mangled front end. There was no one around, no one to tell, so we chucked the Honda in the van and drove back to the Grosvenor. And who was already there but Simpy, wearing an embarrassed grin and surgical gauze over a few bits of missing skin.

It turned out that a woman had reversed out of her drive on her way to work and collected Simpy as he hammered through. He wasn't insured, but she wouldn't make a claim because he'd slid half under the car and she thought she'd killed him until he got to his feet and chirruped something obscene, which is why the police were none the wiser. Placating dad would be trickier. 'It's not too bad,' I lied to him on the phone. He was livid.

From there it went from bad to worse. Although I'd been to the Island lots of times, I'd never done that many laps of the TT course. But I was riding round in practice with people whose names I knew from club racing. I already knew I was miles faster than them on short circuits and couldn't see any reason it'd be any different on the Isle of Man. So I set off on my first practice session, muttering to myself that they'd better not get in the way of this hot new ace from Huddersfield. Even before the bottom of Bray Hill, about 600 yards into the lap, I caught up with an Aermacchi which had set off five seconds earlier. Its rider was wearing an orange jacket, just like me, which I thought simply meant he was a novice. I'd no idea classic racers had to wear them as well. All that entered my head was that no other novice was going to beat me, no way. Little did I know this was probably his millionth lap of the Mountain Course. It was my first.

'Come on, get out of the road you useless newcomer,' I'm thinking, right up his chuff half a mile into the lap. I passed him on the brakes into Quarter Bridge and forgot all about him, until he came thundering under me through Snugborough, then took Union Mills neat as you like, tucked right in on the perfect line. That should have told me something, but it didn't.

The Kawasaki had 20mph on the Aermacchi, so I got in front of him on the next straight, but couldn't get rid of him, although I did some pretty stupid things trying. At most places I was on the wrong line, running up and down kerbs, lost. Eventually I reached Sulby Straight to find it littered with marshals waving flags and about 20 riders stopped in the middle of the road. Apparently a tree had fallen across the track somewhere ahead. So I stopped behind them and killed my engine, the model of the cool professional, only to be nearly knocked off the bike by a huge thump in the back. It's the bloke on the Aermacchi, absolutely fuming. 'You're dangerous…you want locking up…you're going to hurt someone and kill yourself…it's people like you who give this place a bad name. Go home!'

I think you could say he was upset, although I never found out who he was. If he's reading this, can I say belatedly that he was dead right? I spent the evening with a right sick feeling in the pit of my stomach. It actually taught me a lesson. I cooled down a bit after that and knuckled down to learning my way round.

A day or so later after practice, Pete announced that he was going to stick a number plate on his GPZ900 and take Carl for a lap as a reward for being the team gofer. Off they blasted, both wearing just paddock jackets, and – the Simpy business was obviously catching – didn't come back.

By this time we'd developed a well-rehearsed routine. I rang the police station.

'We've lost some mates again. Any accidents on the course?'

'Ah, yes, there's been a big accident on the Mountain. They're in Nobles.'

It turned out they'd had a blowout – or so Pete said – at the right-hander after the Bungalow. Pete, Carl and the whole shooting match had cartwheeled into a ditch. Pete had bust a collarbone and wrist and lost some skin; Carl had also lost a load of skin. They weren't in any danger, but both spent a couple of days in hospital.

At the time, the man of the moment was one Carl Fogarty, riding a Yamaha TZ250J, a purpose-built racing bike. Around the paddock he was seen as a bit of a spoiled rich kid who had the best gear and brand new leathers, while most of us were scratching around to afford the next set of piston rings and living on chips.

I'd no idea he was a hard little bastard, even then. On Thursday afternoon, by which time I was feeling as though I was getting the hang of the place, I set off for a lap right behind him. At the time I'd lapped at around 97mph, fractionally quicker than him, and I wanted to see what this flash kid from Blackburn could do. We found ourselves locked together for the whole lap, riding really close, really hard.

I've talked about that lap with him since, and he certainly remembers it. He couldn't believe a proddy bike was that quick. Afterwards I strolled up to him, saying nothing, just with a smug grin on my face. His Yam was peppered with stone chips from the Kawasaki's back wheel and he looked a bit sick.

Being mugged on the Sulby Straight was by now a distant memory. Proddy 250 beats TZ250 racer? Obviously there was only one conclusion: I was hot stuff on the roads. So I set off for yet another lap, which is where it all went wrong. I ran out of road at the Bungalow, crashed on the gravel and broke my collarbone. I ought to have been disappointed, but all I could think was, 'Helicopter…mint. I'm in for a ride in a chopper!' Unfortunately it was needed more urgently somewhere else and instead, hours later, a creaky old ex-army Bedford ambulance pitched up and they slid me in the back. I was all right apart from the collarbone and a bit of missing skin. I definitely wasn't about to die. Already lying in the Bedford, looking very dazed, was a bloke who was definitely in a worse state than me, but still not on the danger list. As we bounced along the Mountain road on our way to Nobles, I asked him what happened.

'Oh, I can't believe it,' he croaked. 'I remember coming out of Ramsey Hairpin and knowing it was flat to the Gooseneck and deciding I should stop being a pussy.' And it wasn't as though he was on an old nail. He'd been riding a Suzuki RG500.

'What about bleedin' Waterworks?'

'Exactly.'

He and the bike had gone over the cliff. The bike was destroyed and they'd had to physically carry him out through the jungle and brambles between there and Tower Bends, which is why the ambulance took a while to arrive.

Since I'd been concussed, I had a night in Nobles – amazingly the only one I've ever spent. Pete and Carl had only just been discharged. I think the bed was still warm. Naturally the ward was full of beaten-up racers, with bits hanging up on wires and tubes poking in and out. I remember it best for the BBC News, which showed Randy Mamola doing that amazing rodeo stunt on the Rothman's Honda. I couldn't understand how come he could stay on a bike doing that whilst I was in here after a silly mistake at the Bungalow.

The next day we made a token effort to fix the bike and do the race, but it just wasn't on. Foggy went on to win the Newcomers and finish third in the 250 race, as well as setting the fastest lap, 104mph. That's when I first thought the lad could go places. He might have looked scary but even then he was safer than me.

So by Friday, Simpy's the only member of the 1985 Huddersfield MGP Assault Team still operational. Or so I thought. At almost precisely the same instant I was sliding past the Bungalow bogs on my backside, Simpy was having a truly massive crash of his own. Apparently he was hammering along on the Mountain section, went into a fog bank, slowed down a bit but was still cracking on. Then, about half a second before he hit it, he saw a bike lying on its side in the middle of the road. *Kerrump!* He completely knocked the front end off his 600 and slid down the road for miles. When he stopped, he gave himself the usual once-over and stood up, thinking, 'Christ, I've hit a bike, gone down the road at 80mph…and I'm all right.'

Then it occurred to him that somebody might be concerned, hearing all this carnage in the mist. But there were still bikes screaming past him as he stood at the side of the road. So he yelled at the top of his voice:

'I'm all right. I'm all right.'

Nothing.

This was all feeling a bit unreal. He walked back towards all the wreckage, thinking part of this mess was someone else's crash and wondering where they were. After a while he encountered a wrinkled old bloke wearing a white coat and holding a yellow flag, peering down into a ditch where a guy named Dave Woollams was spitting out most of his teeth. Apparently Dave had become disorientated in the fog and run into the ditch. But other than

Dave revising his dentition, nothing was happening. No one had a radio, and the next marshal's post was invisible in the fog. Eventually a travelling marshal arrived on a big Honda and gave Simpy a lift back to the grandstand. The rider definitely knew what he was doing, for Simpy said he'd never been so fast on the TT course, and was never so scared in his life. I think he preferred the crash.

So out of three riders and five bikes, we had four smashed-up bikes, three smashed-up riders, one mangled mate, and a TZ350G that hadn't even been taken out of the van. It probably wasn't Huddersfield's finest hour.

Naturally this didn't deter me in the least from going back to do the TT the following year. Again, I had the problem of not owning an eligible bike. I wasn't enough of an Isle of Man prospect for anyone to be willing to lend me bikes. In fact I was probably better known at Nobles Hospital than for my talent over the Mountain Course.

The only option was to buy a bike, a Mk 3 Suzuki Gamma, a beautiful little thing, brand new. Pete Moore stripped it, checked the squish clearances, ran it, jetted it. It was utterly legal and bog-standard, but it ran well. In those days there were hardly any modifications allowed in the production class; you just put plates on and off you went.

Mat Oxley was the man to beat that year, along with Barry Woodland, Graham Cannell and Gary Padgett. But by then the 400cc four-strokes were taking over from the 250cc two-strokes, so there wasn't a hope of me winning, even if I'd known my way round. The target was simply to be the first two-stroke home, which I managed in 12th place overall, lapping at 99mph. Compared to the mayhem of the previous year it was utterly lacking in drama – the most trouble-free, enjoyable TT I've ever had. And I came away in one piece, learned my way round a bit, didn't get beaten up on Sulby Straight and had a TT replica to put on the mantelpiece.

CHAPTER 8

A PROPER JOB

At heart I've always been a grafter. My dad saw to that. But the thought of regular work appealed about as much as regular trips to casualty – probably rather less, given my later history. But inevitably the time came to leave school and get a proper job. Although I'd done reasonably well academically, partly through mum's influence, there was never a question in my mind of further education. Whilst I did quite well in exams, passing nine GCSEs, including three 'A' grades, I never had an ambition to stay on for sixth form and university. Instead, I always saw myself as a practical sort of bloke. Besides, I liked the thought of being able to get a job and buy things, especially things with engines, rather than being skint for the next five years. Being a teacher, Mum was keen for me to stay on, whilst dad wasn't too bothered either way. In fact the person who applied the most pressure for me to stay was Mr Lenton, my metalwork teacher, who'd told mum at a parent's evening that I'd make a natural teacher. But that wasn't the way I wanted to go, especially as leaving school also more or less coincided with me starting racing. There was no way I could have afforded that if I'd stayed on at school.

Dad found me my first job through his cronies in flying, an aircraft engineer's apprenticeship with Blackpool and Fylde Aero Club, which serviced light aeroplanes at Squire's Gate airport. In many ways it was an excellent job, and in the brief time I was there I enjoyed it. What wasn't so enjoyable was the 70-mile trip each way to get there, the living away from home and – most crucially of all, as it turned out – the difficulty of also finding the time demanded by my new-found other career as a motorcycle racer.

The Aero Club wasn't a big outfit. There was the Chief Engineer, John Dodds, then two qualified engineers underneath him, both lads in their 20s, and at the bottom of the pile was me and another apprentice, Mark Bird. Mark was a Blackpool lad, exactly the same age as me, doing exactly the same things, which meant he was also exactly as unskilled. One of our duties – the only one we could be trusted with, initially at least – was to make the mid-morning and mid-afternoon tea on a week-on, week-off rota.

It happened to be my turn for tea duty after the factory had shut down for a two-week holiday. Naturally – you probably know how sloppy and squalid factory tearooms can be – no one had thought to wash the mugs after they were last used a fortnight before. In the meantime they'd all developed some rather luxuriant furry moulds. The tearoom didn't have much by way of washing facilities, not even a sink, but I took a bit of time washing my mug out, because I'd seen this fungus and no one else had, and I figured that what they didn't know wouldn't harm them. So from everyone else's mug I just sort of scraped out the biggest lumps with a spoon.

No worries. Nobody complained about the taste, so I didn't think any more about it until a few of the staff began complaining about upset stomachs. By the next day two of them had developed full-blown dysentery and didn't turn up for work at all. They never did get to the bottom of it, just assumed some sort of bug had been going through the place. That, it turned out, was my major contribution to the British aerospace industry.

To get across the Pennines I had a Fizzie, a 50cc Yamaha FS1E – except that I'd bolted on a tuning kit and it actually displaced 65cc. It was a brilliant little thing, so much so that a few years ago a bought another one and restored it, which must be even sadder than keeping my first Carnaby programme. Since the Fizzie was supposedly a moped, and I hadn't passed my bike test anyway, I couldn't go on the obvious route via the motorways. Instead, early every Monday morning, I had to use the A-roads through Burnley and Preston.

The journey took an hour and three-quarters, and when winter set in it was bitterly cold. I'd have to stop every half hour or so, just to warm myself up. Mostly, though, I'd try to do it on the move. The

Fizzie was ideal for that, because it had a nice hand-shaped cylinder which you could cup in your palm and try to get back some of the feeling in your hands. Warming your left hand was easy, because you could still hold the throttle with your right. Warming your other hand, holding the throttle and steering with the wrong hand crossed over, was trickier.

Later I got a bigger bike, an overhead cam CB125S, which wasn't all that much quicker but at least meant I could use the motorway to get to work and back. But the travel, and paying for digs, was too much. After about eight months I packed in the job and Blackpool breathed a collective sigh of relief as the risk of a cholera epidemic wiping out half the population diminished.

So for a while I was back home full-time, drawing the dole and bumming around. This period happened to coincide with some friends finishing sixth form and also having nothing much to do while they waited to go to university, so there were pals about. Some of them were also into bikes, so we'd whiz around Yorkshire and generally hang out, and at weekends I'd be off racing. Although I enjoyed the novelty of having nothing to do but mess about and work on my race bike, dad wasn't best pleased. Bumming and scrounging weren't exactly at the core of his belief system.

'You're going to have to do something,' he'd tell me, in between trying to fix me up with a job he considered suitable. After a couple of months I was inclined to agree with him, so, in spring '84, I started looking for work. Eventually I applied for a job as a trainee draughtsman at a local engineering firm, Taylor and Jones. They made, and still do, reamers and cutters – anything hardened for lathes and the like.

Although I got an interview, the job they'd advertised went to someone else. But happily when the guy who interviewed me rang to tell me I hadn't got the position because of this, that and the other, which I didn't particularly want to hear, he added that I'd nonetheless made a good impression and that they'd like to offer me another position that would soon be available. I'd be a shop-floor toolmaker's apprentice, and if I were to take the job it would save them the bother of advertising it.

Taylor and Jones was an OK place. It was kind of old-fashioned, with that lovely aroma of cutting oil and metal. There must have been 50 or 60 people working there, which seemed quite a crowd when you all sat down for your mid-morning break. There was a staff canteen with a couple of women making tea and sandwiches, the usual factory banter with everyone puffing away on tabs.

Most of the staff seemed to have been there forever, which was a novel concept to me, as were some of their habits. Many of them seemed really stuck in their ways. They'd turn up for work with sandwiches their wives had packed, the contents based on what day of the week it was, so that if Bill had corned beef you knew it had to be Tuesday. Then there was the pecking order, which didn't seem much different from picking football teams at school. The very first day I was in the canteen, new and nervous, no sooner had I sat down with a cuppa than I noticed everyone was looking at me. Were my flies undone? Did I have a big bogey dangling from my nose?

'What?' I said. 'What's the matter?'

Apparently I was in John's seat. So I moved. Same deal. That one, apparently, was Steve's. Then Bob's.

'Where the fuck can I sit, then?'

'Oh you've got to sit over there,' they said, pointing to the grottiest corner of the room where all the untouchables used to sit. It all seemed to be part of some unwritten law. I think that when you finally retire from Taylor and Jones they don't give you a gold watch, just your old canteen seat to take home.

Apart from the odd slightly bizarre tradition, the place was all right. I learnt quite a lot, and much of it was stuff that truly interested me. Some of the work was maintenance engineering for the factory itself – fixing machines, installing machines, all hands-on work which was really just a step up from the sort of fiddling-about I was used to at the airfield. It wasn't the most high-tech place. They had a couple of CNC machines and some NC rigs, but mostly it was steadfastly non-computerised, non-digital – just lots of cylindrical and surface grinding machines, with big old-fashioned wheels on the side and a Bill or a John or a Steve who knew how to work out his tables when he wasn't hogging a seat in the canteen. I learnt quite a lot about grinding, turning and other ways of making lots of swarf.

Hardening processes were the plant's big thing, and I learned quite a lot about that too, although the surface treatment plant was the last place you actually wanted to work. The fumes were bad enough, but the names they used to throw about gave me the willies. For instance, they use a lot of cyanide in metal hardening, and even as an ignorant 16-year-old I figured that cyanide probably wasn't so good for you.

When I wasn't being gassed, I was learning about inspection, which was Taylor and Jones's other big thing, since they had to work to such close tolerances. I could bore anybody rigid about comparators and Brinell testing. Overall it was an interesting place to be. As well as practical experience in the factory, they'd have us going to Huddersfield Tech in the evenings, doing what was basically a metallurgy course.

I was kind of looking forward to going to Tech, partly because I knew they had a roomful of nice lathes and mills and partly because I had such positive memories of metalwork at school, but the course was disappointingly dull. It was mainly concerned with the theoretical side of Taylor and Jones's business, so the lathes may as well not have been there. Instead we discovered dendritic grain structure in metals and peered through a lot of microscopes, whilst I wanted to be watching swarf flying off shiny bits of metal. It seemed like a lot of hard work. Maybe if I'd known then that Soichiro Honda, the founder of Honda Motors, had trained as a metallurgist I'd have taken more interest. But probably not.

My position at Taylor and Jones was one of the first under the Youth Opportunity Programme. It was a proper, old-style apprenticeship, except that my wages were paid entirely by the Government – all £27 per week. Some people might be inclined to look back through the rosy mists of time and suggest that was a lot of money back then, but let me tell you, it bleeding wasn't. It was a disaster. When I'd worked at Blackpool it had cost me about £17 a week to live in someone's attic. Because that was such a large chunk of my wages, mum had let me live at home at weekends for free. As soon as I began at Taylor's, it was a whole new deal: 'Right, Mr Apprentice Toolmaker, let's be having it,' and more than half my wage disappeared. Looking back that's fair enough, but it didn't half sting at the time.

I could barely afford to run a bike, let alone buy a van for my race bike, but dad came to the rescue again when he bought me a van after I passed my test, 23 December 1984. It was one of the original Renault Trafics, an ex-Tool Hire workhorse; not that you could tell, because it was dented out of all recognition from being bashed inside and out. It had more dings than Big Ben, but it ran well enough and was exactly what I needed.

Although dad had also paid the first year's insurance, he wasn't keen on me running the Trafic on a day-to-day basis. I suspect he was worried I'd fill it with mates, get pissed and stuff it into a drystone wall. If I did take it out, I'd be bombarded with questions about where I was going and who with – reasonable concerns for any father, although a bit of an arse-ache at the time. But he was more than happy with the idea of me driving 200 miles to Snetterton. He sensed, I think, that by that time I was dead serious about my racing and wouldn't be going crackers with the bike in the back, which was true. But the rest of the time it was probably best that he didn't know what I got up to.

So partly to placate dad, partly because I've always enjoyed riding road bikes, I still ran a bike day-to-day. Naturally that caused me to gravitate towards some of the other younger guys at Taylor and Jones who also had bikes. One of them was called Darren Dewar, although everyone knew him as 'Bone', because he had a big Mohican haircut – a right bone-head. He was sort of an original Gothic punk type, with trousers tucked into big Doc Martens which came halfway up his legs. He looked fierce but was actually a nice lad, except that he was totally crackers on a bike – and fast.

Since I was well into racing by then I was convinced Bone would have made a pretty good racer himself, because he was proper mental, which is obviously the main qualification. He lived at Meltham, a village towards the Pennines from Huddersfield. Although Meltham itself is quite pleasant, the council estate Bone lived on wasn't quite so tranquil. Everyone local called it 'Badlands' because it was a bit rough.

Although my racing took up almost all my money, so I didn't drink very often, now and again Bone and I would go out for a pint, and occasionally he'd come to watch me race. But since the roads to

Crosland Moor and to Meltham were the same for the first couple of miles, the main racing activity would be on our way home from Taylor and Jones. Every single day we'd race each other over the same twisty bit of road, him on his Suzuki GT175 and me on a Yamaha DT175. Our route used to go past the back of a big cotton mill. Soon our little race became a major attraction to the guys working on the loading bay, so every day there would be an impromptu grandstand with guys shouting and waving as we came rattling by, heads down and screaming these 175s for all they were worth. As often as not Bone would be in front. He was every bit as good as me, but even more prepared to take mad risks.

I don't know what he ran his GT175 on, because he never had any money – not a cent. Every penny seemed to disappear into beer and women. He'd never spend anything on his bike, using his tyres until they were mostly canvas. Once he snapped his throttle cable, where the nipple attaches it to the twist-grip, and taped the outer to his handlebar and clipped a pair of Mole grips on the inner. For anyone else this would have been just a get-you-home bodge. But not Bone. True, he struggled with it for the first week or so, but after that he was deadly. When he perfected the art of wheelying the damn thing by yanking on the Mole grips, he decided he didn't need a new cable at all.

For obvious reasons he was also a big fan of a particular MoT test centre, where they'd pass anything a magnet would stick to. I've taken bikes there myself, knowing with absolute certainty that they ought to fail, and they've flown through. If your bike was bad enough to fail an MoT test there then you must have delivered it in a van, because you'd be taking your life in your hands even to sit on it, let alone ride it there.

Meanwhile, in the industrial heartland of Huddersfield, matters were coming to a head at Taylor and Jones. By '85 I was making more in prize money than the factory paid me in wages. Despite this, training and a career seemed the right thing to do, since I had no real thought of earning a long-term living any other way. The trouble was that it was becoming a real bind to get Fridays off, which I needed to get down to meetings for practice. The only times I didn't need Fridays off were when I was injured, which was also pissing Taylors off. Once I broke a collarbone and didn't get back to work until after the other collarbone – which I'd snapped as soon as I could ride again – was healed.

Finally, in June '85 my boss, Mr Roebuck, called me into the office. I was slightly intimidated by him at the time. 'Look, James,' he said, 'we think there's a future for you here at Taylor and Jones. And we have plans for you. But this isn't working. You've got to make a decision: racing or work.'

My first instinct was to say I needed time to mull it over, whilst actually thinking Taylor and Jones could take a running jump. But, being a bit of a chicken and never much of a one for confrontation, I didn't want to burn my bridges. Then I remembered that I'd already entered the Manx Grand Prix, which would definitely mean two weeks off work even if I came back unscathed. I'd no idea how I was going to break that to him, but thought I'd better come clean.

So I told him I needed two weeks off in a couple of months.

'What for?'

'To race at the Manx Grand Prix.'

He gave me that 'you haven't listened to a word I've said' look, before adding, 'It's your choice. But if you go to the Isle of Man, don't bother coming back.'

You can't say Mr Roebuck wasn't true to his word. When I got back from the Manx, there was my P45 in the mail. I've not had a proper job since.

CHAPTER 9

TO EUROPE ON A SHOESTRING

By the spring of 1986 I still didn't really see racing as a career but one way or another I seemed to be on an upward spiral and was more than happy to go where it was taking me. And of course I no longer had a job to get in the way. The most obvious step appeared to be to race in Europe, for which you needed a special licence from the sport's governing body, the ACU. Because I'd had a good year in '85, and had been leading the British championship for a while, getting on their official grading list was no problem. Pete packed in his job to come with me, Simpy took time off from Stork Brothers Mill to come to a few meetings early in the season, and a guy called Martin Wibberly, known as Wibbly Wobbly, but usually Wibbsy to his face, also tagged along. And off we went to tackle the European championship on the MBA. Europe was to prove a paradise for a fun-loving, piss-taking bunch like us.

The first championship round was at Vallelunga, not far from Rome. It soon became clear that having a bloke like Pete in your corner was priceless, because he was not only a pretty good engineer, but had done a lot of racing, so understood the game and understood what was going on with me. Usually he seemed to have more idea of what was going on in my head than I did. By this time the MBA was in its third season – well looked-after and still a sound, competitive machine, but showing its age here and there. In one practice session it just stopped dead. It clearly hadn't seized a piston – the engine was turning over easily enough – but just died. I pushed it back to the paddock, where Pete dived in with the spanners, and the problem was soon obvious. The MBA's ignition had a brass rotor with two pickups which timed the spark, but the rotor had worn to the point where almost nothing was left to hold it onto the shaft. The threads had practically disappeared. The engine had died when the rotor had fallen off the shaft and we were probably lucky it hadn't seized, because it must have thrown out the spark timing whilst it was wobbling about.

Without ignition we may as well have not had a bike. We couldn't find a new one, and probably couldn't have afforded it even if we had, and to fix it properly we'd have at least needed a lathe, so Pete set to bodging it as best he could. Using bits of pop can and Araldite, he somehow persuaded it to go back where it belonged, then used a dial gauge to shim it so that it spun true and with the right clearance on the shaft. Amazingly, it not only lasted practice and the race but a couple more meetings, until we were able to get hold of a new one.

Despite all this I managed to qualify on the front row, third or fourth, which tickled us. The race went just as well. I led for the first seven laps and was dicing for the lead the whole time, but ended up running onto the grass with about two laps to go, dropping to fourth. Overall we were elated. We'd gone to Vallelunga with no idea how competitive I might be, but came away knowing that I had the pace to run with these Continental lads.

A few hundred quid in prize money was also pretty welcome. We'd set off from England with about £300 in cash, a couple of packets of biscuits, a few tins of soup and a damn-you-all smile apiece. '£300,' I'd thought, 'that'll get us anywhere.' But by the time we'd reached Italy we'd literally run out of money and had nothing left for diesel to get home – until the fourth-place prize money came to our rescue.

When there was no prize money, we needed other techniques to stretch the cash. Running a small team in Europe, you learn a lot not just about racing but how to get by. I grew up a lot that year, became more street-wise, especially in the ways of service station foraging. We soon learned never to go anywhere without a long piece of hose and a jerry can. Even some of the circuits provided complimentary diesel. Typically, rather than be allocated a garage we'd be shoved out to paddock five or somewhere equally remote from mains electricity. Instead, power would come from huge mobile generators – with equally large diesel tanks. We had no hesitation in liberating fuel from these too.

On the way out to Italy we'd called into Holland and collected some parts from Bob van de Graf, who'd supplied the 250cc Kawasaki I'd ridden at the Manx Grand Prix the previous autumn. I was still on good terms with Rod Lee, owner of the 80cc Kawasaki I'd ridden the year before and who by now was even helping us with a bit of sponsorship. Rod used to do business with Bob, who supplied grey import motocrossers from a shop in Amsterdam. At some time Rod must have mentioned to him I'd be racing an MBA in Europe, and it turned out that Bob had a stack of trick parts made by the Fokker factory precisely for bikes like my MBA.

So we'd arrived at Europort on the ferry, motored up to Bob's and picked up all sorts of trick race gear – ignition packs and other stuff – paid for by Lee Brothers. Then, two weeks after I finished fourth at Vallelunga, we found ourselves racing at Zolder in Bob's backyard. He turned up to watch. Again, I was dicing in the top four or five, battling with Thierry Fuez on a LCR/MBA, a couple of Team Italia guys, Claudio Borganova and Paolo Casoli, a German bloke called Adi Stadler and three or four others. About eight of us were having a right set-to for the lead, then, late on in the race, my MBA broke a gudgeon pin and completely destroyed itself. Although it was encouraging to have been up with the front-runners again, we were devastated. All that driving, all that effort, with nothing to show for it but a pile of scrap and a bloody great bill. We packed up the van and drove home, feeling low.

Even in the 125cc class, many of the Europeans teams had budgets we could only dream about. The attitude was different too. So many young Continental riders, especially the Italians and Spanish, seemed to regard bike racing as a career, a profession, almost from the off – or that's how it seems by the time you meet them. Brits are different – I think in general, and it was certainly true of me – tending to regard it all as more of a laugh. Most of us seem surprised to be doing it at all, and if we ever do get really serious about it, it's relatively late in the day.

Not that all Europeans are dead serious. We met one guy, a Finn, Ari Ramo, who was doing the 500cc Euro series. He and his brother Kelvi, who was his mechanic, were parked up next to us at Vallelunga with a Suzuki RG500. They were interested in maybe racing in the UK, partly because there didn't seem to be many meetings in Finland. We were already scheduled to go to Mallory for the Spring Cup meeting on the way home, so I popped off to a payphone, rang the circuit, and got him an entry and a few quid in start money. The organisers were quite keen to have a few foreign 'names', even obscure ones like 'Ramo'.

We saw Ari's van as soon as we arrived at Mallory, and had just parked next to it when his side door slid open and out strode the Finn in flip-flops and a bathrobe, with a towel under his arm, demanding to know where the sauna was. And this is March. The best we could offer was for him to come into our van and I'd leave the kettle on.

Despite that Ari kind of liked England – mainly because he seemed to like drinking even more than racing. He and Kelvi took to the post-race booze-up like professionals. Ari wasn't spectacularly fast, just a good lad, and not even as serious about his racing as we were – which at the time wasn't a lot. A year or two later Kelvi was killed when he crashed the van travelling between meetings.

So there's serious professional racing and there's party racing. And then there's luck, although a lot of the good fortune that matters doesn't happen on the track. Who you happen to bump into, who knows who, and the impression you make…these things usually seem of no significance at the time, but can open doors and make seemingly impossible things happen. Bike racing might appear to be a huge, global entity, but in reality it's quite a small, closed word – a world essentially held together by personal relationships.

Bob van de Graf didn't mention anything to us, but he must have spoken with Rod Lee after the Zolder meeting, although I didn't learn of this until several years later. Evidently Bob told Rob flat out that if I'd had a better bike I could definitely have won. From our perspective it soon became clear that because we were doing longer, tougher races, and above all because we just didn't have sufficient money to chuck at it, the MBA was becoming unreliable.

It became dispiriting: Hockenheim…running up at the front again, then the gear lever snapped. Assen…ignition failure. For another round we drove all the way to Salzburg, only for the meeting to be cancelled at the last minute because the nuclear reactor at Chernobyl had just done an impression of my MBA. It was crazy. The meeting organisers were worried about us glowing in the dark, or something, but we were already there, already breathing the air. Bike racing's not like running the 1500 metres. Even if the air had been full of plutonium, we'd have breathed no more of it whether we'd raced or not. The upshot was that we'd spent about £500 we didn't really have getting there, without even the chance of getting any of it back.

Events were a little more encouraging on the domestic front. As well as racing the MBA in the national 125cc races, I had regular outings on a competitive 80 which I didn't even have to pay for. Although we had never really got Rod Lee's 80cc Kawasaki sorted the previous season, it did lead to one good thing. Towards the end of the '85 season I was approached by Steve Wicks, the creator of the British Wicks, a race bike built essentially from scratch in Leeds. Steve had previously made a 250 which Neil Tuxworth had ridden in the North-West 200, but his latest project was an 80, which he wanted me to ride. I suppose I was an obvious choice, being not only up-and-coming but quite local. Leeds is only ten miles up the motorway from Huddersfield.

I'd had the odd go on the Wicks towards the end of '85, then rode it pretty much full time in '86, winning five rounds and eventually finishing the season as British 80cc champion. We also had a run on the Wicks in a couple of European championship rounds. Although it was certainly competitive in Britain, it was outclassed in Europe, and the best finish I had was 13th at Vallelunga. It was flattering to be asked to ride the bike, and Steve was a good bloke. He was a big, cumbersome fellow who you wouldn't guess could be a talented engineer, but he certainly was. He was also a complete crackpot – you'd have to be to try to build a competitive race bike from scratch in your shed – but I really enjoyed working with him.

But to be honest, I wasn't particularly interested in the 80cc class. My focus was very much on 125cc and I loved my MBA so much more.

Our biggest outing of the season was at the British Grand Prix at Silverstone. After getting 17th place in the dry on the Wicks, it rained – bucketed down, as it often seemed to do at Silverstone – for the 125cc grand prix. My home grand prix was probably the biggest moment of my season, and it began so well. I was running in the top five, only to be sidelined when the ignition packed in again.

All in all, '86 was one of those seasons which began with such promise, such excitement at the thought of taking on the Europeans, but just seemed to peter out. By mid-season we'd cut our losses and more or less abandoned the European championship. It cost less, and offered a more realistic chance of decent prize money, simply to stay at home and do the top domestic meetings. Unfortunately missing out the first few British championship rounds cost me dearly, for again I finished the season as runner-up. Even then, I only had myself to blame since I led the standings by three points going into the final round at Silverstone, only to end up on my backside. Winning the national 80cc series seemed slim consolation.

By the end of this rollercoaster season I was a bit disillusioned by the whole racing business. This probably sounds a strange attitude on the part of someone who had just won his first national championship, but riding an 80 – and domestic racing in general – wasn't where I wanted to be. By now I absolutely knew I could run with the European guys and had seen for myself the backing many of them enjoyed, which was in stark contrast to anything a British rider could expect. For me, Europe was where the action ought to be.

Over the autumn it crossed my mind more than once to hang up my leathers and be done with it. This may sound like bleating viewed from a perspective over two decades down the line, but at the time I had no notion of racing as a career. It was still a bit of fun – time-consuming and obsessive, maybe, but essentially I was doing it for enjoyment. So if it stopped being fun, what reason was there to continue? Yes, it had been terrific for a while, and I still loved almost everything about racing. But the steady upward curve that had sustained it over the previous three years seemed to have hit a brick ceiling. A couple of people helped in their own small way with a few quid, some tyres or some oil, but serious sponsorship seemed like a distant mirage. Like scores of racers in similar positions before and after, I was throwing away money I didn't have and seemed to be getting nowhere at all, except even more broke. Even Pete had his work cut out to keep me upbeat.

Then I got a phone call from Mick Grant.

CHAPTER 10

'YOU'RE WASTING YOUR TIME ON THOSE LITTLE BIKES'

A year or so after he'd first told me how to put my career in order, in September '86 – just a few days after my 20th birthday – Granty rang me at the airfield. He wouldn't say what it was about, just that it was important and I should nip along to his place at Lepton for a chat.

'Right,' he said when I arrived, picking up where he'd left off 12 months before, 'I've said it before, but you're wasting your time on those little bikes. You really ought to think about moving up.'

'Yeah, but…'

'Superstocks,' he went on, ignoring me, 'is where you want to be. It's a good class, a competitive class, and relatively affordable. It's not easy but there are a lot of televised races. If you do well, important people can't help but notice. If you're going to be able to cut it at that level, you may as well find out now rather than down the line.'

The British Superstock championship had begun the season before, 1985. Mick had been the first Superstock champion, an impressive feat in the year he finally retired. It was open only to 750cc road-based machines, but with modifications allowed to brakes, tyres and other bits and pieces.

Although Mick no longer worked for Suzuki, he'd enjoyed some good years with their British team and still got on well with them, and especially with Rex White, who'd been his boss and still ran Reg Marshall and Paul Iddon in the Skoal Bandit Suzuki team. Mick had already had a word on my behalf with Rex, as a result of which Suzuki were prepared to supply a GSX-R750 and as many parts and spares as we'd probably need. They'd deliver a GSX-R750 to the house, brand new in a box, and Mick was confident that we could blag most of the expensive extras – wheels, racing exhaust and the like – from kit surplus to the official Suzuki team. All we'd have to do was take a van down to Suzuki's HQ in Crawley and load it up.

'You should be able to build a competitive bike without breaking the bank,' concluded Mick. Since I had nothing in the bank to begin with, this was what I wanted to hear.

It wasn't long before Doug Flather, from whom I'd bought the MBA three years before, heard of the Superstock plans. Because I'd done so well riding his old bike, I imagine he'd taken a particular interest in my progress. He rang up, insisting that moving to Superstock was the biggest mistake I could possibly make. Evidently he'd been trying to scratch together a budget to buy me a new MBA good enough to run in the top three in grands prix. He seemed convinced I could run at that level, and that he could get the funds to run a reliable and competitive bike. It was touching to discover that people I barely knew were not only taking a keen interest, but prepared to put themselves out on my behalf.

We'll never know whether Doug was right, although I'll always appreciate his interest, because I went the Mick Grant route. It wasn't an easy decision. I worried over the options for at least a week before telling Mick I'd follow his advice.

Barely had I made the decision than Mick rang to say he'd got me a one-off ride on a Superstock bike in the last big outing of the '86 season, October's Brands Hatch Powerbike International. This was always a fiercely competitive meeting, with riders keen to put on a good showing with end-of-season contract negotiations ahead – as well as caring less than usual about getting hurt, since they had all winter to recover. Suzuki had put together an extra Superstock bike from spares, and wanted me to ride it...in Skoal Bandit colours, as team-mate to Iddon and Marshall. It had originally been built by Nigel Everett for Neil Robinson, but had been parked when he was killed.

Big team, big audience, big expectations. I was nervous as a kitten. Despite sliding off at Druids in practice, when I got off the dry line and cracked the throttle way too hard – Mick reckoned he knew I was off two seconds before I did – the meeting went well. I simply loved the sensation, or so it seemed after the 125, of having power to burn. I grabbed eighth place in the Superstock race, after a race-long dice with Trevor Nation, a proper set-to. The feature event of the day was the Powerbike International race itself. It rained heavily before the start so most of us opted for full wet tyres, only for the track to begin drying during what would have been about a 30-lap race. Colin Breeze, a lovely, funny guy who had a lot of talent but never much money, just happened to have intermediate tyres on the only wheels he possessed and the drying track came to him. From nowhere early on he took the lead, cleared off, hit a damp patch and slid off. Keith Heuwen won.

When my GSX-R arrived in a box at the airfield a few months later, it was not only shiny-new but monstrous compared to the MBA. Mick and I drove down to Crawley one evening, rooted about and piled a mountain of stuff into the van: wheels, exhausts, sprockets, sprocket carriers, discs, calipers, master cylinders, you name it. I hope Granty really did have permission to 'borrow' all that stuff, because otherwise – sorry, Suzuki – we nicked it.

Mick had raced for over 20 years, many of them as a successful privateer, so knew all the wrinkles, had all the contacts. He set up a deal with Oxford Products for bodywork, which was handy since I tended to get through a lot of that sort of stuff. With his help we converted the GSX-R to total loss racing ignition and bolted on an ex-factory racing exhaust.

In other respects the class rules dictated that the engine had to remain pretty standard – depending on how you interpreted them, for everyone seemed to bend them to some extent. We had it blueprinted, which means that it's built *exactly* as the designer intended, with all the usual mass-production tolerances taken out. The crank was balanced so it would rev more easily and be more reliable, and the compression was increased just a little, and we were good to go.

Throughout his career Mick was always regarded as the rule-bender supreme. Pretty well everyone reckoned he was always up to something dodgy, whether he was or not. Inevitably, because everyone knew that he was associated with it, tongues soon started to wag about the legality of my GSX-R. Hand on heart, I can state that it was absolutely straight. It was stripped several times during the season during post-race scrutineering, and never had any problems.

Even so, doubts persisted. At the Stars of Darley awards night at the end of the season, Trevor Nation gave me one of the best backhanded compliments I've had in racing. I'd raced against Trev throughout the season, and he buttonholed me, convinced my bike had to have been bent for me to go as fast as it had. I was a bit offended at the time, for I knew, if no one else did, that it was totally legit. True, it had a few trick bits on it, things I'd got from Suzuki which wouldn't have been cost-effective for anyone else, like a five grand exhaust – and never mind that I'd had to kick it straight before it would fit. Other than saving a few ounces here and there, most of this kit made sod-all difference to how quick it was.

For the 1987 season we ran the Suzuki in stock colours – red, black, white and silver, a right confection. The arrangement was that I paid all my own running costs, but with the understanding that if I needed something I could go cap in hand to Rex, who'd see what he could slip out of the back door of the official Suzuki truck.

Superstock was an unbelievably well patronised class. The first round, at Brands Hatch, drew eighty entries. Eighty! That's more than two grid's-worth, so they had to run heats. I got on with the bike right away, finishing second in my heat, right up Terry Rymer's chuff. To within a few months, Terry was the same age as me, 20, another up-and-coming youngster. He wasn't nationally well known at the time, but was a Brands Hatch specialist and knew his way around the Indy circuit. He was going well and, being a local lad, got lots of media attention, where I was just left to get on with it. After following him around in the heat, I thought I could maybe beat him in the final, if not actually win. Everything was going to plan when – not for the last time – I high-sided coming out of Clearways.

Rymer went on to win at Brands, his first high-profile result, and really leapt to public prominence. Although he went on to beat me in the championship, he didn't seem to get much faster during the season, whilst I was really coming to grips with the bigger bike and, I thought, getting faster all the time. There was a bit of rivalry between us throughout the season as to who'd finish top rookie in

Superstocks, but after winning at Mallory Park I usually felt I had the beating of him.

After the MBA I was on a big, steep, win-or-bust learning curve, which inevitably meant that I overcooked it now and again and slid off. Yet after the TT in early June I seemed to come to grips with the bigger bike and hardly crashed at all. This was probably just as well after I damn near destroyed it at Oliver's Mount, since there were limits to how much scrounging from Rex I could do.

Mick was hovering around at the time, not actually managing me, but taking a keen interest, offering lots of advice. In that first meeting we had lots of typical Brands Indy problems, particularly decking out, especially at Bottom Bend, which would unload the front tyre and make you lose the front end. Mick set to, pushing the fork legs through the yokes, jacked up the ride height everywhere he could. Very few bikes at the time had adjustable rear ride heights, but Mick somehow came by a lovely Kayaba shock-absorber which had adjustments for everything. He'd fiddle with it, measure the adjuster, then work out what difference that made at the back wheel. When he'd finished, he explained the set-up to me and Butch, who by that time had finished racing and was working as my mechanic. Apparently the shock was now at the absolute limit of adjustment, on the verge of running out of thread for the locknut. He said it would be OK for Brands, but we shouldn't use it like that anywhere else.

From Brands me, Butch and a bloke named Steve Dale drove straight for the Irish Sea ferry to get to the North-West 200 meeting in Northern Ireland. This was my first taste of proper road racing, other than the Isle of Man, but in practice I went pretty well. Luckily the Suzuki wasn't too badly damaged from the Clearways crash – just a smashed fairing and a few other bits and pieces. The North-West 200 circuit uses ordinary public roads between three towns, Portrush, Port Stewart and Coleraine. It's blindingly fast, a big crazy speedbowl, and I loved it from the very first lap.

Friday afternoon practice brought perfect weather, so everyone was going for it, especially me. One of the sections, Station Corner, is little more than a kink: really fast and quite bumpy over a stonechip surface. You drove into it pinned flat/stick in fifth gear – basically as fast as you could get at the corner, a real buzz but no problem. But on this particular lap, just as I'm tipping into the corner, the whole bike suddenly felt as though a wheel had collapsed. It turned out that the shock adjuster Mick had been on about at Brands had been unscrewing itself, until finally it just fell out of the bike and locked up the back wheel. So the road went right but I didn't...and all I could think was that I'm going to die, because the speed was certainly enough to get you properly mangled.

As I hit the tarmac I remember thinking that whatever happens it isn't going to hurt, 'cos it'll be over one way or another pretty fast. Crashing is strange. There's no time for fear because it all happens so quickly, and once it's started there's obviously nothing you can do about it. So what's going through your mind is something ridiculously inappropriate like 'Oh dear,' and a crazy sort of detached curiosity about what's going to happen next. By the time I stopped tumbling I was dimly aware that I'd had a bang on the head and was a bit stunned, but mainly felt really cold. Apparently I'd bounced into a big drainage ditch and surfed out the other side through a bramble bush, so I was wet through, although my only real injury was a badly grazed neck from the bush. I was still tottering about thinking, 'What the hell happened?' when an old boy in a white coat trotted over, looked at me, and yelled back to the other marshals, 'Bloody 'ell, he's alive.' All I could think was, 'Thank fuck for that.'

After a while the medics arrived and shoved me into a battered ambulance. Looking back, the absence of anyone who seemed to know what they were doing, or equipment to do it with, was frightening. Heaven knows what they'd have done if I'd actually been mangled. But I was all right. Mick took me back to his hotel where I got washed, rinsed the mud off my leathers, and sat next to a radiator to warm up.

Meanwhile the lads were working miracles with the bike. At the Irish meetings, if you have a serious problem almost everyone's usually happy to help. One of Joey Dunlop's mechanics, a keen amateur welder, got a TIG unit organised and glued the Suzuki's aluminium rear sub-frame back together. Eventually they got the bike ready to go, although it looked more like a patchwork quilt than a nearly new race bike. Unfortunately, due to my bang on the head, the race organisers wouldn't let me ride, so that was another meeting shit-canned.

Oddly enough Andrea, who would become Mrs Whitham over a decade later, was also there for her first North-West 200, with another Superstock Rider, Mick Preston. Her brother, Allen, was Mick's mechanic. I knew she was local – from Mirfield on the other side of Huddersfield. She was a good-looking lass, funny and feisty, and I kind of fancied her.

The evening before my crash they'd been going for fish and chips when Andrea swerved to avoid an old dear who'd pulled out without looking, rolled the van, and finished upside-down in a bog not even a quarter of a mile from where I'd soon end up in another. And guess who was first on the scene? Me. Mick had told me to get in lots of laps, in a car he'd borrowed from an old racing buddy, Billy McCosh, and as I drove past the scene Andrea, Mick, Allen and Mick's wife Julie were extracting themselves from what was left of the van, spread all over the countryside. Although Andrea will tell you I just waved and abandoned them, John Lofthouse had already stopped and given me the nod that they were OK. Since there wasn't much I could do that he couldn't, I just gave them the thumbs-up and drove past. That earned me no points when I bumped into her the next day in a nightclub. But it was nice of her to practise my crashes for me, don't you think?

There was no one to blame for my crash but me. Regardless of what Mick had said, I'd reckoned that if the shock was good at Brands, it was bound to be OK at the North-West.

The TT, as usual, was just a couple of weeks after the North-West 200, so I arrived on the Isle of Man freshly laundered from my trip through the ditch – and maybe a little more prepared to take Mick's advice. He was around on the Island, just for support and guidance rather than actually running me, but seemed quite concerned that I was going to cripple myself, especially after the shock-absorber incident. He sent me out on my first practice lap with lots of words of caution, talking about there being lots more power and corner speed than I'd been used to on the Mountain Course, telling me to take my time and enjoy it. For once I actually listened to him, and had a really pleasant lap. Despite a standing start and slowing down, Mick timed it unofficially at 100.6mph, and yet it hadn't felt as fast as on the Gamma the previous year.

I did three TT races, Formula One, Classic and Senior, all on my Superstock bike. Race week began with a 17th in the F1, finishing with 13th in the Senior, the same race in which my future team-mate Mez Mellor crashed whilst leading at The Nook, a horrible little place. My fastest lap was around 107mph, which wasn't shabby on the Superstocker, and for the second year running I didn't have a really hairy moment all week.

A few weeks later we were at another place it's not very healthy to fall off – Oliver's Mount, Scarborough. Inevitably, I had another big, big one.

The main men at the Scarborough meeting were guys like Roger Marshall, Andy McGladdery and Roger Hurst. Butch couldn't get time off from work, so another mate, Zac McMillan, was helping me out.

I loved Scarborough – all those wild whoops and jumps through the trees – and was fair stomping round in practice. In general the Suzuki handled and stopped well, but was a bit of a handful over the leaps. You had to hit them absolutely straight and be utterly precise with the throttle – not too little, not too much – to land just back wheel first, with the engine driving as you hit the ground. If you didn't get it exactly right, you were in bother.

I led the race for a couple of laps, but knew 'Reg' Marshall was close behind, and out of the corner of my eye I could see that he was gaining as I accelerated out of Mountside Hairpin. Most of the time while you're racing you're talking to yourself...trying to maintain concentration...telling yourself not to do anything daft. With Reg closing, I was telling myself to push, push, push, but not go silly, just as I hit the big downhill jump on the main straight... leaning over, only a little, but enough. I knew it was going to go badly wrong even before I landed, and it did.

Christ! It was like trying to hang on to a crazy anaconda – weaving all over the road, but fast. After two or three big, wild weaves the bike just chucked me off and smacked into the banking, then went even more bananas with sods and bits of grass and chunks of bike flying in all directions. I hit the same banking, ricocheted off the opposite bank at a nice oblique angle, and was just thinking how my obvious skill and judgement was going to let me get away with it again when what was left of the damn bike landed on top of me and broke my arm. The Suzuki absolutely destroyed itself, but I was all right apart from the arm and a spot more concussion. A St Johns ambulance crew carted me off to hospital, where I was patched up.

Just as inevitable as the crash – this woman was definitely not my good luck charm – Andrea was at Scarborough, tagging along again with Mick Preston's team. In fact I was so un-tuned to my karma that I'd asked her out for our first date on the night before the race. I liked her, sure, but wasn't sure my health could stand having her around – not that I was doing much for hers. After the crash which, for all she knew, had killed me, she'd run back to the van to find out how I was and found Zac shovelling chunks of GSX-R into the back of it. He'd given her a bollocking for distracting me from the weekend's finer purpose, which in his view wasn't chatting-up paddock totty and late romantic nights. Things perked up after that. She lived close enough to Crosland Moor that we could have a practical relationship and, from hanging around with Mick Preston's team, she understood racing well enough not to get in the way. She was soon tuned in to knowing when I needed leaving alone, when I needed geeing up or my confidence boosting, and never got under my feet. In fact the whole racing experience was better for having her as a companion – although to this day I don't understand why she needs so many shoes.

The broken arm meant I had to sit out the next Superstock round at Knockhill, as well as relying on Andrea to drive me whenever we went out. I got on well with her parents, Barbara and Roy, and for the rest of the season Andrea and me were an item. Luckily her bad karma seemed to have gone elsewhere, so I only had a couple of offs, neither of them big bike-wreckers, so maybe she wasn't so bad for me after all. She did seem to think it a bit odd that I always made sure she rang me, rather than the other way round, because I was too tight to put money in dad's payphone. But apparently I amused her and we've been together ever since. I doubt she missed half a dozen meetings in the next ten years.

I probably needed all the support I could get. The Superstock bike was a massive step up from the MBA in power, weight, everything. The riding technique was totally different. 125s are all about maintaining corner speed, where the big 'un is about having it leant over for as little time as possible and having the throttle on as much as you can. On the 125, every extra mph you could carry through a corner was an mph you carried down the following straight. With the 750 it didn't matter so much how you got round the corner, so long as you got the gas on early. And a lot of that, of course, is about finding grip – in other words, set-up.

I realised early in the '87 season that if I tried to ride the GSX-R like I had my 125 and pushed hard, as often as not I'd end up on my backside. It was a big learning curve, but by mid-season we'd got to grips with it, and by the end I felt completely at home on the 750.

As well as Superstock, at most meetings we could also ride in Super One races. Super One was really a transition class. This was the era in which four strokes were taking over from the 500 and even 750cc two-strokes, but there were still plenty of them about, so Super One was created to give the strokers somewhere to race. Other than maybe three or four proper Formula One bikes, everyone else was on some sort of Superstock device, most of them home-built to some degree. It was a right mishmash. The attraction of the Superstocker – other than the happy fact that mine cost me nothing – was that you could do a lot of races with the same bike. Darren Dixon gave the two-stroke its last glimpse of glory when he won the Super One championship on the Padgetts' RG500, but it was near the end of the line. By the end of the season the four-strokes were outpacing him.

By September, when we went to Mallory Park for the Race of the Year, I was full of confidence and flying. The Race of the Year itself was under unlimited Super One rather than Superstock regulations, so we bolted in a big set of flat-slide carbs to give the GSX-R a bit more oomph.

As usual Reg Marshall was favourite to win, along with the American Fred Merkel, who would go on to win the World Superbike title the following year, but the three of us got away from the pack and spent the race dicing for the lead. It was wet, which usually suited me, and the GSX-R was working well. Reg kept getting into a mess over the bumps out of Gerrard's, allowing me to drive under him and beat him to the Esses almost whenever I felt like it. Near the end of the race I tried that bit harder to open up a gap out of the Esses so he couldn't get back at me into the Hairpin, and down I went. I'd hardly got to my feet when, not even a lap later, Merkel crashed out halfway round Gerrard's. The race was stopped and the win awarded to him on count-back, which caused a right furore.

Meanwhile I'm cursing myself for being such a prat, since apart from throwing away a winning opportunity my main race of the day was coming up and I had a bike about six inches long thanks to being shunted into the banking at the Esses. As I'd picked myself up I could hear Mick, stood outside the paddock café, shouting across to the Esses at the top of his voice: 'Whitham, you're a wanker.' And he was right. Worse still, all the Suzuki top brass were there, and we both knew that a sound showing could have done me a lot of good with them.

Since there was no way on earth we could fix the bike, I was sitting in the awning feeling sorry for myself when in strode Mick. 'I've got you a bike', he said, 'although you don't deserve it.' Evidently it was a machine Suzuki had prepared for Kenny Irons, who was away doing a grand prix. 'Get your stuff together', said Mick, and we were out. It was so rushed that Butch was still changing the bike's race numbers as I was letting out the clutch.

I didn't deserve it, but I had a right good do in the Superstock race. After a set-to with Mez Mellor, who was Suzuki's semi-official rider in the class, I came out on top. It was my 21st birthday, more or less, so we went out for a double celebration. Even Suzuki seemed to have forgotten my Esses cock-up, and invited me to ride the Irons bike again, partly to help Mez, who was vying with Keith Heuwen's Loctite Yamaha for the championship lead.

If Suzuki had the idea that drafting me into their squad might calm me down, I soon showed them otherwise. At the next Superstock round, Cadwell Park, I was going well, right behind Mez – who I wasn't supposed to overtake anyway – when I threw the GSX-R away at the bottom of the Mountain. The bike hit some railway sleepers, took off, cleared the medical centre and crashed down in a field next to the official Suzuki truck.

I was a bit hyper, as you usually are after a crash. 'No worries,' I told a Suzuki bloke, 'I've sent your bike back.' Meanwhile Mick's trying to calm everyone down, telling them I'm just young and daft, between trying to convince me I could make a living at this lark if only I'd take it a little more seriously. At the time the likelihood was that Mick would be managing the official Suzuki GB team the following year. He'd made it clear he wanted me to ride for him, but if I made too many enemies at Suzuki that might be difficult. 'All we need,' he implored, 'is one good result before the end of the year.'

By this time I wasn't in a position to win the championship, but there were still three meetings left in the season, three chances to make amends. This was the first year I'd actually been offered start money – a fee paid to crowd-drawers for taking part in a meeting. So as well as the final championship meeting, I'd arranged to race in the Sunflower trophy meeting at Kirkistown one Saturday, immediately after which Butch would drive all night to get us to Darley Moor for the Sunday, where I was also on start money. In the Sunflower we finished fifth and eighth in a couple of anything-goes, 'run wot you brung' type races, against lots of mad Irishmen on all sorts of different kit. At Darley, I had a second place and a win.

I was on a roll – but, as usual, there were hiccups. At Carnaby I blew up an engine in practice, and for reasons which still escape me the spare was back at home. I was sitting by the van feeling sorry for myself, when Mick dropped by. 'At home?' he gasped. 'What bloody use is it there? Go and get it, you dickhead.'

So I did. After that Mick stopped calling me James, preferring 'DH'. The habit even rubbed off onto Butch. After a few weeks I asked Mick what it meant, half expecting it to be something complimentary – Die Hard, at least. The truth was less flattering.

'It stands for dickhead, 'cos you're a dickhead, you dickhead.' It was hard to be a prima donna with Granty around.

All that was left for the dickhead was to contest the traditional finale to the season, Brands Hatch Powerbikes. It was cold, so track conditions were tricky and I knew I couldn't really afford to fall off. Nonetheless, I knew I was riding well, full of confidence, and everything worked out just perfectly. I was back on my own

Superstock bike, which was really sorted by then, and couldn't seem to put a foot wrong. I won the main event by quite a margin. This meant that in the final four Superstock rounds I'd been dicing for the lead at Cadwell and crashed, won at Mallory, won at Brands and finished second at Oulton Park. Heuwen finished the year as Superstocks champion, but by then I wasn't scared of him, Rymer or anyone else. I was 21, on a roll and reckoned I could beat anyone in Britain. There was genuinely no one I feared in UK racing, even guys on bigger or faster bikes in Super One.

Mick was chuffed, too. 'We can do summat now,' he grinned. When he was confirmed as Suzuki race boss for '88, he offered me £5,000 to ride for the team. Five thousand smackers! And I could keep any prize money I won. I spent all winter marvelling at the thought of actually being paid to do this.

CHAPTER 11

A DIFFERENT KIND
OF JOB

Mick had told us late in '87 that the likelihood was he'd be running Suzuki's British team from his home the following season. 'They're sick of throwing money at the job,' he'd said, 'so it'll be a small team, out of vans rather than trucks.' He was perfectly up-front, admitting he couldn't begin to afford to run a recognised front-runner like Iddon or Marshal, but he could afford a relatively unknown 21-year-old like me, living at home with few overheads. But he had a lot of faith in me too. More importantly, this was my chance to move on from what had been a pretty successful season as a privateer and establish myself with a recognised team. There would be a budget, admittedly a tight one, but I'd have competitive bikes and a wage – which was a pretty novel idea in itself. Christ, I was going to be a proper professional racer.

All in all, I didn't need much persuading to sign on the dotted line. Mick got what was left of the kit from the defunct Skoal Bandit squad, a couple of Mercedes vans, a Michelin tyre deal and other bits and pieces here and there. Also in the team was Mez Mellor, another Huddersfield lad who, as a bit of an established name and a TT winner, was paid a bit more than me. As well as the UK stuff we'd both be doing the TT.

In those days teams didn't test all winter in warm places like Almeria or Jerez. Usually even the top teams would make do with a couple of miserable practice days at Mallory or Cadwell. Then off you went racing. Mick had other ideas. 'Played a blinder,' he declared one day. 'I've tagged onto a Michelin test day for Thierry Espié at Nogaro, near the Pyrenees. How about that?' Espié, a decent bloke and a talented racer in his own right, was the French tyre company's test rider.

We set off with one van and three bikes: a GSX600F, a GSX-R750 Slingshot and a GSX-R1100 – all brand new, complete with lights and fresh out of their crates. We'd already christened the 600 'the Teapot', because that's what it looked like. It didn't even look quick. None of the bikes had any miles on the engines when we left England, so Mick decided that the sensible thing to do – he was a great one for good ideas that cost next to nothing – was for me and Mez to run them in on the way through France. We'd just wheel them out of the back of the Merc, stick on any old number plate that happened to be lying around, and follow the van. It was freezing.

Part-way to Nogaro, we checked into a Formula 1 motel for the night, which was ideal because it was cheap. Then the four of us went out for a meal. The menu, not surprisingly, was in French. Butch – who's dad's a butcher, hence his nickname – was intent on showing off how cosmopolitan a maintenance job in a Huddersfield mill had made him. He studied the menu as if he understood it, ordered steak tartare and sat back looking forward to a lovely lump of beef. What arrived, of course, was a pile of raw minced beef with a few herbs on top. Even then he tried to bluff it out, telling the waiter it was underdone and could he cook it some more while the rest of us rolled around in stitches.

Mick's running-in strategy meant that by the time we reached the circuit all the bikes had at least a couple of hundred miles on them, so we were ready to go. Near the end of the first day I went out for my second session on the 750. Nogaro has a long back straight leading into what's almost a hairpin, but on this particular lap I didn't get quite that far. It was one of those crashes where you sit up out of the bubble at 160mph and the instant you touch the brakes…oops, that was quick and you're on your bum.

It was a big one, although it didn't actually hurt much. When I stopped sliding I picked myself up, undamaged, although I was hopping a bit because my arse had been scorched by the friction. The bike – the UK's only example, if not Europe's – had tumbled for miles and wasn't in quite such good shape. I already had a good idea it was buggered because I'd seen bits flying off it as it disappeared out of my view. I limped towards what was left of it, thinking Mick wasn't going to be happy. I didn't really even want to look at it. In fact you couldn't, really. Not in one glance. It was scattered all over southern France in about a million pieces. And we had no spares.

Back in England, one of the championship meetings I most looked forward to was Scarborough, because I knew every inch of the Oliver's Mount circuit and always went well there. This year was no exception for I won both Formula One legs and the Supersport race. The only one I didn't win was the production event which, as luck would have it, was the championship we were doing best in.

It started going wrong when I fluffed the start, and by the time I got to the first corner, Mere Hairpin, there was already a bit of a mêlée. Somebody had toppled over in the middle of the pack, somebody toppled over him, and the rest were a huge jumble as they tried to find a way round. Just as I weaved my way through this traffic jam I was shunted from behind and knocked over, at all of 5mph. I jumped to my feet, drew a bead on the bloke I thought had clipped me – who just happened to be the nearest bloke, sat on a scruffy black Yamaha – and pushed him.

Unfortunately for him he was only a little chap, so couldn't get his feet on the ground. Just as he was teetering beyond the point of no return another rider came past, minding his own business, collected him, and the two of them rolled down the bank in a heap.

'Sod 'em,' I thought, and blasted off up the hill, trying to salvage a couple of points, if nothing else. From there it worked perfectly. A couple of lads had a big get-off at the Esses, three fell off in another mangling session at Mountside hairpin, and before I knew it I'd barely overtaken anybody and yet finished third. Brilliant. That'll do me.

The bloke I'd shoved over, it turned out, was named Rory Thompson. Until that day he'd never scored a single British championship point, but with all the carnage ahead of him, after he picked up his bike he was actually running in eighth place, which was like winning a TT for a privateer like him. Unfortunately he had no signals and no dea he was running that high, so he'd given it up as a bad job and pulled in. For all this, he blamed me. Inquiries revealed that he was a part-time debt collector and door-to-door butcher, apparently. In Glasgow. Oo-er.

I'd just got back to the caravan when who did I see out of the window but Thompson striding across the paddock in my direction, along with his dad who looked even meaner than him.

Knock, knock, knock.

Now, you probably think that bike racers are brave. Sorry to disappoint you. On the track, if we can't see it coming, no matter how blindingly obvious it is to the rest of the world, we don't worry. That's stupidity, not bravery. But put two pissed-off Jocks in front of us, and we come over all clever. Suddenly even we can work out that pain probably isn't far behind.

So I summoned all my courage and hid behind Andrea, who's about five-foot nothing without her heels.

'Tell him I'm not in,' I bleated.

They weren't having it. They were seething. The pair of them ranted and raved while I cowered behind Andrea.

Fortunately I didn't get beaten up. Counter them with a few well-aimed jabs and these Glaswegians aren't as tough as they think: 'I'll buy you a new fairing,' I squealed. 'And you can have some of my prize money, and, and....' So I fixed his bike, compensated him for his lost points, and we became friends. He was a lovely lad – as door-to-door butchers and debt collectors go.

From there things could only get better, and they did, swimmingly. It was a cracking season and for the first time I began to believe that I could actually make a living out of racing.

I won the British proddy championship, came second in the Formula One series and even managed third in the Seniorstock championship – what's known as Supersports today – on the Teapot. I felt as though I'd really arrived, and was in no doubt that Mick had been right to urge to me move onto bigger bikes. Mind you, meetings could be pretty frantic. Most were just two days, so on the Saturday you'd do two practice sessions on each of the bikes, followed by heats for both the Seniorstock and Production bikes. On Sunday you'd have two F1/Superbike races, plus the finals of the Seniorstock and Production. It didn't help that the three bikes were so totally different, so for each corner you'd have three different braking points. At the time it didn't seem especially tough. You just got used to it. Ray Swann, Mez, Roger Hurst and Brian Morrison all had the same sort of schedule. But you hardly seemed to be off one bike or another all weekend.

Mention of the Teapot reminds me to put one story straight, because over the years people have accused me of running big engines and all sorts of other illegal stuff. To my knowledge no team I've ever been with has ever cheated with capacity. To be honest it doesn't always matter what you do or say. Some people believe everyone's cheating except for them – Trev Nation for one, although he's a lovely bloke, if a bit mad. Jim Moodie's also a bit of a conspiracy theorist. But there was, shall we say, a certain artistic interpretation of the rulebook by Mick.

We were generally given good bikes to do the job by Suzuki, but the hardest job by far was with the GSX600F which, frankly, was just a touring bike, a shopping bike, out of its depth racing against proper supersports machines. In fact I could never understand why it would take Suzuki, who had more or less invented the race replica class in '85 with the GSX-R750, another decade to produce a GSX-R600. To make the Teapot competitive – and even then it was flogging a dead horse – Mick and Butch did a lot of work on it, some of which might…ahem…have been frowned on. For starters there was a fair amount of titanium. Mick's a talented engineer who could make things or get them made, so he did. The 600 engine was exactly the same as the GSX-R750 in external dimensions, so lots of factory Formula One stuff would fit. We had titanium gear selector drums, because we had them lying around and they somehow found their way inside. The clutch, too, was a bit exotic. And lots of other stuff. But it was always a 600 – even though it was almost certainly the most illegal bike I've ever ridden.

The first of the Slingshot GSX-Rs, the 750J, was also a touch on the bent side. Most people who began that season on a GSX-R ended it on something else, because they couldn't make it competitive. But not us – although we were obviously handicapped to the extent that it would have been considered slightly bad PR for a Suzuki team to go out and buy Hondas. In essence ours was a stock bike completely, as it had to be for production racing, but we had the suspension totally re-valved, including the supposedly 'non-serviceable' rear unit, with different springs.

If we'd been rumbled it could have been embarrassing, with a lot of corporate egg on faces. Luckily for us, we weren't – even at times when I thought it must be blindingly obvious. For instance, by the time we got to the Isle of Man for production race 'B', me and Mez had spent three months with the bikes and they were well sorted. A lot of other riders got a GSX-R just for that race, expecting to jump on and go, but they didn't – except sideways. There's a video of Ago's Leap and just about everyone on a Suzuki is weaving, going sideways...wild. Then me and Mez come through, fast but arrow-straight, no bother. It does look dodgy. Even the commentator remarked on it.

Otherwise I hardly put a foot wrong all year in the production championship, although it began poorly. At the opening two rounds, Brands Hatch and Donington Park, we got our arses kicked – mainly because we were giving away 300-odd cc to most of the field. Unfortunately, being the official Suzuki team, we were more or less obliged to race with their latest sports model, which was the GSX-R750. Changing to the older GSX-R1100 would not have looked good, although it was always our intention to use the 1100 for the two fastest circuits, Thruxton and Snetterton.

Mainly, though, our problem wasn't power but tyres. The GSX-R1100 ran an 18-inch front rim, while the 750 had 17-inch wheels at both ends. Initially, Michelin – our tyre company – couldn't supply a 17-inch front that gave us any confidence. Finally, at Carnaby, they turned up with a new tyre which I just knew right away was the business. It turned, gripped, gave me all the feedback the previous tyre hadn't. From that moment on I knew I'd be hard to beat. At Carnaby I won on the 750 – ahead of an 18-year-old Ian Simpson on a GSX-R1100 – and never looked back. We eventually wrapped up the championship with three rounds still to go.

The only slip-up came at Cadwell Park on the Woodlands Circuit riding the 750, which was something else on such a tight track. I don't think you ever got out of fourth gear. Early in the race I lost the front end and slid off going into the hairpin. I picked it up – and they took some picking up, those big bastards – fired it up and got going again. I remember going round the bottom of the Mountain thinking I could still salvage some points. Or maybe not, since what I hadn't noticed was that the front brake lever had been wiped off in the crash. I don't think I've ever gone into Hall Bends quite so quick. I sped straight on onto the grass, missed the Armco by inches, before somehow managing to get it back onto the track and retire.

Formula One, which was the premier class, was in some ways the most disappointing. Suzuki had supplied us with four full factory XR81 Formula One bikes, as ridden by Paul Iddon and Reg Marshall the previous year, plus lots of spares. I'm not sure whether it was Mick's decision or Suzuki's, but for the early part of the season we just didn't use them. We raced kitted GSX-R750Js instead, which just weren't good enough. Mez and me practically begged Mick to let us ride the XR81s – which Mick had always planned to run at the TT anyway – but it was only when it became obvious that we were being comprehensively spanked on the production-based 750s that Suzuki relented. From then on we were right on the pace, finishing third in the championship despite the lousy start. In the Seniorstock series I finished third behind Brian Morrison and Ray Swann.

We rounded off the season with a trip to the Far East for the Macau Grand Prix, where again I ran strongly, running second in both legs until the bike broke down. That was the year Kevin Schwantz cleared off on the factory Pepsi Suzuki, doing half of each lap on the back wheel. By then I already had a contract to stay with Mick for '89, including bigger wages. There seemed to be nothing to worry about. I was on a roll and couldn't see how life could be better than this.

The only hiccup in this serene state of affairs was at home. For a while me and my sisters had been aware that not all was well with our parents' marriage. There were no blazing rows, they just weren't getting on so well and never seemed to do anything together. We sensed that mainly they were sticking it out for us kids, although by this time we were all in our 20s. Eventually they sat us down and announced that they were splitting up. I think they expected more of a negative reaction from us, because our main emotion was 'Thank God for that.'

Dad carried on living at the airfield, which was his main livelihood after all. Mum moved out into a not very salubrious rented house. It was a tough time for her, yet none of us were in much of a position to help. It took her about a year to get financially settled and buy a place of her own, and from then on she was OK. At first everything was quite amicable between them. Then the solicitors got involved and there was the usual grief and disputes about the settlement, all that old shit. Dad was always a little bitter about it.

Meanwhile, I was embarking on my second year with Suzuki and my third on big bikes. Again the riders were me and Mez, riding the XR81 in F1/Superbike, GSX600F Teapots in Seniorstock, and the new GSX-R1100 Slingshot in the production class. In F1 we were mainly up against RC30s, which were the bikes to have in the Superstock series – which we didn't contest that year – but the XR81 definitely still had the edge in Formula One.

It was another good year. In May I'd had the best North-West 200 you can imagine, which set us up nicely for the TT. We'd actually begun the season in Heron Suzuki colours in a couple of non-championship shakedown meetings. Then a big sponsorship deal from Durex came through and a big media launch was scheduled for Donington Park on the day after the North-West. Part of the deal was that we had to send six bikes to Donington as props for the launch, but we were already committed to doing the North-West 200. Consequently we were able to send only a skeleton crew to Ireland, just two GSX-R1100 production bikes for Mez and me, on which we planned to do both the proddy race and both legs of the feature event.

It was a meeting that also helped in the battle for local bragging rights. Having a gen-u-ine British champion at the airfield may have impressed a few people, but dad didn't seem to be one of them. At least, he didn't let on, although I think in his own way he was as chuffed as I was and kind of proud of me. He was more likely to take the piss out of me than tell me how wonderful I was. But I knew, from remarks he'd made to other people, that he was pretty pleased with how I was doing – not that he seemed to understand exactly what was going on. For instance, he didn't have a clue what 'Superstock' might be. For all he knew it was some sort of medieval bit of kit for pelting folk with rotten fruit. But he was interested in me. He'd always come to watch me race on the Isle of Man, although usually not on the shorts.

If he was visibly bothered about anything, it wasn't where I stood in the UK pecking order. The bigger issue was whether I was better than Dave Leach, who, you'll remember, was his pal Clifford's son. Obviously it was a really parochial point of view – whose was the fastest local lad, who claimed the Halifax and Huddersfield bragging rights. It was 'My dad's tougher than your dad', but in reverse.

Obviously Leachy had started racing a couple of seasons before I had and had been a role model to me. I admired how tough he was, how he could lose chunks of his body and still carry on as if nothing had happened. He was better than me, earlier than me, at the Marlboro Series, winning on bigger bikes – 250s and 350s – while I was doing well on the 125. Then, when I moved up to the Superstocker, he was on 600s. So, oddly, we never clashed on track and there was no way a comparison could be drawn.

Dad asked me once whether I'd beat Dave in a straight race. Certainly by the end of '87 I was fairly sure I would beat him on a short circuit, as well as being confident I could put a more competitive bike together. Dave's bikes were usually well prepared but a bit pedestrian. At the time he was as good as anyone on the Irish roads, where the locals loved him. For some strange reason they called him Fred and adopted him like an Irish Tyke. So I sensed that Dave would have the edge in Ireland, where, as it turned out, we had our only set-tos.

Anything that didn't handle, anything that you had to stop trying to set up, because it was basically shite and you were never going to make it work anyway, just ride the wheels off it – Dave could ride. He was sensational on the FZR1000 Yamaha, which was an animal. Yet, with a bit of luck, I managed to beat him on it at the North-West 200 in 1989.

As usual I'd got a pretty good start in the proddy race. After a few laps Dave came past and I half expected I wouldn't be able to stay with him, but I tagged onto his slipstream to see what would happen. Any sections where it was just a single corner and you get your knee down, short-circuit style, I was as fast as him; but anywhere flowing, clipping kerbs, he was something else. But my GSX-R1100 was slightly quicker than his FZR.

When he didn't pull away, I thought I might be in with a chance.

So, starting the last lap, I got to thinking. If he's in front of me at the left-hander at Metropole, I reckoned, he'd definitely beat me, because he was mustard up Juniper Hill and along the coast road to the finish, and well prepared to take a risk. So Metropole was where I had to have a go.

I tucked in behind him on the long straight from the Magic Roundabout, then tried to dive up the inside at Metropole. Dave knew I was there and just rode smart: he let off his brakes, aimed for the apex, and parked it. It was a perfectly legitimate move, but caused me to nearly run into the back of him and run wide. 'OK,' I thought, 'I'll have to settle for second.' But he was still worried about me getting back at him, and under the bridge on Juniper Hill he gave it a bit too much power. The Yamaha spat sideways, chucking him up in the air out of the seat. He stayed on, but by then I was past him and there was no time for him to get back at me. So I won.

Oddly, that wasn't the hairiest event of the day. That accolade went to Granty's driving. The timing for the plane to take us to Donington for the Durex presentation was so tight that literally as we finished the main race me and Mez, jumped into the back of Mick's hire car for the dash to Belfast airport. To avoid the traffic, Mick, who's the world's worst driver at the best of times, drove like a lunatic down Ulster back roads as the two of us cowered in the back, glad still to be in race leathers. Eventually, and much to our relief – no amount of sponsorship is worth dying for – Mick's driving attracted the attention of the Royal Ulster Constabulary. There was the usual 'where's the fire?' chat before Mick explained our problem.

'Right, follow me,' said the copper, and gave us the full blues-and-twos to the airport. Only in Ireland.

A few months later me and Leachy had a rematch in the Supersports event at the Ulster Grand Prix. Leachy was on a Yamaha as usual, Phillip McCallan on a factory Honda, whilst I was on that useless Suzuki Teapot. It wasn't very quick, but it had good top-end, which is what you need round a track as fast as Dundrod.

The gloves came off in what turned into a fierce, hard race. You knew McCallan wouldn't be bothered about taking wild chances, because he was always scary – didn't seem to have a lot of respect for his own safety or anyone else's. But Dave, he was just as crackers. What's going on? This is a lad I've known since I was seven, used to play toy soldiers with, and he doesn't seem to care if either of us lives or dies. Not that I can have been much different, since I stayed with the pair of them for the whole crazy race, just pipping McCallan for second whilst Dave won. I obviously hadn't fully realised what a nutter I'd become too.

Ironically, it was later in the same meeting whilst riding under what seemed like complete control that I was slung off the Formula One bike and broke a leg. At the time I was leading the British Production championship comfortably, just leading the Formula One series, and even stood third in the Supersport championship again. By then Mick had bolted even more titanium on to the 600. It was so light that you had to lash it down in the paddock to stop it blowing away in a breeze. As a result of breaking the leg I didn't race again until November's Macau Grand Prix and won none of the championships.

I got on pretty well with most of the people I raced with, although one who seemed to stand for everything I didn't was Steve Spray. He was a bit flash – private number plates, all that crap. And I hated that bloody Norton rotary, even though it clearly brought a lot of people through the gate and was generally a good thing for British racing. It was quick, although probably not the easiest thing to ride, and a frigging hard thing to race against. It'd belch flames into your face and set you on fire going into every corner, then pull 100 yards on you down every straight. I loathed the damn thing.

Spray had one seriously good year on the Norton, winning both the Formula One and Supercup series and finishing the season as *MCN* 'Man of the Year'. He wasn't a bad rider. He rode it OK. But I was convinced I'd always beat him if he was on the same kit as me. Instead I spent most of the year breathing Norton fumes and fuming. Oddly I didn't mind it so much when Trevor Nation was on it, 'cos he was a sound, down-to-earth guy. And quite mad, obviously.

Although I didn't learn of it until later, around this time Gary Taylor, who ran the factory Suzuki grand prix team, phoned Mick to say they'd been keeping an eye on my progress. Apparently they discussed the possibility of me having a test outing on a grand prix Vee-four if I wanted it, and I'd probably have jumped at the chance. But I never got to decide, because Mick turned it down on my behalf. Some time later he told me the tale and gave his reasons. He believed I could do myself more harm than good and, although I was brassed off with him at the time, with hindsight I can see that he was probably right. I probably wouldn't have got a lot of time on the bike, the learning curve would have been too steep, I'd likely have crashed, and that would have burned my prospects for the future. But on the other hand how many chances like that do you get? So few come along in a career, your instinct tells you to grab them when you can.

So If I'd been asked to my face, I'd probably have jumped at the chance. There's no knowing how it would have gone. A year or so later Foggy had a high-profile one-off ride on Frankie Chili's factory Honda and landed on his arse in the gravel trap at Donington. That certainly didn't do his reputation or career any good.

CHAPTER 12

THEN IT ALL WENT HORRIBLY WRONG

My first year at the TT as part of an official team was 1988. The previous year, as a privateer, I'd had a trouble-free fortnight, enjoying myself and learning my way round the Mountain Course. Yet even as an official Suzuki rider, I can't say I felt much pressure to do well. Mick wanted success, of course, but there was never any question of taking mad risks to get it. I was out in almost every race apart from the Junior: Formula One, Senior, a GSX-R 750 in production class 'B' and the GSX600F in class 'C'. Despite failing to finish in both the Senior and Formula One, it turned out to be another fairly comfortable TT, although perhaps in my mind that's only compared to the events of the following year.

A strange thing happened with the Teapot. It wasn't a bad bike to ride, mainly because it was such a gutless thing it was easily managed round the TT course. It wasn't fast enough to get you in bother. I was in the top five on the practice leaderboard, running on a standard fuel tank. On the morning of the race the correct tank, painted by Dream Machine in two-tone blue and white Heron racing livery, finally turned up.

It was obvious on the first long straight of the race that something was amiss – a chronic top-end misfire. Sometimes the engine would cut out altogether. Evidently a chunk of paint-job debris was blocking the breather, causing fuel starvation. Luckily Mick had thought to tape a key inside the fairing, so at least I could open the tank to let air in now and again, and I wobbled home in 22nd place.

The other proddy race went far better on the 750 Slingshot. They were a popular bike that year, but almost everyone else jumped on theirs straight out of the crate, in which case they were evil, wobbling violently over the bumps. I was one of the few who'd been campaigning the bike all season, so by TT time I'd reached a near-perfect set-up, partly thanks to a dodgy re-valving job to the rear shock. Fourth behind Steve Hislop, Brian Morrison and Geoff Johnson was my best TT result to date.

By this time I'd settled into a kind of love-hate relationship with the TT, which I imagine is common for most of the faster guys. On the one hand I kind of enjoyed it, especially after a couple of years without many major moments. But on the other, it certainly scared me. I'd be deluding myself to pretend otherwise. Amongst the whole mix of emotions that accompanied TT fortnight, one always stood out, and that was the huge sense of relief at getting on the ferry back to England under your own steam, because that meant you'd survived it again. You felt, 'Right, that's out of the way, I'm probably not going to get maimed for the rest of this season.' And you'd put the thought of next year's TT out of your mind until the last possible moment, as though it were homework you were constantly putting off.

That's not to say I didn't want to do it. I did, but I was always aware of the dangers. I could never understand people who seemed to see racing through rose-coloured blinkers, riders who seemed blind to the realities even a slaphappy bloke like me was only too aware of. A year or so before there'd been a guy called Chris Slack, an ex-trials rider who started off on a 750 Suzuki at club level, winning everything. People would say he'd never been beaten, won 150 races in his first season, going places, watch this space, blah, blah, blah. He came with such a fanfare, so many whistles and bells and more sponsors than he knew what to do with, that even without knowing him he pissed me off. I just thought, 'What's he done? When's he ever gone out in Superstock?'

Some time in '87 I'd been to pick up some Astralite Wheels, and even the Astralite boss, Tony Dawson, was full of this Chris Slack talk – and Tony could talk. He even started me thinking that maybe this guy was a bit special after all. So I bought into it, and started saying the same as everyone else. A few days later Dave Leach dropped round for a brew at our house. Leachy never said a lot, but when he did open his mouth you listened, because he'd been thinking. He was a pretty shrewd guy, pretty laconic.

So I said, 'What about this Chris Slack then?'

Dave had a sip of tea and just said, 'Oh, aye. Wait 'til he has a big accident.'

And that's the point. Slack was quick, I don't doubt it, but it wasn't going to be until he actually got hurt that the possibility of getting hurt seemed to occur to him. The following year he had everything he wanted, a big van with his name on the side, and started doing the big meetings. But before long he'd had a big crash, broke his leg, and packed it all in. It wasn't even as though it was a particularly bad break.

Bike racing might look from the outside like everyone's delusional or has a death wish, but most of us, somewhere at the back of our minds, know the score. One of the things you realise early in racing is that some of your mates are going to get spannered at some point. But why should something worry you when it happens, when you knew all the time that it was a possibility? Because it's self-evident that it might happen it shouldn't be worrying you any more or less whether anyone else gets hurt or not.

Granty always said he could never understand people who had obviously never sat down and thought that they might get killed racing bikes, especially on the roads. I'm not getting at Slack in particular, but I do find it hard to understand that sort of mind-set. That's sticking your hand in the fire and being surprised when it hurts. You've bought the ticket, so you can't complain when the show goes pear-shaped. I sat on every grid knowing it could go badly wrong, and nowhere more so than on the Isle of Man, where the risks seemed so much bigger. To say otherwise is kidding yourself.

So I was always aware of the risks, particularly because I did fall off a bit – typically four or five times a season. Not like Joey Dunlop, who almost never fell off, and was always going to have a better chance from that perspective alone. Sure, you put it to the back of your mind to some extent – you probably couldn't go out and race if you didn't. But it's always there. In a way, facing the risks head-on contributed to what you might call the gladiatorial element, which was certainly part of the appeal.

There's certainly nothing else in racing quite like the build-up to a TT. Even for a World Championship Superbike race, it's generally pretty cool and there's a well-established routine...the tyre-warmers, the brolly girls, the grid interviews. Yes, you're nervous, but you know that the instant the flag drops it's all going to turn from butterflies into action and aggression. But the TT's more like a ritual, starting with your bike being wheeled along the Glencrutchery Road towards the grid. Then you climb on it, pull on your gloves, fasten your helmet, your mechanics leave you to it – but in a way that carries more gravitas than anywhere else. Then everything goes quiet and you're alone with your thoughts. Because you start at intervals, there's more to come. You'll hear the first bike scream towards Bray Hill, revving through the gears. Then another, then another, until eventually it's your turn to fire it off the line. All the time your pulse is racing, your mouth's dry, you just want to get on with it. It builds and builds, like nowhere else.

Riders differ enormously in how they behave before a TT. Some you just can't talk to, and you know to leave them be. I was always the opposite, approachable, really jokey, as if keeping the grim reaper chuckling might keep him off my case. I'd be happy signing autographs, chatting, anything to distract me from thinking about the race. From the outside it probably looked as though I had nerves of steel, but I was crapping myself as much as anyone else. In a way, that was half of what the TT was about. I can't say I enjoyed the lead-up to a TT race, but because of the pressure, the risks, the knife-edge you were on all week, the sense of achievement was always so much bigger when it was over.

Even Foggy wasn't immune. Just before the '89 Formula One TT I was sat in the van taping tear-offs to my visor when Carl dropped by. He asked if I was shitting myself about the race about to start.

'Why would I be?' I said, trying to be cool.

Fully ten years later he reminded me of that conversation. It had obviously been on his mind for a long, long time.

'Were you serious?' he asked.

'Course not. I was crapping myself too.'

Only then did he admit he'd walked away from the van a troubled man, thinking, 'It's just me...I'm weak...I'm pathetic... what's wrong with me?' Even World Champions have their frailties.

Rob McElnea, a man I respect enormously, says there's nowhere else that ever gave him the same buzz as the Isle of Man. He's long retired now, running the Yamaha British Superbike team. But the other year he was even toying with the idea of racing the TT again, just for fun. True, that was probably his mid-life crisis talking more than his head. I told him he was a daft old git, but I can understand exactly where he was coming from. Even now I look forward to riding in TT parades, lashing down those straights at ridiculous speeds. What biker wouldn't relish the prospect of 200-odd miles on open roads, closed to traffic just so you could go and have fun?

Rob was Foggy's team manager for his last TT race, that epic duel when he just lost out to Hizzy's Norton in the 1992 Senior. He said it was one of the few times he'd been truly impressed by a rider, because he couldn't understand how anyone could ride that Yamaha at all, let alone set a lap record that would stand for another seven years. By the time it finished, the exhaust was falling off and scraping on right-handers, the chain was jumping the sprockets, something had dropped off the rear axle and was sawing it's way through the swing-arm, third gear had disappeared, and so had the clutch for most of the last lap. Rob wheeled it away quickly because he didn't want anyone to see it, it was that trashed.

Years later I asked Carl why he'd kept going on such a shed, but it was obvious. So long as his signals were telling him he was in with a shout of a win – which was all that ever really mattered to him – he'd ride round any problems for as long as he physically could.

A lot's said about the essence of the TT being to race against the Mountain Course rather than against other riders. Sod that. That was a notion I never bought into at all. If someone came past me or I saw someone's arse disappearing round the next bend, I was at it. That was my focus, to the point that I never really strove for fast laps, which for most people is the bottom line at the TT. It's the only circuit in the world where people – riders and fans alike – focus on the average speed. Hardly anyone has a clue what speed the Brands Hatch lap record equates to, but everyone knows it about the Isle of Man. So to that extent, it is the circuit you're racing against, and often the conditions. But fundamentally I just wanted to race other guys. Maybe I wasn't cut out to be a TT racer, although I was still young. Maybe I'd have matured into it, if it weren't for the events of '89.

Of course with hindsight it's clear that I didn't need to have done the TT at all. The culture of racing was changing, and it was no longer an essential part of any rider's job description or CV. The factories no longer insisted you do it, although it was still important to some British teams, and it was perfectly possible to make a living elsewhere. But none of this seemed half so obvious at the time, particularly for a daft 22-year-old still besotted with the idea of actually being paid to race a bike – anywhere.

After winning the big production race at the North-West 200, I quite fancied my chances at the '89 TT, which was just a couple of weeks later. Nonetheless, you were always inclined to worry about the big proddy bikes, because they didn't need asking twice to spit you off. On the other hand the GSX-R1100 had been all right at the North-West, and with a bit of luck would work as well at the TT. The FZR1000 Yamahas were probably the best in the class, but I felt sorry for anyone who had to ride a Honda or Kawasaki, because their 1000s were big, unwieldy buses. Ray Swann reckoned that putting the ZX-10 round the Island at any speed was like steering a half-filled tin bath down a bobsleigh run. They were fast, heavy, and vague on the steering, so half the time you were a passenger with no real idea where you were going. And the CBR1000 wasn't much better. Neither bike was ever really meant to go racing.

As well as the GSX-R, we had the factory Formula One bike, which was the sweetest thing to race and couldn't have been more different from the GSX-R. It went exactly where you pointed, stopped and turned well and landed dead straight off jumps. Finally we had the 600cc Teapot, which, although we always mocked it – as did everyone else, especially when they were accusing it of being bent – was quite a rideable bike. At short circuits like Donington it didn't turn quickly enough, but it was stable and long-legged, ideal for the Mountain Circuit. It didn't have much grunt, but did rev, particularly after Mick filled it with dodgy bits.

So for one reason or another I wasn't shitting myself as much as usual before the TT. In fact I was quite looking forward to it. Little did I know.

As usual, race week began with the Formula One TT, held in good weather. For almost the entire six laps I had a brilliant set-to with Foggy, both on time and on the road, although he just came out on top. I was getting good signals – people were poking out of hedge bottoms with chalkboards all over the place – so I knew exactly how I was doing. The pair of us were dicing for fifth and sixth, and might even have expected to get near the rostrum, but it was one of those races where very few of the top runners dropped out. This was the race in which Hizzy took the outright lap record past 120mph for the first time, actually lapping at over 121mph. I managed sixth place with a best lap at 118mph, which I was pretty happy with.

For a while fifth or even fourth place had looked possible. Going into Ramsey on the last lap I thought I had a couple of seconds on Carl, but even though I reckoned I was pretty hot stuff over the Mountain he still beat me, the bastard. I could say that I was distracted a little by noises from the back of the bike, where it turned out that a couple of sprocket carrier bolts had come adrift and were sawing through the swing-arm. But in truth it didn't hold me up more than a second or so. Foggy must have been flying, and just grabbed fourth place from Graeme McGregor by the end. In later years he insisted that he could pull that amount out of absolutely anyone, even Steve Hislop, over the Mountain, but then he was never unduly handicapped by modesty.

I followed that up with a third in the Supersport TT on the Teapot. Strangely, since it turned out to be my only TT rostrum finish, until I checked I thought I'd placed fourth. Perhaps any fleeting sense of achievement evaporated with what happened next. But it wasn't a bad result, by any means, on a bike which, dodgy as it was, wasn't really in the same class as most of the rest.

For most of the Teapot race I didn't have any problems, and the one I did have was entirely of my own making. Perhaps another way I wasn't totally cut out to be a TT ace was that I couldn't help making a special effort at places like Gooseneck and Quarter Bridge where there were always stacks of spectators. Why, you might well wonder? Me too. Wasn't I a factory rider being paid to do a proper job, not piss about entertaining the punters? Instead, I was usually thinking, 'Hey, guys, watch this,' and stuff it in sideways and chattering. That's probably what I had in mind when I was in the hedge bottom with my knee down at the left-hander before the Gooseneck. I just couldn't help myself. I wanted to look the part. Then, stunt riding over, I'd get back down to business.

For the 1300cc proddy race I qualified about third-quickest, behind Leachy and Geoff Johnson. Luckily the likes of Hislop, Brian Morrison and Swanny were on Hondas and Kawasakis, so were realistically out of the running before they even started. So I thought I was maybe in for a result. In practice the leading riders had been doing 114, 115mph, which seemed hard work and bloody quick. At the time Geoff Johnson held the lap record, 116.55mph, which Nick Jefferies would raise to over 117mph in the race, also on a Yamaha.

During practice I'd seen Leachy setting off on his weird metallic blue proddy FZR, so I dashed out right behind and tried to tag on to see what his secrets were. We were both going pretty damn quick, but he managed to pull out a few yards on me, so mostly I wasn't close enough to see exactly what he was doing. But at Barregarrow, where there's a huge compression at the bottom of the hill, you didn't need to be close. The FZR bottomed out that hard I thought his suspension had collapsed. Sparks and bits of Yamaha flew everywhere. I was convinced I'd get round the corner of the cottage to see him and the bike spread over 300 yards of road. But no, he was still on it, still weaving down to the 13th Milestone. Nuts.

Mez, my team-mate, was also one of the pre-race favourites. I'd known him since '87 as a competitor, and from '88 as a team-mate. He was a funny bloke, a real oddball, not only in the obvious way that he had a lot of health problems and looked unusual, but he and I were never really on the same wavelength. He used to look at me as though I was off my trolley, which half the time I probably was.

So he and I weren't natural mates, although that's often the case in any race squad. But you couldn't help but like Mez, and we got on really well, spending a lot of time together doing open days, sharing hotel rooms, and so on. But it would never occur to me to ring him up on a weekend off racing and invite him out for a pint. He was 36 in '89, so we were from very different eras. Being much younger, I tended to live life at 100mph, whilst he generally preferred a bit of peace and quiet when he wasn't on the track. Our life tempos were totally different, me at 10,000rpm and him just ticking over most of the time. But nothing seemed to bother him, and he didn't care what other people thought of him. He'd probably grown up as something of a loner, on account of his looks. And with all his experience, he wasn't under Mick's wing in the way I was, so he and Malcolm, his mechanic, tended to keep themselves to themselves. Not like me and Butch, who were young and daft and thought life was a big game, so weren't the most relaxing of company. Mez seemed to spend half his time with his eyes rolled up and a resigned 'What did I do to deserve Whitham?' look on his face. Looking back, I was probably the team-mate from hell.

But as a rider Mez was tough and experienced. He'd rarely bother me on the shorts, but on the Isle of Man he was something else. In the big proddy race he started number 10, as usual, with me number 12, ten seconds behind. He was slightly built and struggled a bit on the big, production-based bikes, seeming more at home on the likes of the Padgetts' F2 Yamaha on which he'd had such success. So in the race I wasn't particularly surprised to catch and pass him quite early on, contending for third, with Leachy leading. I was telling myself to settle down, ride intelligently, thinking that if Dave had any problems I was in with a shout of a win. Everything was going to plan. I caught Morrison on the Honda. Next thing, going into Ballacraine on lap two, Mez is outbraking me. 'Bloody hell,' was all I could think, 'I'm going to be stuck behind him right through the Glen Helen section'. Obviously you don't want to do anything silly with your team-mate, especially round there, so I just had to bide my time. And that's when it happened.

Now Mez certainly knew what he was doing round there. He tanked round Ballaspur, over Ballig Bridge, where you roll it a touch into Dorans, a lovely, sweeping bend, neat as you like. Dorans was quite ripply, and quite cambered, so you needed to keep to the left, but Mez drifted off-line, slightly over the crown of the road. The Suzuki's back end stepped out about six inches on the adverse camber, and as it gripped again the front lurched, by which time he was in the gutter. There was nowhere for him to go. His front wheel clipped the kerb and threw him into the wall, then there was a horrible scraping noise of him and the bike cartwheeling between the footpath and the stonework with bits of GSX-R flying off in all directions.

That wall's evil – hard, angular, with sharp chunks like knife blades. But as long as you keep tumbling, you've got a chance. Then Mez hit something, probably a gatepost, and stopped, suddenly. It was sickening, obviously bad, but I didn't know what to make of it. Part of me was thinking, 'That's my mate, probably dead,' and the other part's thinking, 'How often have you got back to the paddock and he's all right, climbing onto another bike?'

For the next few miles I couldn't concentrate…running off-line, all over the shop. By the time I'd reached Quarry Bends I'd given myself a good telling off: 'Get it out of your mind, get on with your job.' Ironically I felt as though that was the point at which I was getting into my rhythm again. Then I clipped the kerb.

At Quarries you go into the first right-hander really quick, by which time you're already committed to the next left-hander, because on the proddy bikes there's only so much you can do to muscle it about and change line – the speed just sort of throws you into the next bit of track. As the bike settled into the left-hander it felt all right, then I felt it scrape and move. For an instant the front wheel was searching for grip, then – *bang*! – it all went down and I hit the floor. I wasn't really worried. There wasn't time for that. But it was one of the only times I've thought I wasn't going to feel a thing, because there's a wall coming up and I'm dead. This is it. There's absolutely nothing you can do and it's always strangely dispassionate.

Luckily for me, because the bike had clung on for just that split second after hitting the kerb it had just managed to get me halfway round the corner and fired me down the straight. As I slid along the tarmac I was dimly aware of a noise from the crowd, then found myself sitting on the white line in the middle of the road, 100 yards or so from where it all started, facing towards Ramsey.

'Bloody 'ell,' I thought, 'I'm all right.'

In almost the same instant there's a huge cacophony of banging and scraping from somewhere behind. 'Christ,' I thought, 'I'm going to get hit by something else.' I leapt to my feet and ran to the side of the road, then looked back, and there's such a commotion – debris, stuff everywhere...bikes, petrol and oil pissing out, bits of fairing, people in leathers lying in the road. One bike had hit the wall and ricocheted right over me, apparently, although I never saw it, and clipped some spectators. One youngster had a broken arm.

At the time I wasn't aware which riders were involved, but later remembered having passed Steve Henshaw and Mike Seward having a bit of a ding-dong. They'd passed me back when I was fretting about Mez, then I'd got my act together and passed them again. The poor bastards would have been riding so close, had so little chance. I think Henshaw was slightly ahead at the time, saw my accident, sat up, and Seward had no time to react, nowhere to go, and ran into the back of him.

It was so clearly a bad one. I looked at Henshaw lying in the road, but was frightened to go over for what I might see, not that I could have done anything useful anyway. Seward was obviously alive but seriously injured, his legs contorted under him, screaming in pain.

I didn't even go back to look at my bike, just walked off in a daze and climbed over the fence next to the Wildlife Park with my helmet under my arm. There was quite a crowd of spectators around, and they just seemed to part, noiselessly. No one said a word. Not a thing. It hardly seemed real. I didn't know what to think.

A local bloke offered me a lift back to Douglas in his old Mini, and it was only during the journey that it occurred to me what Andrea and the rest of the team would be going through. That morning Hizzy had been off at the same place in the Junior TT, but got up and walked away without a scratch. Word of that crash came over the radio as Andrea and I were getting ready to go to the paddock, and I'd remarked that it's about 130, 140mph at that spot. It's a place that you just can't fall off: there's a bank on one side and a wall on the other, and Hizzy's the luckiest man on earth to be alive. And a couple of hours later, the first news she has is that I'm off at precisely the same place, and that the helicopter's on its way. And that's on top of the news that Mez is off. It was another 90 minutes before she got word I was alive.

By the time I got back to Douglas the race was finished. There was no one in our pit so I wandered down to the team's lodgings at Laureston Manor. As I walked up the drive, everyone's sat on the lawn – Andrea, Butch, Mez's mechanic Malcolm – not speaking, just staring into space, almost catatonic. I learned that Mez was seriously hurt but still alive, which I could hardly believe. Then Mick arrived from the hospital, and you knew from the look on his face that he'd gone.

'I can't do this any more. I can't race on Friday,' I told Andrea. We packed up, loaded the car, drove to the ferry and went home. Not much was said. There was nothing much to be said.

It was the most wretched day of my racing career. Obviously I felt bad for Mez, because he was a mate. It seemed unfair that he could die when he'd been so good around the Isle of Man, at the stage in his career where he'd have been thinking about retiring not too far down the line.

And of course I felt wretched too, that in no small way I'd caused another accident where a good mate had been mangled and another I knew fairly well had been killed. No matter how much you try to rationalise it, no matter how often you tell yourself that they knew the risks, and falling off in front of them wasn't something I'd meant to do, the fact remains that I was instrumental in taking a life.

But it's also true that we all accept the risks. If the same thing had happened the other way round, I wouldn't have been happy, but I'm sure I'd have accepted it in that way. This was brought home to me just a couple of months later at the Ulster Grand Prix, what turned out to be my last road race other than Macau and Scarborough. I'd already had a rostrum finish on the 600, and was going well when I had a huge crash on the Formula One bike at Flow Bog Corner, sliding feet-first into a ditch and bank at about 100mph and smashing my ankle to bits.

In all there were nine breaks, some of them compound, from six inches above the ankle down. The other ankle was also cracked, and my left wrist broken. I spent a week at Belfast's Royal Victoria hospital at the top of the Falls Road, with Andrea and mum braving burned out cars and other hairy clutter to visit. The Irish racing community, as ever, rallied round. I hadn't been in hospital a day when Alan Patterson turned up with a telly. Jim Waters, Dave Leach's Irish sponsor, put up Andrea and mum.

I'd no idea what caused the crash, but when riders say that you usually know they've made some sort of mistake. All I knew was that the front wheel had locked and gone down for no apparent reason. When Butch got the bike back he found that one of the floating front brake rotors had broken up, damaging the top-hat fasteners which hold it in place. When they pulled apart the caliper there was a huge gouge on the inside face. Obviously at least one of the top-hats had jammed in the caliper and locked the wheel.

It shouldn't have happened, but it did. It could have happened anywhere and I could have been killed. But there was no point jumping up and down complaining about it – not that I was in a state to do any jumping anyway. It's racing. Things do go wrong.

But in the aftermath of that TT meeting, my main need was to get away from the Island and start sorting myself out mentally. I didn't at that point decide not to race at the TT ever again. I just had a head-full of sausage meat and didn't know what to think.

The 1989 season must have been one of the worst in the history of the TT course. As well as Mez and Steve Henshaw, Phil Hogg, John Mulcahy and Marco Fattorelli were killed during TT practice, and in September a further three riders died at the Manx Grand Prix. But even without that level of carnage, by the end of the year I'd come to the conclusion that I'd be stupid not to take the TT tragedy and the Ulster crash as a warning.

In most walks of life the more you do something, the better you get at it and the better your chances of surviving whatever it throws at you. But on the roads, the longer the tour of duty the shorter the odds are against you. I've heard ex-World War Two bomber crews say similar things. If you keep knocking on that door, sooner or later it's going to open, or so it seemed to me. Looking back it's hard to believe I was only 23 when I rode my last TT race. Maybe I also tackled it when I was too young, too wild, too immature.

So during the following winter I began thinking that maybe I didn't have to go back and do the roads any more. It wasn't so much that I hadn't enjoyed the TT and the Irish meetings, because on the whole I did. Indeed, if I ever have grandchildren, telling them about having raced on the Island will be one of my proudest moments. They're never likely to ask whether I'd raced at Donington Park, but the TT has a special aura of its own. So I'm glad to have raced there.

At the time it had also been shown by a few riders, Terry Rymer in particular, that doing the TT might even be counter-productive. Tel was going really well by then on the Loctite Yamaha, winning a couple of World Superbike rounds. Naturally it occurred to me that maybe I'd missed the boat a little, because I'd been as fast as him not long before. Foggy, and to a lesser extent Hizzy, were pretty much the last men able to do both the TT and short circuits to the same world-class level, and even Foggy's career didn't really take off until after his last TT in '92.

That whole period, apart from the obvious – the deaths on the Isle of Man and breaking my ankle – was one of my happiest times in racing. I was having fun on and off the bikes, and had great mates, guys like Ray Swann and Roger Hurst. Partly because of the interest created by the factory Norton rotaries the British championships seemed to be emerging from the doldrums. Crowds were increasing. There was a mood of optimism in the air. On the track I couldn't seem to put a foot wrong and was doing what I wanted to do, working with people I liked, and Andrea and I were by now an item and getting on well. I wasn't making mega-money, but at the time neither was anyone else in the British championship. Life was good, but it was about to bite me on the arse.

CHAPTER 13

'SO WHO'S GOING TO STOP US?'

This was the lost year, brightened only by the arrival of the world's grumpiest border collie, named Mez after my late team-mate.

At the end of '89 Mick was keen that I stay with him and Suzuki, and I think pretty much assumed that I would. But in the meantime I'd had a phone call from Honda Britain's Martin Marshall which gave me another option. I'd had a chat with Martin at Donington the previous summer, wondering if there were any possibilities of a ride for the following year. He didn't commit himself, but his reaction was positive.

One of the problems with staying with Suzuki was that they didn't have a superbike, at a time when Superbikes was obviously the coming class. Honda, of course, had the RC30, on one of which Fred Merkel had just won back-to-back World titles. The V-four appeared to be the bike to have. Little did we know.

Suzuki's Formula One bike was still good, but not eligible for Superbikes, whilst F1 was a class which seemed to be fading. Carl Fogarty had won the world F1 title the year before, but for 1990 the series wouldn't even be a proper World Championship, just the Formula One Cup. From my point of view there was an even bigger factor: the F1 series also more or less obliged you to race on the roads, which by then I'd decided was no longer for me. Suzuki had been promising a bang-up-to-date Superbike for some time, but it never seemed to happen, and they certainly had nothing new in the pipeline for 1990. On paper the new 'RR' version of the GSX-R750 looked as though it might be the part, but without factory backing it was never going anywhere. Only Suzuki Germany persevered with the 'RR', with Ernst Geschwender and Sven Seidel – who was so mad we christened him 'Sui-Seidel' – but even they never made it really competitive.

Above all, the assumption was that Mick's team would mainly be competing in British championships, rather than in international events. Although I'd had two successful and happy seasons with Mick I was frustrated at not having a competitive machine on which I could move up to world level. Those two seasons had also shown me that I had talent. I knew I could run with anybody. But without a competitive superbike, I felt that I was being left behind by Carl, Terry Rymer, Steve Hislop and the rest. I didn't ask Mick what he thought. I didn't need to. I knew what he'd have said.

I signed for Honda even before going to Macau for what was my last ride for Suzuki that season, although I kept the deal to myself. Shortly after, I thought I'd better ring Mick to tell him. He was stunned. Later he wrote me a letter, obviously upset. I wrote back saying that it was nothing personal, just that I thought the Honda ride was in my best interests. I was fond of Mick and had a lot to thank him for, so it was difficult. In truth, I felt a bit of a shit. What I didn't find out for some time was that John Norman, the managing director of Suzuki GB, had been told by his Japanese head office that they wanted me to ride a factory-backed Suzuki in World Superbikes for the 1990 season. It wouldn't have been a particularly competitive bike, but after two years of scratching around for cash the deal carried a proper budget and would have been an opening onto the international stage. Unfortunately by the time Mick learned of this I'd already signed to ride for Honda.

The Honda set-up, though, looked perfect. This was Neil Tuxworth's first year as team manager, so the squad was run from his hometown of Louth, near Cadwell Park, which was only an hour's drive from Huddersfield. Even before I signed I knew who my team-mate would be: Carl Fogarty. That was an attraction in itself, since by then we were becoming good mates. But on top of that was a competitive edge. 'Now we'll see,' I thought to myself, 'now we're on equal bikes we'll see who's top dog.' Naturally, in my head it would be me who'd come out on top. In fact it wasn't just Carl that I knew I was going to beat. I was absolutely convinced that the RC30 was going to be the best race bike, with the best, most tractable engine, and I was just going to fly on it. After all, if you're good at sports you have to have a bit of confidence in yourself.

The first meeting of the season wasn't going to be some pissy little shakedown, but a big one: the Daytona 200-miler in March. The team had prepared the race bikes, put them in a box and air-freighted them to Florida. Until we arrived there Foggy and I hadn't even seen them, let alone sat on them. Even our new team leathers went straight from the Kushitani factory in Japan to Florida.

Both of us got down to business well, going quicker and quicker all practice week. The bikes weren't brilliantly fast, but on the speed-bowl's fast banking you could slipstream your way past other bikes, so we were definitely competitive. The quick men were the American Jamie James and Scotland's Niall McKenzie, who was doing grands prix at the time. Everyone expected one of them to win, but when the race started they took each other out on the first corner. I saw them both scuttling onto the grass and remember grinning inside my helmet. 'That'll do me,' I thought.

With those two out of the way, Carl, John Ashmead, Randy Renfrow, myself and a couple of other top Yanks duked it out for the whole race. The 200 is a long, long race, with tyre and refuelling stops, which mean that the leaderboard changes every few laps. You'd come in for a pit stop lying second, battle your way back to fourth…then someone would break down and you'd find yourself leading for a while. It was fairly confused but all-action, and both Carl and I held the lead at various points. Then, with about 15 laps to go, Foggy slid off. So it was all down to me.

I was leading when I came in for my last pit stop, put on a new rear tyre and set off in pursuit of Ashmead and Renfrow, who were dicing for the lead about five seconds or so ahead. The start/finish straight is so fast and frantic you can hardly read your signal board, so as well as a board there, Andrea was signalling from the infield. A few laps later she put out 'L11 P3 +1.5', which meant there were 11 laps to go, I was third and lapping 1.5 seconds quicker than the leaders.

'Friggin' 'ell,' I thought, 'I'm going to win…£25,000…what a bloody good do.' I was utterly convinced I was about to become the first Brit ever to win Daytona. Next thing, I'm on my arse. I'd been so busy celebrating I'd not seen the warning flags and slid off on an oil spill.

Yes, we'd blown it, but we'd been quick. Carl and I came away from Daytona absolutely bubbling with confidence. I remember sitting on the Jumbo on the way home when Carl came right out and said one of us was bound to win the World Superbike Championship that year. Even for him, it was quite a bold thing to say.

'Do you reckon?' I replied.

'Based on that performance at Daytona,' said the cocky bastard, 'who's going to stop us?'

He was like a Jehovah's Witness – a bit mad but totally convincing. I believed everything he said and for one glorious day I was Superman. Then reality bit. From Florida we went straight to the first World Superbike round at Jerez in southern Spain. The pair of us strutted into the pits like the second coming of Mike Hailwood, but that didn't last long. I qualified 21st, Carl 15th. We were shit, our bikes were shit, and we couldn't ride 'em. It was a disaster. I sat in the garage thinking, 'What's going on? A week ago I was winning Daytona and now I can barely ride a bloody bike.'

From then on it went from bad to worse. In total I had 14 crashes that season, 90 per cent of them through losing the front end. Even when it wasn't painful, it was intensely frustrating. Previously I'd always raced bikes on which I'd been able to push hard and still retain a bit of a buffer zone. I might go for an overtaking move or an extra-quick lap aware that I might fall off, but I'd still go for it anyway; sometimes I would fall off and sometimes I wouldn't, but it was my decision to go for it, and the bikes had given me enough confidence to try. But with the Honda there was no feedback, no warning at all. The front just let go without any warning…just *bang*, and down you went.

Honda's original plan had been for us both to do a full season of World Superbikes, interspersed with the British championship. But after the first two or three world rounds it was abundantly clear that we were pissing into the wind. Tuxworth became so used to me mangling his bikes he practically used to wince every time I went out. After the first few crashes and crap showings he was quite straightforward about it. He simply said there was no point taking me to Hockenheim World Superbikes, because it would be a waste of budget. I had to agree that he was right. Carl struggled with the RC30 too, although he certainly came to terms with it a lot better than me.

And it wasn't just that I couldn't win on the damn thing. I actually became scared of it. I was like a dog that'd been kicked every time someone walked past, always expecting the next kick. Front-end crashes are strange. They're the ones riders fear most of all, because they're so sudden and almost always end up with you on the ground, even though you usually slide off the low-side and they rarely hurt. Yet every racer is comfortable with rear-end slides, because you usually recover from them. But if you don't, you're looking at a high-side and, often as not, a heap of pain.

By mid-season I couldn't even seem to stay on the bike long enough to high-side. I expected to lose the front and land in a heap almost every lap. I'd arrive at meetings not expecting a rostrum finish but wondering instead where I was going to bin it and whether it'd hurt. I had a few good moments, like running second and breaking the lap record at Snetterton, but then losing the front the next lap. But they were few and far between.

I never understood why I couldn't get on with that bike, and still don't. It seemed to be something like a combination of my riding technique and the characteristics of the RC30 that we simply couldn't fix – even with chassis guru Ron Williams practically camping in our pit. I pondered over it, fretted, experimented with riding styles, bought books about bike set-up, asked people who knew about that sort of thing. Nothing worked. Nothing made the slightest bit of difference, and in the process I was becoming totally freaked by the whole business. By mid-season I was ready to pack in bike racing.

Just a few months before I'd felt on top of the world. Now, all I could think was, 'Is that it? Has it gone? Have I lost it?' I was beginning to think I'd much rather clock in and out of a factory or dig holes in the road...anything that wouldn't lay me open to so much failure and pain. It was that horrible. I'd lost all my self-respect.

Everything I touched that year turned to shite. For instance, I had a lovely Lunar caravan for race meetings. It spent most weekdays parked up at the airfield, where it can get very windy. One breezy day I looked out of the window just in time to see a gust pick it up, roll it over and blow it down the runway. In about five seconds it was smashed into a thousand pieces. There were cups and saucers, plates, cushions, underpants and all sorts of stuff flying the length of Crosland Moor, pursued by what was left of the caravan. It was just another hefty kick in the teeth. 'It's a nightmare,' I thought. 'My life's falling apart. What have I done to deserve it?'

So all in all it was a truly crap season. Eventually I told Tuxworth that if he wanted me to stop riding and turning up for meetings, he just had to say the word. For the most part I soldiered on, getting more and more downhearted, although I sat out a couple of non-championship UK meetings at the end of the season. By that time I'd probably trashed more RC30 bits than the entire World Superbike grid.

Mind you, I was still versatile. I could trash four-wheeled as well as two-wheeled Hondas. For the season Honda had loaned me a Prelude, on the firm understanding that it came back in one piece. In August I rode the RC30 in a support race at the Donington Park grand prix. On Sunday night me, Andrea, Ian and Bill Simpson ended up having a party with a bunch of yank racers. One of them, Kevin Schwantz I think, decided a lap or two of the circuit would be a top idea. Trouble was, the yanks were all in hire cars, while I was in my precious Prelude. And they just went mad. There were wrecked cars everywhere...two on their roof, another on its side. When one stuffed itself into the side of the Prelude, that was about the point that I started to think I couldn't afford to keep up with these boys. Even after the police arrived they were still at it. I ended up sat in the back of a police car next to a pissed-up ex-World Champion, who was still shouting, 'Let's go, let's go,' as police cars chased other hire cars round the track.

But on the RC30 I couldn't even get arrested. At the time there weren't that many riding jobs on offer, and I wasn't exactly my own biggest fan. Who the hell was going to give me a job? I wouldn't even have employed myself, the state I was in. It genuinely felt as though my race career might be over and I'd have to get a proper job.

Nonetheless, I tried to go through the motions, and now and again something would happen to cheer me up. In September I drove down to Donington Park to have a word with a few racing people, see if I could resurrect anything from the wreckage of my career. In the paddock I bumped into Ian Simpson, who'd become a good mate. He'd been having fun, too.

'It's been a disaster,' he said.

'What, bike blown up?'

'No, me dad.'

Now things have a habit of happening to Simmo, and also to his dad, Bill, who used to be a talented racer in his own right – one cold winter night he was abandoned outside a transport caff on the A5 wearing nothing but his underpants. But on this occasion Bill had hit lucky, or so he thought, when he tapped up a woman in a pub near the circuit. Simmo left Lothario to it, driving back to the paddock thinking, 'Good on ya, dad.'

Simmo had a typical Merc van with a couple of bunks behind the cab, then a bulkhead with the bike gear behind. Their mechanic, Fraser – an enormous ginger Scotsman – had the top bunk, about six feet off the floor, with Simmo in the bottom bunk. Bill, returning from his amorous adventures in the small hours, slithered into his sleeping bag on the floor.

Some time later Simmo was woken by a groaning noise, accompanied by Bill croaking that he's in terrible pain. He got up and turned on the light, to see his dad, who's built like a whippet, pinned to the floor by 16 stone of snoring Jock. Fraser had rolled off the top bunk, plummeted six feet onto Bill, and not even woken up. Bill was awake, all right. His collarbone had snapped.

Bill wasn't best pleased but it brightened up the day for the rest of us. Not that Simmo himself was any more immune from accidents than his dad. A couple of years later I was on a fast practice lap at Kirkistown when he wobbled out of the pit lane under my front wheel, the daft sod. We ended up in huge pile, sliding along right quick – at one stage he was actually sitting in my lap – before ending up in a bog. I picked myself up but he was lying flat on his back, looking in a bad way. I ran over to check he was all right, reaching him just as the marshals arrived. As the marshals peered down through his visor he opened his eyes and said, 'It's all right – we're professionals.' I just cracked up.

At the same Donington meeting I also bumped into Mick Grant.

It was a bit tentative, a little uncomfortable, but we'd both had disappointing seasons and wanted to move on. Mine had been an unmitigated disaster, and Mick's results, with Roger Burnett as his sole rider, had mostly been disappointing. I could have my old job back if I wanted it. There wouldn't be a lot of money – where had I heard that before? – but Mick was prepared to give it a go if I was. I wasn't likely to get any better offers, so I said yes and ended up back with Granty and Suzuki for '91.

CHAPTER 14

BACK WITH THE OLD PALS ACT

Being back with Suzuki was like a reunion with old pals. Granty and Butch were still there, much the same if a little older – as were the bikes. The Suzuki Formula One bike had been getting more modified as time went on, most obviously with big air scoops through the screen and tank to the airbox. Although I won on it at Pembrey in April – my first win for almost two years – the old girl was long in the tooth, about five years old, which is an eternity in racing development. I'd thought even before I signed that we might well struggle to compete. Mick knew that I needed something to get me going again, to regain some of the confidence that had been shattered the previous year. So he hatched a plan.

Included in the programme for the big national meetings that year were non-championship races open to almost anything – races like Snetterton Race of Aces and Mallory Race of the Year. Although there was no reason to stick to 750cc for these races, most teams would be running their Superbikes or F1 machines rather than building something bigger just for the odd race. But not Mick. He had a knack of not just interpreting the rules, but sussing out what was going to be competitive and what wasn't. He figured this might be our best shot at doing a bit of winning. There was also the money angle, which he was good about. He couldn't pay me a lot of money, but if I could arrange a meeting at, say, Kirkistown with good start- and prize-money, he'd be happy for us to do it. Scarborough was usually a bit of an earner too.

So Mick and Butch set to turning a GSX-R1100 engine into a race bike. It was nothing very radical, mainly race cams, extra compression, a race exhaust system and big flat-slide carbs which they slotted into a spare factory XR81 endurance chassis. The bike didn't even have a name. It was just a big lump of engine in a super-light frame.

Trouble was, I hated it. It had a power curve like a diesel – the oomph was all in the mid-range and there was no top-end. Yes, it had lots of power, but just seemed to lose interest when you revved it. And there were only five gears, miles apart in a big tractor gearbox. Try as I might on the 1100, I struggled to get within half a second of my 750cc time, so we didn't run it and I sort of forgot about the idea.

Luckily Mick and Butch didn't. Instead, they got plotting again. Somehow they got hold of a set of Cosworth pistons which, when bolted into an over-bored 750cc endurance engine, gave 880cc. We couldn't run any championship events with the bike, but it was totally legal for the non-championship races.

That year's championship was pretty strange anyway. This was right at the end of the TT Formula One era, but the third year of Superbikes. So whilst Superbikes were taking over, there were still plenty of competitive Formula One bikes around. The obvious solution was a race series open to both, so they came up with a hybrid TT Superbike class, although it was actually even more complicated than that. At the time British racing was really struggling for coverage and sponsorship, so when ITV said they'd like to televise the championship, the race authorities jumped. Trouble was, TV only wanted to air a six-round series, but six rounds wasn't nearly enough to keep the circuit promoters happy. The result was two British TT Superbike championships, the TT Supercup and the TT Superbike series, running piggy-back. Both featured exactly the same riders and machines.

Despite its age, our Formula One bike was competitive all year, and we ran strongly in both series. Although I managed only three wins, we were rarely out of the top three, which, after the disasters of the previous season, was brilliant. Not just me, but the whole team was travelling to meetings more or less expecting a good result. In no time all the old confidence came flooding back. Butch and Mick were good to be around and we were enjoying ourselves, off the track and on. The misery of 1990 was soon forgotten. Racing was fun again.

As well as the 750 and 880, I raced an RGV250 in the Supersport

400 series, winning first time out at Pembrey. Compared to the big stuff, these bikes felt like toys – great fun to ride, and seemingly designed for close racing. We had a few good results, including three wins, but by mid-season the new generation of 400cc four-strokes were taking over, and keeping the 250cc two-stroke competitive was hard work. The result was all sorts of mechanical problems – twisted cranks, power valves falling apart – and our championship campaign sort of fizzled out in a pile of melted pistons and broken bits.

The 880, though, was magnificent. The Snetterton Supercup meeting featured two TT Superbike championship legs, for which we were obviously limited to 750cc, followed by the day's finale, the Race of Aces, for which the 880 was eligible. We didn't even use two complete bikes. I ran the same chassis all day, with Butch just sliding in the big engine for the final race. Anyone looking wouldn't have known the difference.

I've always liked Snetterton. It's a bit of a windswept old airfield, but such a speedbowl, and I'd always done well there. Unfortunately our 750 wasn't very quick compared to the Yamahas and – especially – the Nortons. I had to ride my nuts off to get a third and a fourth in the Supercup races, so I was looking forward to having a bit more power. In the Race of Aces I got a so-so start, came out of Sears onto the back straight in fifth place, opened the throttle and just drove past everyone. By the Esses I was leading. It was wonderful. That thing was *fast*.

I was still leading on the second lap when someone slid off and piled into the tyre barrier at the Bombhole. The race was stopped so they could pick up the bits and we all toured back to the grid to await the restart. Rob Mac pulled up alongside me and, as his engine stopped, nodded at the 880 and said, 'What the fuck is that thing?'

I just grinned and said, 'Did you like that?' I certainly did.

When the race restarted, same thing: I couldn't get the 880 off the line very well, but on the back straight just cleared off again. Superb.

As a team we'd grafted for the win and deserved it, on a totally legal machine. Yet inevitably there were a few mutters of complaint, all from people who, according to Mick, 'haven't even read the regulations to see what the cc limit is.'

In fact the first doubts had surfaced at Pembréy, before the 880 was even built. Apparently Ray Stringer had a mate who worked for Cosworth, who'd told him Granty had bought a set of 'big' pistons. Stringer told Barry Symmonds and Colin Wright, who ran Honda and Kawasaki's race teams. They all seem to have put two and two together and made five, concluding that we were running an illegal big engine in the 750cc class. If I won, they told Mick, they'd protest and demand the engine was stripped. 'Be my guest,' responded Mick, who then arranged for *Motor Cycle News* journalist Norrie White to witness the process. When I won, the engine was measured, found to be totally legal – and was pronounced as such in the following week's *MCN*.

For the moment, though, the upshot was that including '88 and '89 I'd won the Race of Aces three times in all. Despite the glittering array of names on the trophy – Hailwood, Sheene, Surtees, just about everyone in British racing history – no one had chalked up three wins before. It had always been said that anyone claiming three wins would keep the pot, but they seemed keen to hang on to it. In fact I was always unlucky with trophies, once winning the Scarborough Gold Cup a few days after it had been nicked. A year or two later, after it had been recovered, I won it again – but still never even got to touch it because by then it was securely locked up in a museum.

In mid-season we had our one European excursion. Mick thought it'd be fun to do the GSX-R Suzuki World Cup, which was supposed to be for non-factory-supported Suzuki riders – anyone who rode a non-factory-supported Suzuki in their domestic championships. In the first one, three years before, me and Mez had gone out to Jerez to act as mechanics for Ray Stringer, Mark Linscott and a bloke called Hodges. Basically, they smashed the bikes to bits, we tried to fix 'em, then we all came home. Other than the fact that Suzuki ended up with about 40 scrap GSX-Rs, the idea even seemed to work for them, so they continued to run the World Cup in future years.

I suspect that Suzuki thought that a team like ours wasn't eligible. Mick thought otherwise. 'Look,' he said, 'you can't call us any sort of factory-supported. There's a factory, and there's us, and naff-all ever comes our way. So let's enter. You like them GSXR

146

750 proddy bikes, you'll piss it – and it's good money.' When he added that first prize was something like £10,000, more than my wages for the entire season, I had to agree.

So off to Hockenheim we trotted for the GSX-R Cup, held at the World Superbike meeting. I qualified on pole, but only just. There were riders from everywhere: three Brits, a couple of Norwegians, Finns, Malaysians, Japanese, Spaniards, Yanks, Mexicans. It was like the United Nations. The British team was Dave Jefferies, *Performance Bikes* journalist Mark Forsyth, and me.

The Japanese always like to put on a cultural show at these sorts of do, so the night before the race, buses arrived to cart all the riders and mechanics off to a fairy-tale castle way up on top of a hill. The theme was medieval, so you'd be sipping your mead whilst a sword fight broke out on your table, surrounded by pigs with oranges in their mouths.

I've never been one for late nights, and fell asleep in the coach on the way back to the hotel. When I finally came round I found myself in complete darkness. Luckily I wasn't alone. Three seats forward of me I could hear snoring, which turned out to be Forsyth. I shook him awake.

'Where are we?' he groaned.

'A fucking bus garage.'

'Oh.'

What sort of driver doesn't check his bus is empty, especially when it's been full of foreign drunks? As well as that, I was also fuming about the sort of pals that leave you snoozing, until I recognised that leaving the pole-setter locked on a bus in the middle of nowhere is a pretty cool racing strategy. We had to break out of the bus. Luckily – or so we thought – the driver was still locking up the garage, but he just shrugged and told us to bugger off. So off into the night we wobbled. Eventually, we reached a village, but that didn't help. Left? Right? Straight on? After what seemed like hours of wandering around aimlessly we finally found a taxi which took us back to our hotel.

The race was typical Hockenheim. It didn't matter how fast you went through the corners, half a dozen blokes would still be in your slipstream on the next straight. After about three laps I decided I wasn't going to get away and may as well cruise around with the bunch and save my tyres. That seemed to be working OK until, with a couple of laps to go, the Malaysian rider shunted me off the track and that was the end of my Suzuki Cup bonus. The winner was a Norwegian I'd never heard of. I wish he'd got left on that damn bus.

Back in the British championship, the top runners throughout the season were John Reynolds on the Kawasaki, Ron Haslam on the Norton, Brian Morrison on the Drambuie Yamaha and Rob McElnea on the Loctite Yamaha. Rob Mac pretty much stitched up the Supercup series early in the year, but I nagged at him throughout the other championship, which was wide open. I wanted it badly and fought for it. At Mallory, when he'd looked completely in control, I'd won after overtaking him at the Hairpin on the last lap. I was getting to him.

By the last meeting of the season, Brands Powerbike, I stood second in the standings, just a handful of points behind Rob. When I placed second, just ahead of him, in the first leg we stood exactly equal on points. This meant that with one leg to go we couldn't possibly tie. The whole championship boiled down to a straight fight in this one race. Whoever beat the other took the gong.

We battled it out for every one of the 28 laps. We were together during the whole race, usually with one or other of us in the lead. We both had fairly average starts, and had a bit of company for most of the race before pulling out a gap with about three laps to go. Rob couldn't shake me, and I couldn't shake him, so the entire championship literally hinged on the last corner of the last lap of the last race. Strangely my memory of it's a bit foggy, perhaps due to the celebrating we did after. I think I slipped past Rob into Druids hairpin and managed to hold the lead to the line to take the win and the championship. So a season which had followed such a disastrous one, on a bike we truly didn't think would be competitive, ended in the best possible way. We had a drink, possibly two.

After such a rewarding season, and after having my backside so badly singed the last time I'd left Mick, there never seemed to be much question about what I'd be doing the following year. Even so, the prospects for the season looked mixed. On the one hand Suzuki were finally bringing out a completely revised, reshaped, water-cooled GSX-R750 'W', for which we had high hopes. On the other, they point-blank refused to let us run the Formula One bike on which I'd gone so well the previous year.

Worse still, these were tough times for British racing in general – and especially for us. The truth was that as a team we were practically skint. All we had was a Renault Trafic, Mick, Butch, me and a few bikes. Because we were the official British Suzuki team, everyone assumed that we had big backing, which couldn't have been further from the truth. As a result Mick got some flak for seeming not to make a big effort about presentation – flashy paint jobs for the van and all that crap. But he didn't have much option. We could barely afford a can of Dulux, let alone a custom spray job. In desperation Mick got dozens of Suzuki dealers to put money into a pot, the idea being that at each meeting the bike would promote a different dealer. It was cheapskate stuff, as well as being hugely time-consuming to organise – not to mention that Butch seemed to spend half his working life changing stickers when what he should have been concentrating on was preparing race bikes.

It was like being a poverty-stricken vagrant, struggling to finance the MBA125 all over again. Mick's entire budget for the season was a piffling £60,000. In practice we were reduced to using John Reynolds' cast-off tyres.

To make matters worse the 750W was a disappointment, and yet again Suzuki appeared to lose interest. We seemed to get next to no technical help from the factory. Nonetheless, the season started well. In the first round of the British championship I was narrowly beaten into second place by Rymer's Norton. That, it turned out, was one of the few bright spots of a difficult season. Mostly we struggled. The bike wasn't very good and generally we got our arse kicked, finishing sixth in the championship.

Still, I didn't crash a lot: I wasn't going fast enough and, anyway, we couldn't afford the repairs. Despite poor results – after two wins at Thruxton in the spring, there wasn't another until Scarborough in September – I felt that I was riding pretty well. Occasionally I might wonder if it was me that was crap rather than the bike, but this wasn't like the Honda year where I clearly couldn't ride for toffee. It was frustrating, but at least it wasn't a weekly kick in the teeth. There were times, though, when I wondered whether I had any feel for racing at all. After practice at Oulton Park I returned to the van complaining that my new leathers were cutting off the circulation to my arms. When Butch helped peel them off my shoulders, a wooden coat-hanger fell out. Suddenly I was 'DH' Whitham all over again.

The 750 wasn't miles off the pace. I was always there or thereabouts, usually lying fourth, fifth or sixth in the championship. I led a couple of races, including in the wet at Silverstone before I pinged myself over the 'bars. But it never had that final few per cent of competitiveness, was never quite good enough. Still, I didn't feel as though I could say right out to Mick that his bike was rubbish. It wasn't his fault, or Butch's – and there wasn't much either of them could have done about it anyway. Throughout my career I've had no time for riders who'd be world-beaters if only they could have some other bike, and when they did get it were often as not no quicker than they were before. So I was careful about what I said. My job was just to carry on riding as hard as I could.

Some consolation for the poor results came from an unusual source. Towards the end of the season a motorcycle magazine conducted a shoot-out comparison of that year's top race bikes, track-testing my Suzuki against Rob Mac's OW01 Yamaha, Simon Crafar's RC30 and a Kawasaki. Of several test riders, ex-racer Graeme McGregor was the one not to mince his words: 'How the fuck Whitham's doing what he's doing on that,' he said, 'I've no idea – because it's slow, doesn't handle, doesn't steer. It's a pile of shite.'

To be honest I didn't care what Mick thought of that, because it didn't come from me. But it was just what I wanted to hear. It gave me the confidence that the fault truly lay with the bike and not with me. Not that the fault was Mick's either. If the entire Suzuki factory couldn't come up with a competitive piece of kit, what chance did a bloke in a workshop in Huddersfield have?

The 750 did have one major impact on my career. It was such a long, slow-steering device that we christened it 'The Ironing Board'. That's how keen it was to turn into corners. Whatever you did, however you set it up, it wanted to run wide everywhere. Before '92 I'd had my own distinctive riding style, but nothing that really stood out from the crowd. The Ironing Board changed all that. To get it to tip into turns at all you had to practically chuck yourself into the corner and drag it round after you, really holding it into the turn. That's where I developed my hang-off technique. I eventually got rid of The Ironing Board, but I could never get rid of the style. To me, it's not important. Style's a thing you shouldn't be noticing because you should be concentrating on going as fast as you can, not worrying about how you look. Some bikes need a particular technique – like using a bit of back brake into turns on a two-stroke – but that's different. What you look like on a bike shouldn't be an issue. If you're quick, that's all that matters.

I had another ironing board too – a proper one, in our new home. My sister, Susan, had noticed a pair of stone houses for sale at Healy House, a lovely spot in a valley bottom close to the mill Bone and I had raced past nearly a decade before. She'd told mum, who was also looking to buy a new place, who'd told me. Both houses were much the same, although I gazumped mum on the one with the bigger garden since I needed the land to build a garage. Mum ended up next door.

By late season, I was still upbeat about life and racing in general, but frustrated about the direction – or lack of it – of my career. There was never any doubt in my mind that moving up to the bigger classes had been the right move, but ever since I had it seemed to be a case of one step forward and one back. At the age of 26 I was conscious that I ought to be near the peak of my craft, rather than messing about like this. The clock was ticking yet I still wasn't making much money. It didn't even look as though there would be a budget for Mick to run a team at all the following year.

Then along came an opportunity made in heaven. Or maybe one just too good to be true.

Late in '92 Mick was approached by a bloke called John Stratton. He'd become a bit of a regular at British Championship meetings, turning up in a flash £100,000 Bentley and buttonholing people. He was some kind of big wheel in The City, he said, was dead interested in bikes and intent on running a team the following year. Later he drove up to Yorkshire to discuss his plans with Mick.

At the time, Yamaha had released factory race engines in a move to improve entries for 500cc grands prix, through the likes of Harris and ROC. I'd actually raced one at Magny Cours, in Padgett's colours, when their regular rider Simon Buckmaster was injured. Ninth place had been a pretty good result. Although they later lagged behind in development, at the time these 'customer' bikes were quite competitive. Stratton told us he had a lot of money coming from a big offshore deal in the Far East, and he was going to sponsor a team of Harris-Yamahas, run by Mick with me and Foggy. There would be all the money we could possibly need.

We just sat there, stunned...until Mick started doing back-flips. We wanted to believe this, it was all we'd dreamed of, so we did believe it. At the time Rob McElnea was waiting for me to sign for the Fast Orange Yamaha squad for '93, but with this GP deal in the offing all I could do was keep putting him off.

Stratton seemed to have all the right credentials – flash cars, the lifestyle – and he talked the talk. He decided the perfect launch would be at the Macau Grand Prix in November, so he arranged for two bikes from Harris and Padgett's. He even sorted paint jobs from Dream Machine, the livery based on a new credit card. 'No one's heard of this card yet,' he explained, 'but it's going to be bigger than Visa and Diners put together and in two years you and everyone else will have one in their wallet.' The way he told it, the card would be called Royal Express, in metallic green, gold and silver, embossed with a picture of a prancing horse. The bikes arrived, the Royal Express bodywork arrived. We crated them up and shipped them off to Macau, pleased as punch.

By Wednesday, the day before practice began, there'd been a bit of communication between Mick, Harris and Padgett's, and it was becoming apparent that Stratton hadn't actually paid for any of this stuff. Padgett's didn't want to let us down but didn't want the race costing them thousands either, so they insisted we couldn't fire up the bikes without their say-so. The Harris brothers were stuck in the middle and didn't know what to do. Meanwhile Stratton was telling us there was no problem, just a technical snag with the bank account and this, that and the other.

He was a massive name-dropper. One day he told us he'd 'been on to my man at Coopers and Lybrand.' I didn't have a clue. He may as well have told me about his man at Cow and Gate, but Mick seemed impressed. But still no bills got paid. Eventually, at about midnight on the eve of practice, when I was convinced we weren't going to be riding, we got the green light. Apparently, Stratton had put a classic car up as collateral against the cost of Padgett's running the bikes, so Clive Padgett – despite probably thinking it was a rum way to go racing – gave us the go-ahead. To be honest, I daresay Clive wanted to see us ride them, anyway. Obviously he has to balance his books, but at heart he's a terrific race fan and was probably as excited as we were about me and Foggy screaming those Yamahas around Macau. In any event, Mick came off the phone to tell us he'd no idea what was going to happen, but we were definitely riding.

All these dealings mattered less to me than riding the bikes. They were so bloody trick, almost brand new with semi-factory engines. I couldn't wait to ride one. And everyone apart from us would be on four-strokes, which wouldn't have a chance around a place like Macau. Me and Carl were practically divvying up the winnings when we walked into the paddock – and there's another 500. This one's a proper factory job in Yamaha colours – white and speed-block red. Bugger.

Carl and I were still poking around this YZF when the rider, a chap called Toshihiko Honma, turned up. He was a former 250cc grand prix racer who'd become Yamaha's development rider. Double bugger.

But in practice he didn't seem to be a problem. In the first session Carl was fastest, me second, with Honma some way behind. Second session…me quickest, Carl second, Honma fourth, but still way behind. Final session…Carl by two-tenths from me, with Honma a second and a half back.

No problem. We're thinking there's no chance Honma's going to pull back that much, so it's going to be between me and Carl. The two of us sat by the pool on the night before the race, nursing a pina colada or something else with a brolly sticking out of the top, and sorted out the result. 'Right,' said Carl, 'I don't fancy having a right set-to round here, do you?'

Definitely not. Macau's a hairy old place.

153

'Right. I'm perfectly prepared' – this is Carl Fogarty, a man who hates losing more than being chopped to bits with an axe – 'for you to win one leg and me the other.'

We kicked around a few other possibilities until one win apiece became The Plan, but still putting on a show for the fans. Foggy, who seemed to be chairing the meeting, rounded off business by announcing that if anything went wrong, if either of the bikes broke down, 'we'll split the prize money down the middle'. If the Stratton business seemed strange, actually hearing such stuff from Carl's own mouth was positively surreal. We shook hands and moved confidently to the next pina colada.

The next morning on the grid I couldn't wait to get going. Man, were we going to put on a show! Off we went…and who the hell's that but Honma, right up our chuff. A lap later he's still there. Third lap, closer still. Then he dived inside the pair of us.

That was where the entire bloody plan fell to pieces. It was every man for himself and the race went nuts. Me and Carl lapped two seconds quicker than we ever had in practice, but this bloody Japanese went three and a half seconds quicker – every single lap. We were running wide, up kerbs, bouncing off walls, all on these raging two-strokes. I was shitting myself, but you couldn't stop, couldn't back out. I don't know how – I don't know how I survived, let alone finished – but Carl won, I was second, Honma just third, but you could have thrown a tea towel over the three of us.

Obviously all bets were off for the second race. That bloody Japanese would probably be even quicker with a race under his belt. Carl said, 'May the best man win,' by which he usually means 'May you enjoy the privilege of finishing second to Carl Fogarty', but I was determined to give it a go. The Macau result is decided on the aggregate of the two races. I felt that all I had to do was beat Carl over the line, and since I'd been barely a bike's length behind before, that should give me the overall win.

The second race was just as crazy as the first, each of us getting faster and faster. Crossing the finish line with about two laps to go, I thought, 'It's now or it just isn't going to happen. Stuff it inside Carl at the first corner, mess him up, then go like stink.' So I ducked out of Foggy's slipstream going into Lisboa and…and it nearly worked.

I knew right away I was going to run wide, but kept on it. But something, probably a foot-rest, hooked one of the Hessian bags the straw bales were wrapped in. The wrapping was loose, like a baggy jumper. I accelerated away but the bale accelerated faster, chasing me down the track and thwacking me off the bike at about 40mph, probably the weirdest crash I've ever had. Foggy and Honma cleared off, and although it took forever to untangle the bike from the bales and I just tootled the last two laps, I still finished third. I don't even know who came out on top, although Carl won overall.

Everyone was chuffed with the result – even Padgett's, who ended up underwriting the whole thing, since it later turned out that the car underpinning the deal hadn't even been Stratton's to sell. Yet despite the cock-ups, he still seemed keen as mustard about his big grand prix idea. 'I'm really sorry,' he told us. 'I've made you look idiots, I'm embarrassed about the whole situation. But it's happening, it is happening.' He seemed so convinced himself, and so convincing. If he'd come to us saying 'Look you just give me £10,000 and I'll give you £100,000 to run a team next year,' we'd have smelled a rat. But as far as I knew the money he was talking about was all one-way. If he was conning, we couldn't see what his incentive was.

Both Carl and I had other offers on the table – me from Rob McElnea, whilst Carl was fighting off Ducati offers after his first World Superbike win at Donington the previous summer – but we all wanted to believe this Stratton bloke. We had doubts, of course, but most of them disappeared at a meeting to thrash out the final deal. He came right out and said he'd pay us £50,000 each to ride for his team. Yippee! After years of scratching around, at long last someone was going to pay me proper money: brilliant. Then he popped in the clincher:

'BMW will supply the team cars, and you'll all get one apiece.'

'Can I have a 325?' says Carl.

'Of course.'

'We'll sign.'

Call us shallow and mercenary if you like, but we signed and off we went to Tenerife on holiday – me and Andrea, a mate, Sedge and his wife, plus Simmo and Fiona.

But even in the Canaries, there were still lingering doubts. I seemed to spend half the trip ringing Mick to try to find out what was going on with the deal. When I wasn't stuffing pesetas into a 'phone box, I had Rob Mac in my ear, telling me I had to make my mind up or he'd have to sign Moodie or somebody else for Fast Orange, although I'll never know whether he was bullshitting. The long and the short of it was that nothing happened. Stratton just seemed to disappear.

And that's the nearest I ever got to a season on a grand prix Yamaha.

CHAPTER 15

OH DEAR –
HE'S GOT A PLAN

So after the Stratton debacle I ended up with Rob McElnea after all. For the 1993 season, Rob took over from Steve Parrish as manager of the Loctite Yamaha team, but in the orange and green livery of Loctite's new hand-cleaning compound, Fast Orange. I already knew Rob well, we got on, and he'd been really keen for me to join the team. For '93 Yamaha would have a new race bike, based on the YZF750 road bike. Rob reckoned I'd like the YZF, a rideable bike, more 250-like than any of the other 750s. He felt it would suit my style.

I was almost scared to be away from Mick and Butch, because leaving them to switch to Honda had been such a catastrophe. And although '92 hadn't been a great year for results, it was still a good, matey season, almost like a bunch of pals club racing from a Transit van. On the other hand I'd been racing against Rob for a couple of years, and sometimes beating him, and he was already a mate. We had similar interests, talked a similar language, and I also got on well with the Fast Orange mechanics – and even with Sharon, Rob's missus. Andrea and her got on like a house on fire.

Overall this was a pleasant time to be racing: just before you needed a bigger truck for your hospitality than you did for your bikes. At the time Rob's hospitality suite consisted of a small gazebo outside the garage, with Andrea and Sharon making sandwiches and tea. The focus was on the racing, fair and square. It all had a nice, homely feel with everyone wanting the same thing and pulling the same way.

The only thing that did seem to be growing was the team truck, which was the same old horse transporter Parrish had been using for years but got bigger every year as sponsors changed and it got yet another coat of paint. None of this mattered to me. I honestly couldn't have cared less if my race bike turned up in a wheelbarrow, just as long as when I sat on it on the grid, it was what I needed. I didn't give a stuff how it got there.

To turn the YZF into a Superbike you bought a factory race kit, of which there were two types. The A-kits were reserved for hotshot teams Yamaha thought were going places, which wasn't us. So ours had a B-kit, which was a quite modest selection of engine and chassis parts. Our first outing was for pre-season testing at the Paul Ricard circuit in the south of France. Maybe the bike was only a B-kit YZF, but it worked right out of the truck. I hadn't done more than a couple of laps when I thought, 'That's what a race bike should be like, that's what it should do.' It steered and stopped exactly how I wanted it. We clicked. Everything did what it should.

Amongst the guys deemed worthy of A-kits was Terry Rymer, who planned to contest the entire World Superbike series with a Galp-sponsored YZF. In January I bumped into Tel at the Ally Pally Racing Show. Having been on the Norton rotary in '92, he couldn't wait to get back on a bike that handled, and was full of it. '145bhp on the dyno,' he smirked, and I believed every word he said. A week or so later our B-kit arrived. The mechanics bolted it on, and off we went to Micron's dynamometer near Derby. All day we tweaked it, re-jetted the carbs, fiddled with ignition timing, all to no avail. 127bhp was the most it was ever going to give. 'That's it,' I thought, 'we're knackered.'

Our first meeting of the season was the 'Irish' round of the world Superbike series at Brands Hatch in April. In practice I happened to hook up with El Tel early on…and my 127bhp was exactly the same as his 145. 'Either he's got a very tuned dyno,' I thought, 'or he's full of shit.'

For race day the weather was especially Irish so the track was practically underwater. It tipped down, although this didn't bother me because I'd always been pretty good in the wet – or so I thought. In the first leg I hit a river at the bottom of Paddock Hill and slid off. In the second, I was plugging around in third or fourth, in very good company, when I slid off right under the press box at Clearways and watched the rest of the race from there. In fact almost everyone fell off, except Giancarlo Falappa, who was inspired on the works Ducati. He just buggered off from a world-class field. That sometimes happens, but this was different. I simply had no idea how he was doing what he did. Every lap he'd come round and do things I could maybe get away with for two or three corners before going tits-up, and he did it all day long – really aggressive and fast, with lots of mid-corner speed, yet never seeming to have a moment. He won both races and made everyone else look daft. It was one of the most impressive performances I've ever seen, from one of the bravest riders you'd ever meet.

Despite my two crashes, I'd been competitive all weekend and came away from Brands a contented man. I just loved that YZF. From that moment on we just gelled. In the British championship, I couldn't put a foot wrong all season. Whatever I did it always seemed to work out for the best. I'd bin a bike and write it off – but always in practice. It'd snap a chain – but just crossing the line to take a win. In all I had 20 wins, better than any other year in my career.

This was also the year in which I first came good in World Superbikes. Although Rob rode in a couple of the early World rounds, eventually he just came along as team manager. Not that he didn't have his moments. He damn near beat me early in the season at Albacete, finishing 12th to my 11th when I struggled with a knackered tyre for the last few laps.

With all his experience he was good to have along. We drove his car to Anderstorp, a right balls-ache of a trip, but Rob reckoned the circuit would be right up my street. And it was, cock-on – a big airfield circuit like Snetterton, but with banked corners, and fast. The corners were so cambered that instead of going in on the brakes and feathering it in, you could just nail it into the apex, tipping it in with the brakes still hard on, and know you weren't going to lose the front end. I think I could have even ridden that bloody RC30 fast round Anderstorp.

It suited me so well that I qualified for the front row, which fringe teams like ours almost never did. Alongside me were Foggy on his factory Ducati, Scott Russell and Aaron Slight on their works Kawasakis, with Rymer a row behind and Falappa somewhere in the mix. In the race Carl cleared off, with Falappa chasing him, but there was nothing in it between third and seventh places...me, Russell, Fabrizio Pirovano, Rob Phillis and Slight all going for it, lap after lap. It was a brilliant race to be part of, and fifth was a good result.

The second race was following the same script until the bike shat itself in catastrophic fashion halfway down the long straight. There was a huge metallic *bang*! and the engine just prolapsed, everything dropping out of the bottom – oil, water, con-rods and bits of piston. It was a mess. Although this was before bikes had a catch-all in the bottom of the fairing, and the back tyre was blathered in oil, there was lots of room to slow down gently, so I was in no danger. Unfortunately Aldeo was.

His full name was Aldeo Presciutti, a fat little Italian who looked like Mussolini in leathers. Aldeo was filthy rich and just liked the idea of racing, so every year he bought an ex-factory Ducati and spent his summer weekends getting lapped. But he was one of the original Superbike characters and a lovely bloke, so we liked him. Before my engine let go, Scott, Aaron and the rest of us had just duffed him up on the infield, punting him onto the grass. As I wheeled my bike off the track and threw my legs over the Armco, behind me I heard the thump-thump of a big Vee-twin and...oh dear, that'll be Aldeo. There was nothing I could do to warn the poor little sod as he hit my oil and launched his Ducati, which tumbled down the track in a ball of flames with the wheels falling off. Totally destroyed. Sorry, mate.

Sadly Aldeo's misfortunes didn't end there. Not long after he was killed in a car crash. He was such a nice fellow, an old-school gentleman racer with never a bad word for anyone. We missed him.

Assen was good too, although heaven knows how. The previous year, you'll remember, Andrea and I had bought our first house, and when I wasn't racing I'd spent most of my time building a garage. In the process I had to modify a metal drain cover with an angle grinder. Just like dad, who sometimes arc-welded wearing an old pair of sunglasses, I used naff-all eye protection and got a hot metal spark in my eye. It hurt like stink but we couldn't get it out, so I sort of hoped it would just go away. By the time we reached Assen it was infected. I could barely see, let alone ride, and couldn't even sleep for the pain. So, while Rob

ABOVE LEFT: *Riding my Noddy chair, May 1967, aged eight months. The hang-off style was some way ahead. (Whitham Family Collection)*

ABOVE RIGHT: *Don't blame me for the bow tie. Mum made it. Sax section, Colne Valley Wind Band, aged about ten. (Whitham Family Collection)*

BELOW: *On the MT125 Honda in my second ever meeting, Elvington, York, July 1983. I had the strange notion that turning my socks over my boots might make me quicker. (Mike Dowkes)*

ABOVE: *Wearing distinctive 'No10' ex-Grant leathers and blagged Kiwi helmet, Mallory Park Esses, 1985. (Peter Wileman)*

BELOW: *Wheelying the MBA over the Cadwell Mountain, 1986. What a good little bike that was. (Gordon Kinnaird)*

ABOVE: *On the Superstock Suzuki having just won the Stars of Darley meeting at Darley Moor, 1987, with MCN's Norrie Whyte and the rather more petite Andrea. (Trevor Yorke)*

BELOW: *Ahead of Trevor Nation, Pete Dalby and my future team-mate, Mez Mellor, at Druids, Brands Hatch, 1987. (Whitham Family Collection)*

ABOVE: *Pratting around on a Durex Suzuki GSX-R750RR road bike, Brands, October 1989. The happy snapper in the background is Bill Simpson. (Whitham Family Collection)*

BELOW: *With Honda team-mates Phil McCallan (centre) and Carl Fogarty, 1990. This is obviously an early season shot as my leathers are still in one piece and I'm smiling. (Whitham Family Collection)*

ABOVE: *On that cursed Honda RC30 at the 1990 Sunflower meeting, Kirkistown, chased by Rob McElnea and Brian Morrison. Miraculously, I stayed on in all three races. (Whitham Family Collection)*

BELOW: *Back in Suzuki colours being interviewed by yet another well-nourished journalist, Chris Carter, Thruxton, April 1991. (Mac McDiarmid)*

ABOVE: *On the old but still sublime XR81 Formula One Suzuki in the British GP support race, August 1991. (Mac McDiarmid)*

BELOW: *I could never understand horses, but the lasses seemed to like 'em. Andrea (left) and my sisters Jane and Mary, in typical weekend pose aboard Sydney, Chips and Hatty. (Whitham Family Collection)*

ABOVE: *Steaming around Donington's Redgate Corner on the GSX-R750 Ironing Board, April 1992. (Mac McDiarmid)*

BELOW: *Chatting with burley team-mate Rob McElnea (centre) and Norton's Jim Moodie, Mallory Park, 1993. Jim wasn't so happy later in the day. (Whitham Family Collection)*

ABOVE: *Donington World Superbikes, May 1994. I was being deservedly 'shot' by Carl Fogarty after qualifying second, then breaking my wrist at Goddard's Hairpin. (Mac McDiarmid)*

BELOW: *Twelve months later I made amends with third place in the WSB event. Here I'm leading Aaron Slight and Piergorgio Bontempi as we peel into Goddard's. (Mac McDiarmid)*

ABOVE: *The more chemo you get, the more weird you look. Battling Hodgkin's disease, September 1995. (Mac McDiarmid)*

RIGHT: *Mum, Pat, looking fairly pleased with herself. (Whitham Family Collection)*

Yamaha's factory WSB team and their British poor relations, Brands Hatch, World Superbikes, 1996. From left: Colin Edwards, Wataru Yoshikawa, me, Niall Mackenzie. (Mac McDiarmid)

ABOVE: *Tipping the Cadbury's Boost YZF into Mallory Hairpin in 1996. The meeting produced yet another double win, but Mackenzie's superb consistency prevailed. (Clive Challinor)*

BELOW: *Trying the old levitation trick on the GSX-R, Honda Corner, Phillip Island, ahead of Peter Goddard (left) and Troy Bayliss, 1997. As usual, it didn't work. (Whitham Family Collection)*

ABOVE: *The Full Monty at the post-race Brands WSB charity party, 1998: Slight, Whitham, Foggy and Captain Pugwash. (Mac McDiarmid)*

BELOW: *Drumming with the Po' Boys at MCN's Skegness weekend, 1999. Dave 'Coddie' Caldwell is on the left. (Mac McDiarmid)*

ABOVE LEFT: *Andrea and Michaela Fogarty wearing the race pants and, for once, free shoes. (Whitham Family Collection)*

ABOVE: *The aftermath of the Brno crash. Dr Smith's hands-free titanium cup-holder failed to catch on in the market. (Whitham Family Collection)*

LEFT: *Andrea's dad, Roy, had passed away the previous year so at our wedding in 2000 my old fella was honoured to walk her down the aisle. He's the one in the suit. (Whitham Family Collection)*

RIGHT: *Celebrating a win in customary style in Belgarda's back-yard, Monza, 2001.* (Whitham Family Collection)

BELOW: *'There are no lights at floor level guiding you to an exit, nor is there a whistle for attracting attention.' My beloved RV6.* (Kel Edge)

ABOVE: *Poacher turned gamekeeper. Sharing a joke with fellow Eurosport commentator Jack Burnicle at Silverstone in 2006. (Paul Bryant)*

BELOW: *At home with my two best results ever, Andrea and Ruby, January 2008. (Mac McDiarmid)*

sorted out signing-on and scrutineering he packed me off to the local hospital.

Keeping quiet about it was a dumb thing to do. Getting the team to Holland had cost a fortune, and now it looked like it was all a wasted effort. The medics cut out the chunk of swarf, wrapped a huge patch over the eye, and sent me back to the circuit with instructions to keep it on for a couple of days. Rob was livid, and he was never a bloke for not letting you know what he thought. 'Stupid wanker,' was one of the more flattering highlights.

By this time I'd already missed the first practice session, but took off the patch and went round for a wobble in the second. It was perfect. I'd been there before so knew where the track went... all those straights that aren't quite straight, all those lovely sweeping kerb to kerb, camber to camber lines. The bike was ace right out of the truck, and all I had to do was keep it on the grey bits. I don't think we touched an adjuster yet I qualified fifth, right up with all the big boys.

Not that there was ever any chance of staying with Foggy. He was unreal at Assen, with double wins almost every year. So in the race he headed off into the distance whilst the rest of us squabbled for second place – Pirovano, Russell, Slight, Piergiorgio Bontempi and me. The YZF didn't quite have the legs on the factory bikes, but I made a lot of ground up on the brakes, diving under them and tripping them up until the back tyre went off and I started struggling for grip. With my style of riding, if you don't have a tyre you can't really compete, so I was trying harder and harder on the brakes until I ended up going on the grass a couple of times, although not losing a lot of ground.

I'd been desperate to beat Pirovano on the full factory Byrd Yamaha with our B-kit version, but didn't quite manage it, scoring a fifth in both races. But, again, that was a good result. Not that my performance endeared me to everyone. Afterwards, Aaron strolled up to me.

'Here's the thing,' he started, 'if you sat behind me, we'd go quicker than if we kept tripping each other up. How's that?'

'What's good for the goose,' I thought. 'Why don't you sit behind me and we'll see how that works?'

'Wanker,' he muttered, and walked off.

He didn't seem to realise that with less power and less grip, the only way I could stay on terms at all was to make ground anywhere I could – on the brakes – which inevitably meant I'd hold him up. Sod him. It was such a good meeting. Although fifth place maybe doesn't sound like a huge deal, in that company it was a bit special, and a few people noticed. One of the French bike magazines ran a double-page action photo of me on the Yamaha, although maybe my radical new 'Ironing Board' style had as much to do with their choice as the result. But all in all we came home really chuffed, with a sack-full of brownie points.

After that I fancied a full season of World Superbikes. After all, I seemed to be able to run with those boys easily enough. Monza was disappointing in that the bike broke down in both legs, although up to that point we were running strongly. Our next World Superbikes outing was my home round, Donington Park, where Yamaha Italy lent me a proper factory YZF. I wasn't aware of it at the time, but after the Assen result they were already thinking of offering me a ride with them for '94.

Donington could not have been better timed. By then the British Superbike championship campaign was pretty well running itself, almost stitched up, so I could give the meeting my full attention. The Byrd Yamaha was all they said it would be. It revved so quickly the tachometer needle could barely keep up. The chassis wasn't very different from the bike we'd been running all year, so we just put our Donington settings on it and it clicked right away. In the first race I was running second when the front tyre went flat. I didn't fall off, but that was my race over, a huge disappointment. In the second, I finished third behind Russell and Foggy – my first World Superbike rostrum. Chuffed to bits, again.

The British championship was going even better, with double win after double. The main opposition was Jim Moodie, Steve Hislop and Michael Rutter, plus Rob himself, although by then he was probably past his best and maybe had too much on his plate managing the team as well. When he'd come back from grands prix onto British Superbikes he had it. He just took the bull by the horns and rode really well. But by the time we were team-mates his best years were behind him and he'd maybe lost a bit of that edge. He'd come in from practice putting on a weary old bloke act,

'Bloody hell, I'm getting on a bit for this.' But you sensed there was a hint of truth in it too.

He was also affected in a big way when Wayne Rainey, who he knew well and respected immensely, was paralysed at Misano. I suspect it was harder to take because Rainey was such a perfectionist, unlike, say, Kevin Schwantz who was always more of a loose cannon. Although Rob never admitted as much, I think it gave him pause...if someone that good, that precise, could get hurt, then who couldn't? Rob certainly didn't want anything like that happening at that stage of his career.

On pure talent, Hizzy was my most formidable rival. He'd been promised – or thought he had – a trick factory Honda, but when it arrived it was a fairly swanky RVF chassis which had seen a fair bit of action and a pretty stock RC30 engine. It wasn't even as quick as my Yamaha. He was riding well, although at that point I was riding my package better than he was his, but it never seemed to happen for him and all the luck seemed to go my way. Hizzy never needed much encouragement to feel the world was against him, so spent most of the season under a cloud of frustration. We all know how quick he could be when things gelled for him, but that year they gelled for me.

Even when I did slide off, it was usually in practice. At Cadwell I lost the front into Chris Curve, really travelling and driving hard. When the bike hit the grass it flipped and started tumbling, somehow climbed over the perimeter fence, and slammed down onto the bonnet of a parked car with an almighty crash. The old couple who owned the car were sat next to it eating sandwiches – and never moved. They just sat there frozen in mid-munch. I could tell there wasn't much point going to the bike, so just wandered back to the paddock.

'Where's your bike?' asked Rob.

'Sorry, it's a bit of a mess. But don't worry – I've got an old couple looking after it.'

Then there was Jim Moodie. I'd raced against Jim on and off before, but only knew him a little and hadn't often found myself near him on the track. I tended to see him as a bit of a hard-faced aggressive supersport rider who didn't have the experience to set up a bike on slicks. You knew he was always going to be a hard rider, but that wouldn't necessarily translate into being fast. He was on the Norton, which was quick but, to be fair, probably wasn't easy to ride and certainly not as good an all-round package as the Yamaha.

Despite that Jim rode it hard and got close a couple of times. Previously I'd bought into the rock-hard Glaswegian Moodie image. Off the bike it was certainly true. A right little terrier, he'd fight anyone for £1 – and still will. But on track we had a couple of dos where I just shoved him out of the way, and was a little surprised that he let me. I began to wonder if maybe he wasn't quite as tough on the track as his billing, which is the only excuse any racer needs to push even harder the next time.

It all came to a head at Mallory Park. I'd won the first championship race from Rob, although Jim had been up there mixing it and was going well. In the second leg I was stuck with him the whole way round. I was miles in front in the championship and didn't want to get involved in a massive incident, but I also thought I ought to be stamping my authority and beating him. With three or four laps to go he barrelled inside me into the Esses. I sat behind him for the next lap but couldn't see an obvious way past, so settled down to wait and see. On the final lap I had a bit of a go at Gerrard's, then again into the Esses, but Jim was up to it, toughed it out and held me off. With just the Hairpin to go, the race seemed to be his – unless he cocked-up.

He knew I'd try to dart up the inside into the Hairpin, since that was the only chance left. So instead of taking the normal out-to-in line, he ran the Norton up the inside – but so far inside that he almost had to stop dead in order to turn. In the process he ran about two feet wide, which was all the invitation I needed and I chucked the YZF into the gap. Then it became a first gear drag-race into the next corner, the Bus-stop chicane.

At this point I knew I had it. His front wheel was level with my leg. Everything I'd learned in racing told me the race was mine. Whatever he did from that point, he couldn't possibly come off better than me. He had to let me through...but he didn't, he just kept going. 'If that's how you want to play it,' I thought, 'fair enough. I'll squeeze you onto the kerb and that's job done.' After all, any club racer knows that when two wheels come together, the back one always aces the front. Pretending otherwise can only have one result.

But Jim still wasn't having it. He was still aiming for the bit of tarmac I was already on. There was a bit of a bump and I looked over my shoulder to see him hurtling into the tyre barrier. As I cruised over the line, he was being extracted from the wreckage. 'Poor Jim,' I thought, but he only had himself to blame. He could have stopped it at any point.

Jim has a talent for fuming at the best of times, of which this definitely wasn't one. After dusting himself off he put in an official protest. A few minutes later I'm summoned to the jury room to face a kangaroo court of wrinkly old blokes in blazers. Every few minutes they'd traipse in a few marshals as witnesses. Everyone was so obviously partial, it was comical. Some were clearly Moodie fans, some JW fans, and each interpreted it how best suited that. They got even less sense out of Jim, who was threatening to rip my head off and burn down my house, which probably didn't do his case a power of good. By then I'd worked out that whatever the jury decided I was probably going to get my head stoved in, but Jim calmed down eventually. The officials decided it was simply a racing incident and let the result stand.

Since then we've made up. As well as being a hard, talented rider, Jim's actually a bloke I have a lot of time for, a good friend, a good man to have in your corner.

I don't know what it was about me and Mallory, but there was an even bigger kerfuffle the next time we went there, for the penultimate round of the British Superbike series. By then I'd wrapped up the championship, but Rob still had his sights on second place. As usual, Jim Moodie was running strongly, so Rob hatched a plan. I should have told him that me and plans never really got on.

'Look,' he said, 'Jim's going well but it'd be good for us to get a championship one–two. How about giving me a hand?'

'What do you want me to do?'

'It depends what happens when the lights change,' said Rob, 'but if I can get in front and you can hold him up a bit, it'll give me a chance to get away.'

I still hadn't quite wised up to the fact that when I'm involved, plans usually end in tears, so I agreed.

In the first leg, it started perfectly. As ever, Rob was good off the line, took the lead and started pulling away. Within a couple of laps he had about a second and a half on me and Jim. But Jim hadn't given up. He was on it. He passed me and even though I passed him back, Rob's strategy just wasn't working. As we caught him up, Jim got a good drive out of Gerrard's, dived under Rob into the Esses and started pulling away from the pair of us.

It seemed obvious there was no point me finishing behind Rob when I'd take more points off Jim by beating him. But to do that I had to pass Rob, who wasn't having it. A lap later he came flying back past me. 'Bloody hell, mate,' I thought, 'just give me a lap clear to get after Jim. So I went back at Rob into the Esses, hit the bump and lost the front end.

I slid clear, no problem. But my bike collected Rob's and he got sort of tangled up with the two cart-wheeling bikes and smacked into the barrier. I was a bit concussed, but alert enough to see that Rob was badly hurt. He was well knocked about and his femur was broken. For a few moments it was critical.

Rob wasn't just my boss and team-mate. He was a mate. So I felt bad about the whole deal. But it was typical. You can't have a plan in bike racing, certainly not anything that intricate. Sure, if you're in a position to help someone by letting him past, fair enough. But there are always so many variables beyond your control – even more so when one of them's called Moodie. Rob recovered, but that was his racing days over. It was a bad end to what had been a perfect season, both in the British Championship and the one-off World Superbike rides.

CHAPTER 16

HOSSING AROUND
THE WORLD

At the end of '93 I was hot off a near-perfect season, riding as well as I ever had, British champion, and with a growing reputation abroad. I was also not young any more – not exactly old at 27, but aware I shouldn't be wasting time if my career was really going to take off. Most of all, I was keen to do World Superbikes full-time. I'd already shown I could run with the top guys, even without a truly competitive bike. I was hungry for more of the same taste.

After getting badly hurt at Mallory, Rob Mac never actually announced his retirement, he just didn't bother racing again. Despite me being partly responsible for chucking him into the barrier, by this time he was not only a mate but a bit of a mentor. We discussed my options a lot, but there didn't seem to be all that many, despite all the positive noises from Yamaha the previous year. Yes, I had offers from virtually every team to ride in Britain, but we both believed that I ought to be riding in World Championships rather than dicking about with the same old stuff. About the only firm approach I had at that level came from the Ducati factory, through Moto Cinelli, their British importer. The money wasn't great, but Ducati had already done well in World Superbikes with their 888cc V-twin winning from 1990 to '92. For '94, I was told, they'd have a new bike and it was going to be the dog's bollocks. 'It's going to be like nothing you've ever seen,' they promised.

Like most Brits, the first time I saw the bike was at the Bike Show at Birmingham's National Exhibition Centre. As you walked into the hall the Ducati stand was one of the first you passed. I must have still been 40 yards away, took one look at it, and just stopped dead. This thing was so bloody gorgeous. It was the 916.

Like almost everyone else who visited that show, I spent half the day just drooling over it. All I could think was how beautiful and tiny it was...supposedly a road bike, but really a proper little race bike with lights. Obviously I had all sorts of questions, but I knew at once the 916 was what I needed to be on next season. The factory later told us there would only be eight of these bikes available at the top racing spec at world level and that we could have a pair. Foggy and Falappa would have two factory bikes apiece, and two would go to someone else.

That someone else turned out to be Fabrizio Pirovano, which was very interesting – or would have been if we'd known earlier. At the time we'd also been talking to Belgarda Yamaha, who were then still called Byrd – Belgarda Yamaha Racing Division. I already knew them well from the ride at Donington the previous summer. We had a lot of mutual respect, I adored the YZF, and I think they would have offered me a factory bike if they could. In fact they told me they'd love to put another bike on for me but didn't have the budget to run two riders, and already considered themselves committed to Pirovano – who, it turned out, must already have been negotiating to go elsewhere. He was a good rider, definitely, but I'd been the equal of him on my own bike, and would surely have got his place if only we'd bided our time. Instead, it looked like it just wasn't going to happen, so Rob and I went ahead and pushed for the Ducati ride.

Our Ducati had to be run through Moto Cinelli – in other words through the owner, Hoss Elm. The factory simply wanted to give us the bikes, a spares package and engine backing, but everything else would be down to Hoss: our own truck, mechanics and the rest. The factory were still secretive about the mystery fourth rider. Obviously they were up-front about Falappa and Fogarty, but it was some time before we heard that Pirovano had jumped ship to ride the 916. It surprised me, because Fabrizio had always been Yamaha through-and-through. He lived near Monza, practically next door to Byrd's headquarters, and had always ridden their bikes.

Mmm. No sooner had I heard the news and thought 'Who's going to be riding the Yamaha then?' than the phone rang. It was David Brivio, who's now Valentino Rossi's manager but in those days was hooked up with Yamaha Italy.

'*Ciao*, Whitham,' he said. 'How are you doing?' There was a load more blah, blah, blah, before he got right to it. 'We want you to ride our bike next year. No bullshit, we want you as our rider. Pirovano's gone and we want to know what you're doing. We have contracts ready for you to sign.'

He was effusive. He offered me £80,000 for the season, to ride a bike I already loved, compared to the £15,000 I was getting from Moto Cinelli for riding a stunning-looking pig in a poke.

My reply tasted like sand. 'Sorry, David, I'm already spoken for. I've already signed.' They eventually put Paolo Casoli on the Byrd Yamaha.

I was disappointed, of course. But at the back of my mind I still thought the 916 was going to be the bike to be on, and that was more important than the money. Hoss was fuming when he heard they'd approached me, although he'd no real reason to be. I was awash with conflicting emotions...frustrated and disappointed in a lot of ways, ecstatic in others and, I suppose, flattered to be so sought-after for a change. It was a bit of a rollercoaster of fortune, but racing's often like that.

One obvious issue was that Byrd was an established team I knew I could work with, whilst I barely knew Hoss at all. I'd seen him and knew of him, because he'd already been involved in British racing. He obviously loved bike racing, and with a bit of factory help had previously put together a pretty good 888 Ducati. Having been promised things by Suzuki that never quite seemed to happen, I was curious as to how he'd work with the Ducati factory. It soon became pretty clear that the boss Italians loved Hoss, because he'd been the man who saw a little niche to make a few quid out of the brand when no one else wanted to import Ducati spares.

It's hard to credit now, but at the end of the '80s and even the very early '90s no one was interested in Ducatis. Importing them was very small scale, most bikers thought they were unreliable, and getting spares could be a nightmare. So Hoss would whiz down to Bologna in his Transit van, fill it with parts, drive home and advertise them mail-order in *Motor Cycle News*. That grew to become Moto Cinelli, which was just a name Hoss made up to sound Italian. For all I knew it meant fishbowl, although it's also the name of a Milanese bicycle manufacturer. When Ducati started to come good again Hoss was already on the first floor, right at the forefront of their resurgence. And fair play to him: he's a good shrewd businessman who's worked hard.

I knew a little about Hoss's racing in '92 and '93 when he ran a couple of riders in the British Championship, including Foggy now and again when Carl had a gap in his World Superbike calendar. I remember Carl high-siding in the wet out of the chicane at Oulton Park and refusing to go out for the second race. But when Carl wasn't binning it that 888 was a good bike. I think he actually won on it at the North-West 200. In '93 Phil Borley rode the same bike a couple of times. And that's about as much as I knew of Hoss, other than the fact that he always seemed very dapper, smartly dressed, with olive skin, a big cigar and a shop called Moto Cinelli. What else could he be but Italian?

So to begin with I just thought of him as this very sophisticated Italian gentleman – until later, when he arranged a trip for the two of us to the Ducati factory in Bologna. We met the race bosses and Claudio Castiglioni, who was then the boss of the whole Ducati/Cagiva shooting match. It was a good trip. But something hadn't quite clicked. Hoss and I had met up at Stansted Airport. Climbing the steps onto the Alitalia plane, the stewardess greeted me with the usual 'Good morning, sir.'

'Morning, love.'

Hoss was right behind me and, like everyone else, the stewardess clearly thought he was Italian, giving him a cheery 'Buon giorno.'

'Er, yes, buon giorno,' replied Hoss, although it didn't seem to roll off the tongue so well. Even during the flight, the cabin crew carried on at him in Italian, and he still seemed to be struggling a bit. Italy…airport…hire car…toll booths. Still struggling. Over dinner – more struggling – I was dying to know what was what. Eventually, 'Are you that ring-rusty with Italian, or what?'

'Oh,' he says, 'I've never been able to speak Italian.' This seemed a very strange thing to hear from an Italian with an Italian bike shop running a race team for an Italian factory.

'So where are you from, then?'

'Persia.' Oh. You don't get many of those to the pound in British racing.

'Bloody hell,' I thought, 'it's going to be an interesting year.' His family history turned out to be quite interesting. His dad was the Iranian Ambassador to the UK in the days of the Shah, but couldn't go back after the revolution – not and stay healthy, anyway. So Hoss was largely raised and educated in England, from a well-to-do family. A very posh lad.

But even if Hoss had been Venusian, when I'd traipsed down to Northampton to sign the contract to ride for Moto Cinelli I thought I'd best clear up one thing from the start. I already knew from speaking to Borley and Foggy that Hoss didn't much like crash damage. He'd actually stormed off when Borley dumped the 888 at Cadwell Park – just jumped in his limo and drove away in a cloud of cigar smoke.

'Look, Hoss,' I said. 'I'm going to have to tell you there might be a bit of sort of collateral damage here, because I will fall off a bit. And I'll try hard, I'll give 100 per cent every time and we'll have some results, I'm sure. But there might be a little fairing repairing to be done here and there.'

'Oh yes,' he said, 'no problem. I can accept that.' There was a bit more fat-chewing, and I went home quite content with the whole deal. And even after the Yamaha phone call from Brivio, I was happy that I'd done the right thing. Hoss did take a bit of getting used to, though. He's a devout Muslim, which doesn't bother me at all, but it meant that he had his own way of doing things which often wasn't the way I'd been used to in other teams. He could also be pretty hot-headed, but since I'd originally thought he was Italian anyway that was only par for the course.

The upshot was a strange year, all told. We had the bikes, no question of that. Our 916 was every bit as good as Carl's, every bit as good as Pirovano's, and I never once felt that I was being shafted by anybody. We got engines when we needed them, fairings and other bits when we needed them. We generally didn't get a lot of set-up help from the factory, but then we weren't the factory team. The main thing was they never forgot about us and were always there if we asked. People sometimes take the piss out of Italian factories, but Ducati were always as good as their word, never complained about anything, and overall the results were all right.

Our first meeting was a shakedown at Donington Park for a British Championship round in late March. Until that day the only 916 I'd ever seen was the one at the Birmingham Bike Show, and that one had lights. I'd never even sat on one. And I still didn't, because the only one there had been trucked over specially for Carl to have his own shakedown ride. I was on an 888, which was a bit disappointing until I actually went out on it. It had already done two seasons, but was well looked-after and well set-up, and I loved it. It just pulled like a train. You hardly had to change gear. After the Yamaha, which was a right peaky, revvy thing in comparison, you just gave it some throttle and off you went – fast, but easy, relaxing. 'Bloody hell, if the 916 is even better than this,' I thought, 'we're away. It's going to be a wonderful season.' In the race Carl and me had a right set-to, but it was cold and I didn't want to crash Hoss's baby before the season had even begun, and he won both races, just ahead of me.

A few weeks later we were at Donington again, this time for the opening round of World Superbikes. Again it was a bit last-minute. We'd done no testing at all on the 916, and neither had Carl apart from the previous Donington outing. The first time I saw the two bikes I'd be racing all year was about ten minutes before the first practice session.

Some of the Ducatis had serious traction problems getting out of Donington's slow corners, but although we were on similar Michelin tyres to the others we seemed to be all right. As usual I'd have preferred to be on Dunlops, partly because I was still wincing from that bloody awful year of losing the front on the RC30. But for me there was always an issue with Michelin rears too. They had plenty of grip but you never got the warning you got with Dunlops, that sort of 'stop leaning over now, because it's about to go badly wrong'. The only warning they seemed to give me was a big *ping!* and I'd be flying over the high-side to the medical centre.

It may have been possible to run Dunlops, but the problem was that no one had run them on Ducatis before. Other than Doug Polen's, the factory bikes had always been Michelin-sponsored and Michelin-shod, but more than that there seemed to be a belief that Ducatis simply wouldn't work with anything else. Later Gregorio Lavilla and one or two others came along, started running

Dunlops on an 888 Ducati and did really well. The truth was that Dunlops worked just as well but nobody, including the Ducati factory, thought that they would.

After a couple of sessions at Donington, I didn't care. Michelins, Dunlops – they could have put Barum knobblies on it for me, I was going that well. I qualified second to Scott Russell – in front of Carl, in front of everyone – and knew I had lots in reserve, because I'm never that quick until race day. And Scott had been riding his Kawasaki for at least a season, whilst I'd only just met my Duke. 'This is mine,' I thought to myself, 'just wrap up the World Championship and I'll pick it up at the end of the season.' I honestly felt that good, that confident. I don't think I'm particularly big-headed, but to do that, first time out, was special – unlike what happened next. In the second lap of Sunday morning warm-up, coming out of Goddard's, the 916 high-sided and pitched me over the top. I broke a wrist and couldn't even race.

By the time I'd recovered we'd missed Hockenheim and headed off to Misano. After going so well first time out I arrived full of confidence, but struggled horribly. The bike spun up the rear every time you drove out of a corner. There seemed to be no grip, I had no confidence, and even placing 11th was a battle.

By then the 916's rear grip problem had become a big issue. Most of the bike magazines seemed to have a lot to say on the subject, although things have to be pretty desperate before you start looking to them for an answer. The plain fact was that some bikes seemed to be able to lay down all the power they had out of a slow turn, but the 916 only wanted to spin up and slide – but not at every circuit. I became convinced that the fault lay in the single-sided swing-arm and the way the suspension linkages were laid out. But then again, this wasn't really my territory and all I knew for sure was that it could be an absolute bitch to ride.

Whatever the problem was, it wasn't consistent. At the next round, Albacete, we ran really strongly all weekend and came away with two rostrum finishes. Carl had been struggling too, but came good there, winning both races, ahead of Andy Meklau and me, and Slight and me. So to that extent the 916's problem seemed to have gone away – except that this was the meeting where Falappa high-sided off the other factory Ducati and smashed himself out of racing. It was a nothing crash, really slow, but he suffered an embolism which starved his brain of oxygen, and he's never been the same since. It was a truly shitty end to what had been looking like a great career.

That bike was baffling. After Albacete I sort of looked back at Misano as a horrible fluke and thought we'd bounced back where we belonged. Then the next meeting – Zeltweg – we struggled again, with just one seventh place. It was one of those seasons when you thought you'd just got to grips with the bike, found a base setting from which you could develop the bike anywhere you went, only to find that at the next meeting it would be only so-so, and the one after that back to square one. As a result there seemed to be no rhythm to the season, nothing you could fall back on and say, 'We know this works, let's go from here.' Not doing much testing didn't help either.

Hoss, though, was so flipping keen all year, although he had some peculiar theories about race bikes. One of his eccentricities involved his tablets. They were red and shiny with some kind of gold writing, but more than that I don't know. He was right secretive about them, but they were obviously important to him and had some kind of religious or mystical significance. As I was putting on my helmet before a race, he'd stand by the garage door, not saying a word but holding these precious things. The mechanics would be taking off the tyre warmers, knocking the bike off its stand, I'd be revving up the engine – and as I drove out he'd kind of wave these tablets over me like a blessing.

I'd no idea what was going on and Hoss would never say. But that was fine – in racing you need all the help you can get, and I'd have done Voodoo dances if it would have taken half a second off my lap times. The first time it happened me and the mechanics exchanged funny looks, but after that it just became an odd part of the usual racing ritual – a bit like Joey Dunlop turning up at a meeting with a bunch of Celtic Druids.

Another thing most people didn't know, but I did from sometimes sharing a room with him, was that Hoss had a leg missing from the knee down. Ordinarily you could hardly tell because he coped so well. He didn't rush about, but had a sort of purposeful stride about him. He made no secret of it, but obviously it wasn't something he'd blab about either. I got to like Hoss, became fond of him despite his little quirks. One day I asked him what happened to the leg, assuming it'd be something like a bike crash.

The story was really tragic. He'd been driving his Transit on one of his trips to pick up Ducati bits. In the middle of the night on a foggy Belgian motorway he hit some black ice, spun the van and clattered into the central reservation. He was totally unhurt, but the front of the van was bashed in, so he clambered out and sat on the hard shoulder wondering what to do. Then he noticed that the van was still partially sticking out into the carriageway, so he went back to move it a few feet. Another car came screeching out of the mist, clobbered him and smashed up his leg.

Although Hoss was the boss and nominally the manager, which he was very good at, he wasn't all that clued-up about the technical side of racing at that level. He was organised, but not always in the sense that a race team needs, which is often minute-by-minute stuff…a flap here, a tweak there, something unexpected happening with the bike. Sometimes I used to wish he'd just leave us to it. 'Christ – sorry, Hoss – we're in enough trouble without you helping.'

So effectively we didn't have a manager in the sense that, say, Rob Mac or Granty had been. Technical decisions used to be down to me and the crew, Paul 'Plug' Hallet and Martin Bennett. At the time Plug was just a 16-year-old kid, but he's gone on to be one of the top Moto GP mechanics. Martin Bennett, a former racer who'd finished sixth in the Marlboro Clubman's series on the same day in 1985 that I'd finished third on my MBA 125, later worked with the Suzuki World Superbike and Grand Prix teams before becoming chief mechanic for Kenny Roberts. Hoss certainly picked a good crew.

Other than occasional spats with Hoss, their dodgiest moment came on the way to Albacete when they were robbed. The first either knew about it was waking up in a car park with a headache and all the team clothing missing. Apparently they'd been the victims of what for a while became a regular scam. The thieves introduced some sort of poison gas into the truck while they slept, then made off with their swag while they were unconscious.

Luckily nothing was taken from the back of the truck, where the real valuables – the bikes and spares – were kept.

Otherwise it was all good fun. We all mucked in with everything. I helped with the bikes, they helped with booking ferries, stuff that mechanics would almost never do. Despite the flash factory bikes – and they were truly flash, absolute jewels when they weren't trying to spit you off – it worked more like a small private team. We had a good truck and a bit of money; we were all right and had some good results. Other than the grip problem, the most frustrating aspect was the 916's unreliability. This was the year they used to lunch crankcases for fun, which happened to me a couple of times.

For me, the big result that year was my first World Superbike win – my only win, as it turned out – at Sentul in Indonesia. Sentul went well right from the start, apart from the trots. Naturally we were told only to drink bottled water, but I didn't listen, as usual, and ended up with the raging squirts. As bugs go it wasn't a bad one. I didn't feel especially ill, there were no stomach aches or fever. I just couldn't stray far from the porcelain.

Maybe having to get back to the loo in a hurry makes you quicker. Whatever the reason, we qualified pretty well, top five or something. In the first race Carl took off, which was becoming a bit of a habit, then broke down, which was also not uncommon. That left me, Simon Crafer, Russell and Slight in the leading bunch. The four of us diced it out for most of the race, but with a few laps to go Aaron and me dropped the other two, and then it was just me and him. To be honest, from then on it was nothing to do with which was the better bike or better rider. I won because I had more tyre left than Aaron at the end.

I was following him and could see that his back tyre was finished. The conditions were wicked: 40 degrees, 100 per cent humidity, truly stifling. It was hard to breathe, let alone race. The tyres were bound to struggle in that heat anyway, but the surface was rubbish, really chewed-up tarmac, which made matters even worse. I had more tyre left, and knew from following Aaron that I could get a better drive onto the main straight. For a couple of laps I hung back before the previous corner so I could make a practice run on him, and both times easily made up ground. So I bided my time until the last lap, knowing I could make a move and he'd have no way of getting back at me. I nipped inside him, got my head down, and went.

Pleased, or what? On the wind-down lap I did all the usual waving and wheelying before pulling into the parc fermé. Now it's fair to say there wasn't that much love lost between Hoss, Martin and Plug. I always liked Hoss and still do, but he wasn't the easiest bloke to work for. He wound the mechanics up a bit. The pair of them came tearing over to the parc fermé, beaming like idiots and completely flipping giddy, slapping me on the back and generally going daft. After a minute or so of being battered, I asked, 'Where's Hoss?'

Without even pausing, Martin told me 'Oh, he's had a heart attack,' like it was no worse than a blister.

I was still buzzing myself, but, come on, this is serious. 'He's had a fucking heart attack? What are you on about?'

'He's down the medical centre. I don't know, he's had a heart attack.'

Later I got the full story from people who'd actually witnessed it. Like most team personnel, Hoss watched the race from the pit lane wall. Over the last couple of laps he was apparently pretty excited. Then when I crossed the line to take the win he seemed to go into some sort of trance, shouting 'Yes, yes, yes.' At some point in all the hullabaloo he'd fallen over, his false leg came off, and there he was on the floor, hyperventilating and going blue. They carted him off to the medical centre, where he came round and was right as rain, if still seriously hyper about the result.

Other than that my biggest regret was that Andrea had to miss out the Sentul and Sugo rounds to work. So although we were always together at the European and Australian meetings, she missed my one and only World Superbike win. Apparently, at the time Hoss was collapsing, she was watching the race on telly with Sedge and his wife, Michelle, jumping up and down so much they broke the settee. In the second race I came fourth after Carl cleared off, leaving me, Aaron, Scott and a few more of the usual suspects fighting over the minor places.

The previous year Rob McElnea had got me interested in playing golf, not that I'd had much choice. With Rob it was a sort of pre-requisite: if you raced in a team with him, you could be a crap rider

193

but you had to be prepared to ruin a perfectly good walk with a little white ball and a set of clubs. This was probably because he was good at it and always beat you. During the Moto Cinelli season I used to spend quite a bit of time with Brian Morrison. Even to a Yorkshireman he's the tightest man in the world, without any question, but I liked his company. And he liked golf. So we ended end up playing golf everywhere, just to pass the time between meetings.

At Sentul we found a really posh local golf course and hired clubs, clothes, caddies, the whole nine yards. About halfway round the course the trots set in, urgently. It was miles back to the clubhouse and the nearest loo, and I was in a bad way. Luckily I remembered that we'd just passed a big, steep-sided bunker that ought to at least give me a bit of privacy. So I hobbled back to it, dropped my shorts, crouched down and did the necessary while the caddies had kittens about this unusual turn of events. Obviously there wasn't a loo roll handy, so I slipped off my socks and wiped myself with those. Then I back-raked the bunker, and on we went to the next hole. I apologise now to any golfer who's had the misfortune to plug his ball in that sand trap.

Sentul also gave me an altogether more agreeable whiff. I'd got my first win under my belt, and, I reasoned, was obviously on the up-and-up. It followed that after years of scratching around with tuppence, I would soon be very rich. Obviously. Now I'd always wanted a BMW – one of the reasons the Stratton fiasco had been so attractive – and at this time my particular love object was a brand new 325 turbo-diesel. So when I got back to Huddersfield I drove down to my local BMW dealer and there it was: £23,000, no bother. That's what I'll have.

'Right,' I said to the showroom bloke, 'I'll take one of these.'

At first they tried to shoo me out of the door, but after about ten minutes finally started taking me seriously. One of the staff happened to have seen a write-up about me in the local paper, which helped convince them I wasn't a derelict on the make.

'Oh, you're the bike racer bloke. What do you want?'

'One of these. In the metallic blue.'

So we went through all the specs and options and I told them I'd be back to square up the deal within a couple of weeks.

Other than at the British World Superbike rounds, our race

bikes were the only full-factory Ducatis in the country. People used to queue up just to get a glimpse of them, let alone see them race. Obviously they were a bit of a draw, so Mallory Park asked if I'd do their Race of the Year meeting. Even rolling those 916s out of the truck cost a fortune, so I left them to negotiate with Hoss. There was a bit of appearance money on offer but, better still, £5,000 for a win. I loved Mallory and had miles better bikes than anyone else who'd be there, so I thought it was as good as in the bank.

Hoss agreed a deal with Mallory, and off to Leicestershire we went. The only riders I thought I had to worry about at all were Ray Stringer and Mat Llewellyn, and even they shouldn't see where I went after the first lap. As I was driving down to Mallory I was already counting the money and imagining myself in the nice metallic blue 325 turbo diesel it was going towards.

In practice everything went as it should. I was about a second and a half quicker than Llewellyn and Stringer, and a second and a half around a fiddly little place like Mallory is like a month anywhere else. Sedge and a couple of other mates had come down to watch from the motorhome roof. 'It's going to be a doddle,' I told them, 'just watch and learn.'

Well, they learned something all right. Race of the Year...flag drops...so-so start, but the Ducati's a rocket ship compared to everything else. By the back straight I'm in the lead and already counting my 5,000 smackers. Esses...that'll be £1,000...Hairpin... another grand...Bus Stop...oh shit! Only 24 laps to go and I lost the back coming onto Devil's Elbow. The 916 just pinged me off. I wasn't hurt, although I took a lot of skin off the back of my hand, but I'd destroyed Hoss's bike. We were both fuming – him at me for wrecking his pride and joy, me at me for being such a pillock.

World Superbike winner? I should have been shot. It was a classic schoolboy error at Mallory. The Elbow's the first left-hander where you're giving it much throttle, so the tyre's bound to be cold, and a Michelin, especially, is going to need care for a couple of laps – not some moron with his eyes on a BMW. I was absolutely gutted, mad with myself, but my mates thought it was all a huge joke. I was so furious I couldn't even speak at first. When I calmed down a bit Sedge said he knew exactly how I'd damaged my hand.

'How?'

'We could see it all. As you came off the bike you were holding it up like they were about to put five grand in it. That's how it got smacked on the ground.'

After the high of Sentul, the season petered out disappointingly. Frankly, the back half of the season was rubbish. At Donington the bike broke down in the first leg and I chose the wrong tyres in the second, expecting it to dry out when it didn't. At Zeltweg the crank went when I was running in the top five.

My final fling of the season – literally – came in practice at Phillip Island at the end of October. I lost the front over a ripple through a fast left-hander and slid for bloody miles. As usual, there wasn't a lot going through my mind at the time, except the reassuring knowledge that there was lots of run-off – I think Tasmania would have been the first hard thing I'd have hit – so I wasn't all that worried. In its way it was a fitting end to a rollercoaster of a season, but character-building stuff, as they say. Working with Hoss was sometimes hard work, although we've still always got a smile for each other and no one can take that Sentul win away from either of us – although he did skank me for the trophy.

'Can I have it in the shop for six months of the year,' he asked after Sentul. 'Then I'll send it back.'

Yeah, sure, Hoss, I couldn't have done it without Moto Cinelli. I haven't seen the damn thing since. So Hoss, old pal, if you're reading this, it's my turn now.

And 1994 was also our first year with a motorhome, a monstrous American thing. For me and Andrea, having the time to cruise around Europe in comfort was an utter novelty. If we didn't feel like driving home between races we just had a holiday. We spent time in the South of France, which isn't hard to bear, usually travelled with the Fogartys, Scott Russell, or Aaron and Megan Slight. We also hung around with Doug Polen, who was also doing World Superbikes that year. He'd been World Superbike Champion on a Ducati in '91 and '92, but by then seemed to have shot his bolt on the track. But what a lovely bloke he was. You didn't care how slow he was, he was just a smashing guy to have around. Completely mad, him and his wife Diane, but great company.

In that respect it was a terrific season. We had a lot of fun and toured the world. But the bottom line wasn't quite working. It was obvious that we needed better results to keep the factory ride, and as the season drew to a close it seemed inevitable that I wouldn't be doing World Superbikes again the following year. But Hoss, bless him, was really keen to carry on and hatched a deal to do British Superbikes instead.

I moved back to British racing with mixed feelings. Clearly I'd have preferred to be racing at world level. But on the other hand I was back with old friends. Rob Mac took a year out of his Yamaha thing to run the Moto Cinelli Ducatis from his usual workshops in Scunthorpe, so we ran Hoss's bikes but with Rob calling the shots. No more tablets, no more blessings. If Rob was going to wave anything over you it'd probably be a nine iron whenever you dropped one of his bikes.

That was also the year I first went into the bike business on my own account. I'd already been instructing at a few track days as hired help, and a bloke named Shoey – Paul Shoesmith – seemed to be at every one. One evening he rang me up. The gist of it was that doing so many track days was costing him a fortune, so why didn't we team up to organise our own and make a few bob?

'Speed Freak', our track day operation, began the following year, and did pretty well until the cost of hiring circuits escalated out of sight. Because of my contacts in racing it was easy to hire top-class instructors like Cal Crutchlow, Paul Young, Steve Plater and Tommy Sykes. Mick Grant also became a regular, helping customers set up their suspension. I enjoyed the atmosphere, enjoyed helping riders improve their technique.

Inevitably there were plenty of offs, some of them weird. At a Cadwell day I came across one guy lying in the middle of the track on Park Straight. I parked my bike and trotted over to him. Like a lot of non-racers, he wasn't used to falling off and was a bit freaked. He'd damaged an ankle, but was otherwise all right. Then I noticed he didn't seem to have a bike, which is generally a prerequisite for falling off one. And what's he doing falling off halfway along a straight anyway?

'Er...where's your bike, mate?'

'Gooseneck.'

197

Gooseneck? That's miles away.

Apparently he'd gone straight on there, the bike had buried itself in the tyre wall and flung him about 40 yards through the air. That was some get-off. In 20 years of trying, I don't think I ever flew that far.

In the '95 British Championship Steve Hislop and I had a titanic battle, both riding 916 Ducatis. Hizzy was riding really well that year and by mid-season we were neck-and-neck in the standings, with him just a point or two ahead of me. No one else was getting a look-in. I'd been riding well, but was losing weight. Something seemed to be wrong with me.

I'd never been obsessive about training, unlike Neil Hodgson and James Toseland, both of whom are fitness freaks, but I did a bit of cycling, a bit of running, went to the gym and kept myself in good shape – certainly better than the likes of Carl and Scott. Foggy was that good he never had to bother, and Russell always preferred a party to working up a sweat. The previous season I'd got into the habit of joining Aaron for a cycling session regularly after practice, and tried to keep up the same routine in British Superbikes. But, almost imperceptibly, I found myself getting more and more tired every time I went out. At first I told myself it wasn't happening. Then I went on a trail-riding holiday to Spain with a bunch of mates, and every evening while they were drinking and joking I'd take myself off to bed, worn out. It was pathetic even for a bit of a party-pooper like me. In a few weeks I went from someone who couldn't keep still for more than two minutes to someone who couldn't be arsed to do anything at all.

Something was obviously wrong, but at 28 you take it for granted that it can't be anything major, can it? It came to a head after Rob arranged for me to ride a 500cc ROC Yamaha at the Donington Park grand prix. A few days before the race we went to Mallory Park, where he'd organised half a day's private testing. Now those 500cc two-strokes were animals, but this was something else. I just I couldn't cling on to it, couldn't concentrate, couldn't get my act together at all. I actually felt physically sick on the bike. When I got off it I was totally knackered and had to go and throw up.

This was no bloody good. What was wrong with me? The day

after Mallory I took myself along to my GP. I'd had a little lump on my neck since the year before. Although Andrea had kept telling me to get it checked out I'd just gone 'Yeah, yeah,' like you do, and done nothing. Checked out? Me? I'm a fit young lad, what can possibly go wrong with me? Besides, dad's family had a history of fatty lumps. His brothers were sort of lumpy-headed people, so I just put it down to that. I didn't exactly like the idea of being lumpy-headed – who would? – but I'd never been an oil painting anyway, so what the hell.

The doctor did the usual prodding and poking and gave me a load of spiel. 'Basically,' she told me, 'you're anaemic. If you want to race we can do something to get you through the weekend and make you feel better. Then we'll do some tests next week.' She scribbled a prescription for iron tablets, sent me to hospital for a blood transfusion, and told me to come back after the weekend.

I don't know whose blood it was, but it definitely wasn't Michael Doohan's. At Donington I just couldn't cling on to the ROC Yamaha. By then people were remarking on how pale and thin I looked. I was down to less than ten stone and felt weak all the time. I just wasn't right. When I fell off the Yamaha at Redgate in practice I was almost relieved. The penny finally dropped that I was properly ill.

I didn't even ride in the GP but drove straight home and trundled down to my doctor's surgery first thing Monday morning. Ever since I'd begun racing seriously I'd always had a positive approach to medical issues, although all the previous ones had been through knocking myself about rather than something weird going on inside. My reasoning was always that the sooner I recover, the sooner I can race, which is what I do. So that was the mode I got into.

'Look,' I said, 'something's badly wrong and I need something doing, right? I want you to refer me to somebody who might be able to start doing some scans or whatever you need to do, or do blood tests or...'

She was way ahead of me. 'Yes,' she said, 'I think you're right,' and referred me to a haematology clinic at Huddersfield Royal Infirmary.

CHAPTER 17

HODGKIN?
HODGKIN WHO?

Dr Carter later told me he knew exactly what was wrong with me as soon as I walked in the door of the clinic, but they can't give you a diagnosis until they've done the tests. Since he knew pretty much what was wrong, he knew what they'd probably be doing about it, although it was all a mystery to me. I think I was probably the last person in the entire West Riding of Yorkshire to know what I'd got.

'You were the classic Hodgkin's case,' said Dr Carter much later. 'Everything, every symptom pointed one way, and all the tests came back as I'd expected.' But before that, he had to run the tests. He was a nice fellow, and always told me what was going to happen next, but never what was at the back of his mind.

'Right,' he began, 'we'll give you a scan. Then we want to do a bone marrow biopsy. Plus we'll do a biopsy on that lump on your neck.' The results apparently, would take about a week or ten days to come back, by which time we should all know the score. 'We'll admit you as an in-inpatient,' he added, 'then we can do what we want,' which sounded a bit ominous to me, although I didn't know the half of it. The bone marrow biopsy was pretty bloody uncomfortable, let me tell you. They put you into a foetal position, then go in with a little drill. You can't feel so much because you're numb, but you know what's going on and can smell bone burning, which isn't so nice. Then they did a lumbar puncture to see if whatever they're looking for is in the brain stem. That's not much fun either. But at least something was happening.

Over the next few days they did this and that while I sat there baffled and let them get on with it. After about a week I'm sat up in bed watching daytime TV, which was almost worse than being sick, and in walks Dr Carter with a nurse and an A4 folder.

'Right,' he began, 'we know what's wrong with you.'

'Ace,' I thought, 'they'll give me a pill and I can go home.' But he sat down next to the bed, looking a bit serious.

'You've got a form of cancer...'

He said more than that, but all I heard was the 'C' word and went blank. I thought he was telling me I was going to die, which obviously came as a bit of a shock. I imagine he gets this sort of reaction a lot, so was still there when I came back to my senses.

'It's not as bad as you think,' he went on, explaining the ins and outs, although not much of it sank in. 'I'll leave you a bit of time to ring the family and your girlfriend and whoever else you need to tell.'

I rang home, rang dad, mum, Andrea's mum, all the family, Rob Mac. Within an hour or so the ward's full of people trying to put on a brave face but in reality looking glum and regarding me as though I'm a goner. After they'd left I just sat there, numb. I just didn't get it. Here I was, only 28, never smoked, never really drank to excess, looked after myself apart from knocking the odd bit off, and I've got fucking cancer. I suppose I was suspended somewhere between rank fear and disbelief. And there's no appeal. You can't go to the stewards and demand a rerun. Nothing prepares you for times like this.

I think, from what they later said, that a few friends and family had an inkling from the type of tests they were doing that something like this was on the cards. But not me. I was gobsmacked. Dad, too. Like many folk of his generation, he had a fairly old-fashioned notion to anything with the dreaded word 'cancer'. It was all some people could do to whisper the word. To him, they may as well have taken me round the back of the hospital and despatched me kindly, like a knackered old horse. He was really knocked sideways.

Cancer was already only too close to home. Andrea's mother, Barbara, was terminally ill. In 1992 she'd been diagnosed with ovarian cancer. They'd operated, but the tumour was too large to remove, and every six months since then she'd undergone chemotherapy. All the treatment could do was prolong her life, not cure her, but she'd been wonderfully stoical and upbeat about the time she had left. In one way, I suppose, it was an example of how to handle major illness with dignity, but to me at the time it was just another example of how bloody heartless life could be.

Later Dr Carter came back. I think he'd told me a lot of this same stuff before, but I'd been too freaked-out to hear. 'Whatever you're thinking,' he said, 'it isn't as bad as you think.' Apparently what I had was Hodgkin's disease, a form of leukaemia. Once it had usually been fatal, but with advances in treatment the odds had changed dramatically. About 80 per cent of Hodgkin's patients actually make a full recovery, and even half of the rest don't die, they just go on with it a bit longer and sometimes it recurs. Only in around 10 per cent of cases is it fatal. 'It's not bad odds,' he added, before telling me what he proposed to do about it, and for the first time I saw a glimmer of hope.

The treatment's somewhere between high-tech and black magic. I wasn't exactly a stranger to hospitals, but this was different. If you have a broken leg, they'll X-ray it and the surgeon can say 'right we're going to pin this' or 'we're going to plate that' or 'we're just going to leave it in traction', or whatever. It's more like putting a bike back together – fairly black and white, easy to understand. Chemotherapy seems to be a bit suck it and see…a bit of this and a bit of that…all rather mix-and-match and hocus-pocus, with fine-tuning as you go along.

On the Thursday they announced that they were going to begin chemotherapy on Saturday, but there was one job to get out of the way first. 'Are you intending to have kids or have you got kids?'

'No, I've no kids. I think at some point I'd like kids.'

'Righto. We'll make you an appointment at the assisted conception unit at Leeds. You've about a 50:50 chance of not recovering your fertility after the chemotherapy, so you're going to have to make a couple of deposits at the sperm bank.'

Well, at least my genes had a future, even if I didn't.

They weren't taking any chances. They sent me across to Leeds in an ambulance twice, two mornings on the trot, on the days before starting chemo. Embarrassing, or what? They lock you in a side-room with not so much as a page three pin-up to look at. You're not feeling well, you've just been told you might be dying and there you are, feeling as sexy as double pneumonia, chugging away trying to fill a little test tube.

By Saturday Dr Carter had already told me what drugs I'd be on, although as usual most of it went in one ear and out the other. Whatever it was, there was a lot of it, a right pharmacist's cocktail. Because people's reactions to the drugs vary so much, they'd monitor how I reacted to each of them, which they could do on an outpatient basis so long as I didn't take a turn for the worse. I was given a long list of dos and don'ts and packed off home. Pubs were out, because my immune system would be buggered and I stood to pick up every bug that was going. Then the fun stuff: 'You might have liver failure. If so, ring us' – as if I wouldn't. 'Your heart might stop, your hair will probably fall out, you might turn green, your face will puff up, you'll probably vomit a lot but we'll give you something to help with that, but it'll probably give you a limp...' All in all, it wasn't the cheeriest of chats, but better forewarned I supposed.

Dr Carter rounded off his little pep talk by asking if I'd like to see the wig man.

'Wig man?'

'Yes,' he went on, as though he was recommending his tailor. 'Because your hair's going to fall out. We can get you measured up and you can get it all in-house.' Sod that. A shiny head was the least of my problems.

The chemo was in three-weekly cycles. Basically, they're trying to poison you. The cancer cells are more susceptible to the poisons than the rest of you, but everything suffers to some extent, and they pump in absolutely as much as your body can tolerate. So every three weeks they pour you full of chemicals, after which you feel like crap for the first week, so-so for the second week and pretty much all right for the third. In the bad week it was all you could do to lie around feeling wretched and throwing up, but the rest of the time I managed a reasonably normal life. By the 'good week' in the second cycle of chemo, I actually felt better than I had for months, so knew myself that I was getting better, which took away some of the fear.

Meanwhile, there was still a British championship going on. I put on a brave face and went to Cadwell Park just after starting my first chemotherapy cycle, looking more like a ghost than a championship contender. I practised but felt so weak I was a danger to myself and everyone else, although I didn't know the full extent of it until Diane, Robin Appleyard's wife, stomped over and demanded to know what on earth I was thinking of. No one at the hospital had explained to me the full effects the chemo, assuming, I suppose, that most patients go home and watch videos rather than race motorbikes. Diane, who's a nurse, explained that if I had a big smack I might bleed to death. Since I was feeling half-dead anyway, not racing seemed the easy way out. From there I knew I was going to have to sit out the rest of the series, so just went back home and more or less forgot all about racing.

With me out of the way, Hizzy went on to win the championship, getting a fair bit of stick along the way. Some of the things that were said and written were daft. It wasn't his fault I got Hodgkin's. It was just par for the course: championships are often won when someone gets injured, and one of us could as easily have broken a leg and handed the title to the other. It happens.

To be sure the drugs are working, you're constantly tested through every chemotherapy cycle. It's common for some of the agents to disagree with you, so the clinic monitors your reactions, quizzing you about how they're making you feel, and doing blood tests for white cell counts and other mystic stuff. One of the agents made my eyes go funny. For a while I couldn't see a lot, which I was told could lead to permanent eye damage. So they tinkered around with the drugs to settle on a regime that wouldn't upset me in quite the same way.

It was strange – a bit like when, as a kid, your mum tells you that because you don't like something, it must be doing you good. That's exactly how it is with chemo. Every time I went back for a new cycle, they'd run their tests and be delighted when they found I was in better shape than the previous time. They'd positively beam – because that meant they could pile in even more drugs and my body would still just about cope. In a perverse way I began to feel the same: if I'm feeling this bad, it must be working. That's what you associated it with. You almost welcomed it.

What the medics didn't warn me about was the cards. Thousands of them, mostly from people I'd never even heard of, and an amazing number from people who'd recovered from Hodgkin's themselves. You couldn't move in our kitchen for mountains of cards and letters. It was mad. Even Barry Sheene wrote, which is ironic considering that he died of cancer a few years later. He sent a hat. There were lots of hats from folk taking the piss, but nicely. Another mate, Steve Parrish, sent a hat with a wig fastened inside, covering both bases.

This was a huge, huge boost. It wasn't just that so many total strangers actually gave a damn about what happened to me, which was touching; the biggest tonic was the experiences of other Hodgkin's patients. Sure, Dr Carter had said the odds were in my favour, but to actually hear from people who'd been in my shoes and recovered was amazing. This wasn't just a bloke with a white coat and stethoscope reading off 'Ah, yes, you have a 82.37 per cent chance of recovery,' whilst I'm working out that's a 17.63 per cent chance I'd die. These were real people who'd gone through what I was going through, knew how I felt, knew how shitty the chemo made you feel. 'Yes,' they were saying, 'we've been there and it's crap, but you'll be fine.' For the first time I really began to believe that everybody survives this disease. But now and again I thought the statistics might be a bit skewed: 'Hang on, the dead ones probably won't have written anyway...'

Whichever way you cut this, it wasn't a good time. The disease was always there, hanging over you, along with the thought that it might go badly wrong and you might not survive. I was scared – more scared by miles than I've ever been on a motorbike.

After I recovered it sort of came full circle. Every now and again a letter would arrive saying something like, 'My brother-in-law has gone down with the same thing, can you give me any advice.' Sometimes they'd be from people who knew someone with a totally different form of cancer, but hope I might be able to do something to perk them up. I've had phone calls out of the blue from strangers with some sort of semi-terminal illness, who have the idea I might be able to help in some way. Having spent most of my first 28 years giving this sort of thing hardly a thought, it's shocking just how much illness is about, but I always try to respond. It's almost like being in a kind of club.

While I was being treated I had no interest in learning more about the condition. If I'm injured I'm always curious about what's happening to me – about the details of the treatment, how long I'm going to be out of action. But with Hodgkin's there didn't seem much point in bothering about the ins and outs. All I could do was report to the clinic whenever they asked and do exactly as I was told. Probably it was also something I didn't *want* to think about. Rather than dwell on it, I tried to push it to the back of my mind, get on with everything else in my life – just keep going. The worst times are when you're alone. Having the distraction of friends and family usually took my mind off the worst possibilities, but even so there were times when I'd just burst into tears.

I now know, because I've looked it up, that Hodgkin's is what's called a lymphoma, cancer of the white blood cells in the lymph system – hence the swelling in the lymph glad in my neck. The average age to get it is around 28 and around 1,400 people are diagnosed with it each year in the UK. I was almost 29. In most cases no one knows what causes it and it doesn't even run in families. Of the two main forms of lymphoma, Non-Hodgkin's is about five times as common as Hodgkin's, generally affects older people, and the chance of successful treatment is usually less. If you have to get lymphoma, Hodgkin's is the one to have.

Trying to live as normal a life as possible – or what passes for normal at the Whitham household – was the key to getting through it. Andrea and I managed to get out now and again, and in the good weeks I felt up to going trail riding. Crashing into Welsh bogs probably wasn't Dr Carter's idea of therapy, but it did me a power of good. Around November I even felt well enough to do a 24-hour enduro in France with the guys from *Superbike* magazine.

Trail riding's always been a passion for me. There's nothing like getting out in wild country with a bunch of mates, razzing about on dirt bikes – the perfect diversion from chemotherapy or anything else. Sometimes, though, it wasn't always plain sailing. We've been caught out in blizzards, had bikes break down miles from anywhere, buried up to our necks in putrid green bogs, you name it. When the bikes weren't playing up, the trailers were, because it seems to be a trailer's role in life to be abused and totally neglected. Once a wheel fell off near Coniston. Kingy ran back to fetch it, to find a bloke emerging from his driveway in the pitch dark, carrying the wheel. 'It's lucky,' he said, 'it only clipped me.'

Another distraction was the band.

In late '93 me and a few mates – Dave 'Coddie' Caldwell, Zac McMillan and the same Carl Toffolo we last encountered in Noble's Hospital on the Isle of Man – had begun messing about jamming in one of the hangars. The previous winter I'd bought a drum kit second-hand through an ad in the local paper, and used to bash hell out of it. We'd half got to grips with a few rock standards – *Smoke on the Water*, that sort of rubbish – but just for our own fun. Then we heard from a lass called Jenny, who was organising an end-of-season racers' party at The Watermill at Pately Bridge. As much for a joke as anything, we said we'd play. That meant we needed a name, so we came up with RBM, a sideways tribute to REM, except that it stood for Random Bowel Movements. It was pretty appropriate, considering how crap we were. Coddie had some RBM T-shirts made up, and the Watermill bash turned out to be a pretty good do.

We never thought the gig would be anything but a one-off, until later that winter when I was invited as guest of honour to a bikers' charity night at Chickenly, near Wakefield. During the evening a bloke who'd heard about the Watermill gig buttonholed me. 'You want my mate,' he insisted, 'he's the best singer in the world.' 'Great', I thought, 'just what we need: a Foggy on vocals.' So, as much to shut him up as anything, I said we'd be having a band practice the following Wednesday and if he was as good as his billing, this guy should come along.

And he did. His name was Jep, and he could sing – really sing. He'd been in bands before, knew what it was all about, and before we knew it he'd taken over...not aggressively, just moving this collection of musical misfits along. A week later he turned up with another mate, a lead guitarist named Dud, and before we knew what was happening, we'd started getting serious.

After each band practice, we'd pop down to my local, the Sands House, for last orders. We were casting around for alternative names to RBM when someone noticed Po' Boy sandwiches on the Sands House menu. 'What about the Po' Boys?' No one objected, so that's how we came to be named after a catfish sandwich from Louisiana. It's not another piece of Huddersfield toilet humour, as some folk seem to think.

Once we got going, Jep got into the gig circuit and sorted out a booking at Davitt's Theatre Bar in Allerton-Bywater, near Castleford, which became a regular spot for us and our dodgy repertoire of anything from Sex Pistols to Wet Wet Wet, but mainly punk. By mid-'94 we'd begun fairly regular gigging in local pubs, and by the time I was diagnosed with Hodgkin's were well established locally. I managed to keep playing through most of the chemotherapy, although sometimes another drummer, Mick North, stood in for me. Playing with the band was not only fun, but another useful diversion to keep my mind off worse things. Mind you, the audiences weren't always sympathetic. As we were tuning up for our first gig after my hair fell out, some wag yelled, 'What's the scores, George Dawes?' It's funnier now than it was then.

Before my hair had a chance to fall out, I'd cut it short. For a while what was left didn't show much sign of falling out. Then one night I was drying it after a bath, and it fell away in lumps into the towel. Lots of guys were shaving their heads by then, so that wasn't a problem, but it was so inconsistent. There were polished bits and hairy bits dotted all over my skull. It looked like a bad case of mange.

We were due to go out for a Chinese meal with Mary, my sister, about half an hour later, so there wasn't time to muck about. I told Andrea to get a Bic razor and shave my head – and arrived at the restaurant looking like she'd attacked me with a machete, with bits of bloody toilet paper stuck all over my skull. As if that didn't give people reason to stare, because of the steroids I was taking I couldn't stop eating. I must have eaten my own weight in noodles and ginger fried beef. The food was served from one of those revolving tables which I had spinning like a merry-go-round. No one else could get a look-in. The other customers just gawped at this bald food-crazed glutton in their midst, until Andrea told them I wasn't always like that, it was just the drugs.

Naturally everyone felt really sorry for me. They'd arrange little parties to cheer me up. Usually they were very tentative: 'We'd love to have you round if you feel up to it…' The fact was, much of the time I felt all right.

In total I went through six chemotherapy cycles, in a period of less than five months. I'd been diagnosed with Hodgkin's disease on 12 August, my last treatment cycle was the day before Christmas Eve, and by mid-January I was told I was in remission. There'd be further periodic tests over the months and years ahead, but effectively I was in the clear.

As far as I was concerned, that was my ticket back to racing. When word got around that I'd got the all-clear, some people seemed to half assume that because I'd had a life-threatening illness, that was me done with flinging myself round race tracks. No way. I couldn't wait to get back to it. For the previous ten years or so I'd had a job where accepting an amount of risk had been part and parcel of the whole set-up. On a personal level, assessing a risk and deciding whether to accept it was an almost daily event. That's how it should be. You can't bury your head in the sand pretending you're never going to get hurt, as some riders have done. You've got to tell yourself, 'I can get hurt, I probably will get hurt at some point,' and if you're not prepared to accept that you shouldn't get on the bike. To me, that's responsibility.

On the other hand dealing with Hodgkin's did change other priorities. Wanting the latest car and the other flash stuff suddenly didn't seem very important. What mattered now was your missus, your dog, going out for a nice walk of a Sunday morning – the simple things in life you used to take for granted but had almost been ripped away from you. One of the first things to go was any thought of that BMW 325. One day I wandered into the showroom and told them I wasn't bothered any more. I got a Peugeot 306 diesel instead. Great little car. Yet within a year a year I'd obviously forgotten about the simpler things in life, because I went and bought a 50-grand Honda NSX. It was a lovely bit of kit, and probably the most expensive mistake I ever made.

The new mind-set even affected the way I regarded racing. I reasoned that if something like this, that I didn't invite or encourage in any way, can sneak up behind me and try to kill me, then how scary can racing be? So racing itself somehow lost a lot of its fear. 'Sod it,' I thought, 'what's the sense of worrying? If something happens, it happens.' When I finally got back on track it was obvious that people were asking themselves if I'd be as quick as I used to be. Meanwhile I'm thinking the opposite – almost fatalistic, convinced I'd be even less bothered about harming myself than before. At least I'd have some control over it, unlike that stupid, random disease.

I even had a job to go back to. Rob Mac was running Yamahas again for the 1996 British championship and wanted me in the team alongside Niall McKenzie. At the time I didn't look much like a racer. I was still bald as a coot and chubby-faced and had been off bikes for what felt like an age. But I was definitely raring to go.

CHAPTER 18

THE BOOSTY BOYS

Rob Mac's new race team was to be chocolate-powered: for '96 we'd be Cadbury's Boost Yamaha. Cadbury's don't make motorbikes, but they had a new choccy bar on the market called 'Boost', which is presumably what they hoped we could do for their sales.

The team, with new bikes and new livery – but the same old horsebox, with yet another coat of paint – first appeared in public at a swanky reception at London's Café Royal. It was a big, daft razzmatazz, but obviously you're happy to go along with that sort of nonsense because it's paying your wages. For the official presentation, the three of us were in a kind of hole under the stage – Rob in the middle, with me and Niall McKenzie on either side, sat on our race bikes. The idea was that some sort of mechanism would lift us through the stage floor to a fanfare of big, booming music and fireworks. As our heads got to stage level, Rob and Niall were all right – they had hair – but the poor bald git on the left was getting his skull burnt by all the sparks. All I could think was that I couldn't wait to get back on the track. It's a lot safer and not half so dippy.

With the new sponsor, people didn't need much encouragement to christen Niall and me the Boosty Boys, after the Beastie Boys rock band, although I looked the part more than Niall, since he's a skinny little thing whilst I still looked like I'd spent the previous three months carbo-loading on chocolate. Thanks to the after-effects of the chemotherapy I looked more like a cartoon tortoise than a racer, with a chubby-faced bald head poking out of the neck of my leathers.

The championship seemed likely to be a fight between us and Team Old Spice Ducati, which was being run by my old mate Hoss

Elm. Their riders were Chris Walker, in his first year on a Superbike, and Terry Rymer, who I'd been racing against for almost ten years on and off. The pre-season pundits were touting Tel as the man to beat, with maybe each-way bets on Niall, then me. To them – to everyone, I suppose, except me – I was a bit of an unknown quantity after the Hodgkin's.

Although I wasn't short of confidence – I'd been riding as well as ever when I'd been diagnosed – we didn't do much testing so I didn't have a lot of time on the track to get into the swing of racing again. When the championship started I hadn't ridden in about eight months and had only recently been able to do any fitness training. I had no doubt I'd be on the pace eventually, but it might take me a while to get up to speed. In my mind, if I could just hang with the other guys for the first three or four meetings I was confident I could get my season rolling.

Our first meeting was at Donington Park. In the first leg Rymer and McKenzie both went well, but I wasn't far off the pace and ran a solid, safe third – until the gear lever linkage fell apart. A poxy 6mm bolt had sheared.

So with a DNF in the first race I was especially keen to get a good result in the second. I'd already figured that Rymer might blow a bit hot and cold over the season as a whole, although right from the start he did seem to suit the Ducati. But McKenzie was always going to be the big threat. He was not only fast, but a really canny, solid, experienced rider who knew how to set up a race bike and wasn't likely to miss out very often. I knew even then that I couldn't afford to have many non-finishes against this man, because he might go through the whole season without any at all.

So for the second race I knew I had to push hard. It started, like the first, with me, Rymer and McKenzie in a bunch at the front. Then Rymer dropped off a touch and it became just me and Niall for the lead. It was going well. 'I can win this,' I thought. But I was probably riding a bit too hard for the amount of testing we'd done and the physical condition I was in. And Donington on a cold day in April isn't the ideal place to be pushing your luck. Coming out of the chicane the back end stepped out, big-time – it damn near did a 180 – and pinged me off the high-side.

It was just like old times. As the Yamaha flicked me into the air, a couple of things crossed my mind. One of them, obviously, was 'Oh, bollocks.' The other was that at least I was going to find out whether the old bones were still strong enough to stand up to all this shit. 'In about another half a second, mate, you're going to hit the floor fairly hard.'

Bang! I landed mostly on my hands, giving them a mighty slap on the ground. You'll know what it's like when its cold and you bang the palms of your hands. They both went completely numb for a second, then started stinging with pins and needles, but at least nothing broke. I limped off the track shaking my hands back to life, went to pick up the bike, then thought, 'Sod it' and tramped off back to the pits. I was gutted. Rymer had two wins – he'd somehow got back at Niall in the second race. McKenzie had two second places. And I had nowt. On the way back to Huddersfield in the motorhome, I said to Andrea, 'That meeting is going to come back and haunt us. Against Rymer riding like that and against McKenzie, that's cost us the championship.' And it did.

The second championship meeting was at Thruxton on Bank Holiday Monday. Rymer was hot not only from his double at Donington, but from having won the Le Mans 24-hour race the day before. In order to do Le Mans he'd done hardly any practice at Thruxton, but flown backwards and forwards to France to qualify and race there. Then he only went out and won the first race at Thruxton too.

Rymer made one big mistake that day. I liked him a lot, but he was a typical Londoner and could be a right cocky bugger when things were going his way, which could grate a bit. But you had to take your hat off to the way he rode – he came steaming past from the back of the grid and cleared off, smoked the lot of us. He'd had hardly any practice, hadn't seen the place for a year, and he'd been up all Saturday night winning Le Mans. That's toughness. I didn't like it, but it was truly impressive stuff. You couldn't knock the man – until he wandered into our garage after the first race and told us, with a smirk on his face, 'If this bike keeps going, if it doesn't blow up, I'm going to win every single race in the championship.'

In racing, you never tempt fate. You might not be at all superstitious, but you never brag in public about what you're going to do. As soon as he said it, I thought, 'That's it. You've just doomed yourself. Even if you think it, you just don't say anything like that.' In the very next race something went wrong with his bike and McKenzie won. I came away with two second places, my first finishes for eight months, which I was more than happy with. 'Not too bad,' I told myself, 'we'll do all right.'

In other ways it was a tough time. Ironically, as I was getting better Andrea's mum had declined rapidly since November 1995. Although she'd bravely managed to get to the British championship round at Donington, we were all only too aware that her days were numbered. A month or so later at the Donington World Superbike meeting, Andrea got word from her brother, Allen, that their mum was fading fast. Rob Mac drove her home, where she was with her mother when she finally lost her fight on race day morning, aged 71. I wasn't told until after the meeting, and even though we'd all been expecting this, it was hard to bear.

Ever since me and Andrea started going out in 1987, her parents, Barbara and Roy, had always been really supportive, travelling to watch me race almost everywhere in Britain. They hardly missed a meeting for years. After my parents split up in '88 and I broke my leg at the Ulster, I spent a couple of months effectively living at their house. Andrea was still working at the time, and her mum looked after me, almost like a nurse. She was a lovely woman and I'd become very close to her. Life seemed cruel. But, as always, for the rest of us it went on.

After Donington World Superbikes – I pulled in with a brake problem in one race, placed tenth in the other – the British series moved to Oulton Park. I've always loved Oulton and had a feeling I could go well. 'I might do all right this weekend,' I'd confided to mum, so she came to watch and offer moral support. The bike was perfect and I was right back on song with a win and a second place, sharing the results with Niall, although Rymer was still going well.

It was a watershed. I was doing what I used to do and seemingly doing it every bit as well as I had before. Chemotherapy and the misery of the autumn were forgotten, gone. My hair was growing back, I was training again and feeling fit. From there on in everything worked as though I'd never been away. Next time out, Snetterton, two wins. Then Brands Hatch, ditto. Knockhill, two seconds; Cadwell, another double; Mallory Park, the same…bang, bang, racing was easy again. Everything was flowing and we were on a roll. Every weekend we seemed to be clawing back the points I'd thrown away at Donington.

Trouble was, Niall was riding exactly how I'd thought he would back in April. After every win I'd ride into the garage and my first words to Rob would be, 'Where did Niall finish?'

'Second,' always seemed to be the reply.

Or I'd ask, 'Who was behind me?'

'Who do you think?'

McKenzie, always bloody McKenzie. Doesn't this man ever fall off?

By this time Rymer's Thruxton words had come back to haunt him, and me and Niall had both pretty well seen him off in the championship. As you'd expect, Tel rode well at Brands, which was where he'd cut his teeth and always seemed to be his favourite track. In the race the two of us got away from the field. He did all the work, while I just tagged onto the back of him and bided my time. I sort of had a plan, although – ask Andrea – as often as not that would end in tears. The Yamaha had quite good top-end power compared to the Ducati, which was better lower down and drove better out of corners. So I figured my best chance would be to go deep into the last corner, Clearways, on the last lap, turn it hard and just open the throttle and straight line it to the flag. Terry knew I'd be coming at him, so was driving for all he was worth, but hit the bumps on the exit, got out of shape and lost traction. I was coming, coming, coming…and beat him over the finish line by about half a wheel. He couldn't believe it. Even going round for the parade lap in the victory car, he was still absolutely spewing. 'That'll teach you to say you're going to win every race,' I thought to myself, 'you cocky sod.'

About the only break I got from that pest McKenzie came in mid-season when I heard from my old friends at Belgarda Yamaha. Colin Edwards, their regular World Superbike rider, had fallen off and would miss a couple of meetings with a broken wrist. With less than a week's notice, they wondered if I'd like to ride his bike at Monza.

Bloody right, I would, so me and Andrea jumped on a plane to

Italy. The bike was a full factory version of the YZF I was racing in Britain, so it was just like hopping onto an old friend. Practice went well, apart from one incident: on the first flying lap of the first session, as I hammered over the start line, a brake disc exploded. I heard a big *bang*, then noticed I had no brakes – because that's the sort of finely-honed practitioner I'd become. I hit the chicane at about a million miles an hour, bounced over the top of the kerbs, gravel traps, everything and somehow stayed on the bike. I tootled back to the pits, no problem, just using the back brake.

The pit crew weren't expecting me back because I'd only just gone out. They trotted over from the pit wall. 'Whatsa wrong?' they asked.

'I don't know,' I said, totally deadpan, 'but I think maybe there's something's not quite right about these brakes.'

They looked at the front wheel, which was obviously missing some quite important bits, and just stood there, slack-jawed. To this day I don't know whether they think I'm just crazy, or that I hardly used the front brake. They were still goggling when I went out on the spare bike. The rest of the session was hunky-dory.

At the time I had some skin missing after a practice crash in England. It wasn't a problem except that in the Italian heat you'd sweat up under your leathers and the dressing would fall off. After each practice session I had to go to the *clinica mobile* for a fresh dressing, so that's where I took myself after I'd been debriefed. As I sat in the waiting area I could hear someone groaning in the treatment cubicle, obviously in great pain. This was strange because so far as I knew, no one had fallen off.

Being a nosey git, I popped my head round the corner for a look. Stranger still. I didn't recognise the bloke and he wasn't wearing leathers, just a tea towel wrapped round his hand and a look of intense pain on his face.

'What's up with him?' I asked the circuit doctor.

'Oh, he's…how you say?…a marshal. He pick up brake disc, is very hot. He burns all skin off his hand. Very painful.' Good job I didn't tell him who I was, then. Later Kel Edge, the superbike photographer, told me he'd seen the marshal pick up the red-hot disc, then try to let go of it, fast, but it had sort of welded itself to the poor sod's hand.

After that everything went to plan. I qualified high up on the second row, then rode well, running strongly with the leading runners and finishing sixth and seventh. This didn't do us any harm at all with the Yamaha factory, and probably helped to dispel any lingering doubts about my condition. Most of all, it cemented my relationship with Belgarda Yamaha and paid dividends a few years later when they invited me to join their World Supersports team. They were a good bunch of blokes. I liked them and we worked well together.

After another couple of British championship rounds, we headed off to World Superbikes again at Assen, this time on our Cadbury's Boost bikes. Again I qualified on the second row, having been on pole after the first day's practice. In the first race I ran off the track but recovered to sixth, but had a rubbish ride in the other, finishing 14th.

The final European fling of the season was my first 24-hour race, the Bol d'Or. Yamaha France had phoned Rob Mac to see if I'd be interested in taking part. In the previous few years quite a few Brits had done well riding for French endurance teams – Rymer, Brian Morrison, Hizzy and even Foggy. Endurance racing had never been a particular ambition, but I was curious about it, it sounded fun, and I was keen to give it a go. The money wasn't bad either.

That year the Suzuki teams were the ones to beat. Their 'A' team included Doug Polen and Terry Rymer, two really quick men. I was partnered on a factory YZF, a really trick little tool, with Jean Marc Deletang and Adrian Morillas. Paul Ricard, where the Bol d'Or used to be held, is a brilliant circuit and I got on with the bike, qualifying fastest in our team by quite a margin and second overall to Rymer. Because I'd been fastest, the team decided I'd be the man to start.

This was the first Le Mans start I'd ever done. Basically, the bikes are lined up on one side of the track in qualifying order. All the riders stand on the opposite side of the track and when the lights change you run like hell, jump on and roar away with another 60 pumped-up idiots. Before that there's a huge build-up, with bands and stunt riders, huge crowds, all live on national TV. I was scared witless.

I'd rehearsed the dash across the track in my head...only 25 yards, it shouldn't take long...but it's nothing like that in reality. The race started and the world slowed down. I'm supposed to be racing, but here I am running uphill in treacle. I don't know who's legs these are, but they can't possibly be mine...

The race began at 3:00pm Saturday, and by Sunday teatime I'd just about got to my bike. Luckily, it must have been the same for everyone else, because I actually made a good start. Rymer was first away, but I managed to scrabble past him – barely under control, like this was six laps round Carnaby – in the twisty section before the Mistral straight. I didn't know at the time, but Rob Mac had a few mates round to watch this on TV at home. 'That's it, Whitham,' he groaned while I had the YZF tied in knots, 'only another 23 hours and 59 minutes to go, you knob.'

Still, I stayed on for the first session, handing over the lead to Morillas. Then it became frustrating. By the time I got back on the bike two sessions later, we'd dropped to about third. Later we had a brake problem which dropped us further back, to fifth, but got that sorted and clawed back to second. Then we got a lucky break. As Polen was taking over from Rymer on the leading Suzuki, the bike was accidentally knocked into gear with the wheel half-in. The chain snarled up around the swing-arm and bent it. Sorting the mess out put them well behind, so we now stood neck-and-neck with the all-French Honda team. Although their riders weren't particularly quick, they were going well through slick pit work, good reliability and not making any mistakes. We'd ride our nuts off yet seem to make no inroads, because our pit work just wasn't as well-drilled.

Then it got dark. I'd never raced at night before, but was surprised how fast you could go, because by then you're into a groove and you could lap quickly almost with your eyes shut, more or less working on instinct. Then it suddenly got chilly, the wind picked up and the circuit was hit by a monster electrical storm. Lightning crashed about, then came the rain, lashing down like a monsoon. When the course car came out to slow us all down, I nipped into the pits for wet tyres, then straight out again with a full tank of fuel.

We were running Michelins, whose new wets I'd never used before. The grip they gave was unbelievable. Conditions were horrible, but I couldn't wait to give them a proper go. When the course car pulled off I got cracking, just stomping round with this unreal level of grip…enjoying it, loving it. I was lapping a couple of seconds quicker than anybody else, thinking you just can't go wrong with these wets, with about three laps to go in my stint. The Honda was just ahead, ridden by Alex Vieira who was getting on by then but had been a god in endurance racing for years. 'If I can just push him', I thought, 'I can hand over in the lead.'

Being new to this long-distance game, and being with a French-speaking team, I wasn't quite sure about the pit signals they were giving me. There was something like 'P2 -4 +3'. The 'P2' was obvious, but I was baffled by the rest…four seconds back? Four laps to go? I'd no idea. What they actually meant was that I was three seconds quicker than anybody else. The next lap they put out 'slow', but I didn't get that either. If I am slow, sod 'em, because I can't go any quicker. But the minus figure had been coming down, so I half-imagined that was how far the Honda was ahead, but I wasn't sure.

It didn't matter anyway. I was still pushing on when the back end came round driving out of the Flip-Flop chicane, pitched me off and clattered my right wrist. I was pretty certain I'd broken the scaphoid, because I'd done it before and knew the feeling. It's sort of painful deep inside when you try to grip something, but otherwise not dangling about and giving you lots of grief. Apart from being brassed off about that, all I could think of was the team's instructions: 'Whatever happens,' they'd stressed, 'get the bike back. Even if it's been on fire and smashed to bits – get it back.'

So I hefted the bike back onto its wheels, which wasn't easy. It didn't actually look all that bad. It fired up on the button and luckily it wasn't far back to the pits. The crew were ready. I pulled into the garage and they physically lifted me off the bike – quite gently considering I'd just trashed their bike – and put me on a stretcher where someone started attending to me. It didn't even seem two minutes later when Deletang roared off into the night.

Christian Sarron, who I'd been a big fan of when he raced in grands prix, was running the team. 'I must go to the hospital,' I told him. 'I've broken my wrist. I'm fairly certain it's the scaphoid.'

Christian put his head in his hands and asked if I was sure. Yes, yes, I was pretty damn sure.

'What about you have some injections for the pain? And we have a small brace for the wrist. If we take you straight to the hospital, the race is finished for us. But maybe you can ride?'

'No, no,' I gibbered to my childhood hero. 'You don't understand, you nutter. It's broken. I won't be able to brake. I've tried to ride before with a bust scaphoid, and you just can't do it.'

Christian sighed, shrugged, and that was it. They took me to hospital, confirmed my cod diagnosis and potted it up. I was back in the garage long before the race had finished. Deletang and Morillas had slogged their way round and finished fourth or fifth I think, a good show. Even though I'd been a bit frustrated that they weren't super-quick, they were good lads and really toughed it out.

After the race the team held a big debrief. I was sure I was bound to come in for some stick – the only Brit letting down a French team which had battled bravely through the night to rescue...blah, blah, blah. I was ready for a right old slating.

Sarron stood up. 'Here it comes,' I thought, squinting. Unbelievably, he started firing into everyone else, letting them have it with both barrels. 'You,' he said, pointing at Deletang, 'and you,' pointing at Morillas, 'you're useless.' This was all in French, but it was obvious he wasn't inviting them for a romantic stroll on the seafront at Bandol. Then he pointed at me. 'Oo-er,' I thought, 'now it's my turn.' But he said, 'This man only fell off because you are so slow, so slow, four seconds off the pace. For him it was impossible.'

I walked out of the debriefing feeling about ten feet tall. I can't think of anyone in racing, except perhaps Kenny Roberts, who could have got away with that. To the French, Sarron was almost a god. He could say what he liked and they just had to sit there and take it. Even without him leaping to my defence, I liked Sarron a lot, although he was as mad as a badger. Typical French womaniser, too – always giving your missus the eye, not that Andrea ever complained. I suppose he was good for both our egos.

It was not so good, though, for my British championship aspirations. The Brands Hatch round was just a week after the Bol d'Or, so there was some serious healing to be done. Four times that week I carted myself off to Ipswich to see Brian Simpson. Every day he'd shove me into a hyperbaric chamber, manipulate my wrist, zap it with magnetic beams, all sorts of Flash Gordon shit. I'd no idea if it would do any good, but was pretty sure it wouldn't harm. Brian made me a special lightweight cast to support the wrist, and off we went to Brands to try to salvage the odd point.

It was a messy meeting. The weather had even less of a clue than me – one minute bright sunshine, the next pouring down. We seemed to spend more time changing wheels than actually riding. Somehow I managed a fourth and a fifth, amazing under the circumstances. McKenzie didn't do much better and we came away from Kent with one round to go, absolutely level on points. It was perfectly set up for a big finale.

Although we'd been fighting head-to-head all season, Niall and me got on well. In fact the whole team was like one big happy family – no animosity, no jealousy, no tantrums. We didn't try to push each other off the track, there was no bitching to the press. Everything was above board and fair. If I couldn't win the championship, I was quite happy for Niall to win because, assuming the bike ran OK, the outcome was entirely in my hands. If I didn't come out on top it would be because I wasn't good enough – as simple as that.

Naturally, *Motor Cycle News* wouldn't have it that way, preferring to build the final round up to some big grudge match. They got us together for a photo session. They even produced a couple of guns, wanting us to look like gunslingers facing off.

'Can you look across the table and stare at each other?'

Me and Niall just rolled about. We couldn't sit still for laughing.

Going into Donington I knew that whatever Niall did, a first and a second place would give me the championship on count-back, since I had about twice as many race wins as him – nine of the first 18 rounds. He'd won five, with Rymer and the rest sharing the other four.

The long and the short of it was that I cost myself the championship by cocking up on a tyre decision. Neil always had an edge with tyres. He was such a smooth rider he could always get away with running a softer tyre than me. All through practice I ran a tyre which I knew was borderline for lasting the full race distance, but choosing the next grade harder would have meant using a tyre we hadn't tried for full race distance all season, so that would be a stab in the dark too. All I knew for sure was that I could do the same lap times as Niall on the same tyre, but he could probably make it last a bit longer than me. Rob Mac tried to talk me out of it, but I was adamant: 'Just put on whatever Neil's got on. I want a level playing field here. I don't want to be thinking about anything else except me and him.'

Rob kept on at me and I eventually agreed to go with the harder tyre. But it was my decision, the final say was mine. In the race it just didn't work. I never got any feel, never developed any grip. It just didn't work for me, so I slogged round lapping a second slower than I knew I could do on the softer rubber, finishing third. Niall won, with Sean Emmett second a few seconds in front of me.

This gave the advantage to Niall, since even if I won he could finish second in the final race and win the title. By then I had nothing to lose and put the softer tyre back on. It worked perfectly and I won, fairly easily – although there's no telling whether Niall could have been closer if he'd needed to be. He was British champion and I'd been agonisingly close – but no cigar. Like all championships there were pivotal moments where events could have taken a different turn…the tyre choice in the last round, crashing in the first. That's the way it goes. Get used to it.

I was disappointed, of course, but in some ways it didn't matter. I was alive, which I hadn't been able to count on 12 months before. And Andrea's mum wasn't. Racing results are insignificant compared to realities like those.

Around the same time there was another death, although this one had its funny side. For ages my dad had been seeing a lady called Pam. When my parents split up, which had been on the cards for a while, he moved Pam in at the airfield pretty sharpish. In 1990 they got married, then Pam fell ill with a brain tumour. Dad nursed her at home for a while before she had to go into a hospice. It was a very sad time, very hard for dad.

Pam was cremated. She'd known she was dying for quite some time and had told dad she wanted her ashes scattered over the valley at Wainstalls, where I was born. Apparently dad always saw the area as his spiritual home and had often taken her there. They'd go for walks, have picnics, and even talk about the land they were going to buy and the house they'd build there one day. You couldn't help but be moved.

Anyone else would have just jumped in the car with the urn, driven up there, shed a tear and shaken the ashes over a drystone wall. But not dad. No, he had to have a grandiose plan. So he rang his old mate Ron Oldham, who had a flash helicopter, a Hughes 500. A couple of days later Ron pitched up at the airfield, took off one of the helicopter doors, and off we flew to Halifax. Dad was directing Ron on the intercom: 'Left a bit, right a bit...this is the place, Ron, can you just hover here?'

It was a ridiculous idea. There we are – me, Ron, dad and Pam, hovering 50 feet up in the air, being battered by the wind and the rotor wash as the Hughes revved its nuts off. Dad cradled the urn with a little tear in his eye, croaked 'Goodbye Pam,' and tipped her out of the door. There was a big 'whoosh' and half of Pam came flying back into the chopper in a cloud of ashes and dust whilst the rest rattled off the rotor blades. Ron was blinded and couldn't see where he was flying, so the whole shebang started bucking about with dad desperately trying to sweep his sweetheart off the seats to her final resting place.

I like to think I'm as sympathetic as the next man. Yes, it was awful. Dad, bless him, was distraught that he'd made such a Horlicks out of something so important to him and never saw it as anything but a horrible tragedy. But it was funny, bloody funny. Even as it was happening I sensed that in a couple of years we'd be pissing ourselves looking back on it. I could almost see it on the telly with Michael Palin in the lead role.

CHAPTER 19

FACTORY SUPERSTAR

Towards the end of the 1996 season, the Boosty Boys had taken in the World Superbike round at Assen. The Dutch circuit was always one of my favourites, and I'd stood pole after Friday's first timed session, ending up fifth on the grid. At the time the Harris brothers were running the factory Suzuki Superbikes with Kirk McCarthy and John Reynolds, but had struggled so far in their first season of World Superbikes. Their engines seemed to have reasonable power but they appeared to have lots of handling problems. Whenever I'd ridden the factory Yamaha Superbike I'd beaten them by a distance. I'm not casting aspersions on either rider – they were clearly struggling with the bikes.

Naturally both Steve and Lester Harris were at Assen and by this time in the season were casting around for riders for the following year. Unbeknown to me, Granty had already been telling them I was the man for the job. When the brothers invited me and Rob Mac out for a meal on Friday evening I thought nothing of it, although I was obviously pretty chipper since I was standing provisional pole at the time.

To me – missing the big picture, as usual – it was to be just a pleasant night out in good company. You can't not get on with the Harris brothers. They're right into their racing and good at what they do. Halfway through dinner they announced that they would definitely be running the factory Suzukis for the next two years, that everyone was disappointed with how badly it had been going so far, but that the commitment was total – both from them and from the factory. Then the bombshell: would I be interested in riding the bike?

Do high-sides hurt?

This was a pukka factory set-up, real factory machines and real money – at long last. Other than '94, almost everything I'd ever done at WSB level before then had been one-off rides with nothing much to lose: everyone was dead impressed whenever I got any sort of result, and no one bothered much either way if I binned it or didn't run with the top men. So the prospect of a full season with full factory backing scared me a little. There was going to be a lot of pressure for results and nowhere to hide if it went wrong. Part of me went a bit wimpish, but both Mick and Rob reacted to my cold feet in exactly the same way: 'This is what you've said you wanted for all these years, so either piss or get off the pot.'

So I signed a contract and settled down to life on Suzuki's pot. The extra cash, apart from going towards a retirement nest-egg that hadn't grown much in previous seasons, meant that Andrea could at last give up work and be with me at every meeting.

The team were brilliant people to work with. It was a full-on factory effort, with everyone knowing they had to work hard and put in lots of test miles. One of the mechanics was Trevor Nation, whose elastic hand had so scared me all those years before. Another was Granty's old spannerman, Nigel Everett, a brilliant guy who I also knew fairly well. Although neither were big team players, both knew race bikes inside out. Trevor, a big gorilla of a bloke, actually surprised me by his talent for putting an engine together.

Suzuki were keen to start testing well before New Year. Although I was still under my old contract until 31 December, Yamaha UK kindly waived it and released me so I could go to Phillip Island. Ever since Assen I'd assumed my team-mate would be John Reynolds, and it was only later that I learned they'd signed a Texan, Mike Hale, who'd had a couple of World Superbike rostrum results as a wildcard rider at Laguna Seca. In November we all went to Hamamatsu to meet all the Suzuki bigwigs before flying on to Australia. It was only at this time that it became quite clear that Harris had exerted a lot of pressure on Suzuki to get me in the team. I wasn't their choice, but Hale was – their golden child. He came with a burgeoning Stateside reputation and, like most Yanks, he talked the talk.

In Japan we did half a day of testing on the old bike around Ryuyo, the Suzuki test track, followed by a tour of the factory and

R&D shop, which was hugely impressive. Along the way we met all the bosses, including Mitsuo Itoh, the chief exec, who'd become the first Japanese rider to win a TT in 1963 and amongst other things was supervising the restoration of his old 50cc race bike. Every so often he'd descend in a business suit from his office and poke around at his old toy. Dealing with company executives can be difficult, especially if they've not raced or been involved in racing, but Itoh had been right at the sharp end of racing. He was a decent sort, easy to get on with.

One evening we were taken to an exclusive Japanese restaurant. There was splendid food, Kobe beef and all the rest of it, and several types of sake – rice wine. I hate sake, but sipped it to be polite, while the head of R&D and a bunch of other bigwigs were swilling it down like pop. When it came time to leave, two of them couldn't actually stand and we had to half-carry them out. Traditional Japanese restaurants are divided into separate rooms by screen doors made of matchsticks and tissue paper, half of which were destroyed as we lugged out these two dead-weights. Despite the carnage, the owners were typically polite – bowing and apologising to us for our wrecking their restaurant. 'That's a good start,' I thought. For once, something was trashed and it wasn't me who'd done it.

This was my first experience as a full factory rider, other than riding one-off meetings as a stand-in when someone was injured. It was a different world. You might be testing at Eastern Creek and decide that you needed a suspension linkage with a different geometry than anything you'd used before. A fax would rattle off to Japan, the new part would be machined at the factory overnight, and the following day a private jet would be landing with it at Sydney airport. Even in Huddersfield we never had this.

It was the most hectic off-season I'd ever encountered. That winter we tested at Eastern Creek, Phillip Island, Shah Alam, South Africa, then at Laguna Seca, twice, in the spring. I barely seemed to spend a moment at home all winter. The bike felt quick. It had a lot of power, especially at the top-end. It wasn't peaky, exactly, but didn't have much bottom-end, and the drive out of corners would prove to be its Achilles' heel. The only true indication we got of our competitiveness was at Phillip Island, where the times weren't very impressive compared to other teams who'd tested there.

In those days the capacity limit for four-cylinder superbikes was 750cc, not 1000cc as now, so the bike was based on the GSX-R750 roadster. The 750cc fours always struggled against the 1000cc twins and, as it turned out, '97 was the only year that a 750 – Honda's RC45 – won the manufacturers' title. For all its problems the GSX-R was a trick little thing, a lovely piece of hardware. It gave me a buzz just to look at it. But with race bikes it's performance first, second and third, and looks about 20th. Even before the first round I thought the coming season might be hard work. Firstly, we were on Michelins, which wouldn't have been my first choice. Although they were a lot better than they'd been in 1990, they never seemed to give you the degree of feedback provided by Dunlops, which would usually let you know before they let go. Stability in general was also a problem, especially at high speed. Normally, you'd expect a bike that was unstable to change direction easily, but the Suzuki wasn't particularly flickable either. It was a bit of a conundrum.

The team tried stacks of different things to iron out the steering issue. Nothing was too much trouble. At one stage we thought the chassis was maybe too stiff, and in no time a frame arrived like magic from Japan which was outwardly identical but made from a more flexible alloy – not a cheap thing to do.

So we struggled, especially on twisty circuits. There was no shortage of effort from everyone involved. We did a lot of work, but whatever we tried, the results were crap. It began well enough in the wet at the opening round, Phillip Island, where I was in the top five and in good shape for a result before flipping myself off. A pair of thirds at Hockenheim and Monza – two quick circuits which suited our bike – flattered to deceive. Typically, I was riding my nuts off to scrape into the top ten.

We just happened to have the perfect bike for Hockenheim. Because it had such good top-end, you'd just unleash it onto those long straights and listen to it scream through the gears. It even worked all right through the infield, and if someone did make a bit of a break I seemed to be able to slipstream back to them. In the second race I placed third behind Foggy and Akira Yanagawa. It was the bike's first rostrum in one and a half seasons.

The team was delighted, as you'd expect. They were always very professional up to the race, but most of them liked to party afterwards and, naturally, they were going to have a good one to celebrate our result. Unfortunately Andrea and I had to return Niall McKenzie's Pace Arrow motorhome, which we'd borrowed for the weekend. It was an enormous thing, with an equally huge engine, a 7.4-litre V8 petrol-guzzling lump, so for once we damaged the environment instead of ourselves.

That was the last time we borrowed that damn Yank tank. After collecting it from Donington I pulled into a gas station on the M42, then me and anyone who happened to pass by spent fully 45 minutes looking for the filler cap, which turned out to be hidden behind the rear number plate. That was the easy bit. I put the nozzle in the filler and clicked it on. After 100 litres it automatically knocked off, and I had to give the cashier a credit card. Another 100 litres, same thing. At the time a normal tank of petrol cost around £25. Eventually the bill reached £300 and the tank still wasn't full.

A few days after the Hockenheim result a letter arrived from Japan congratulating us on our third place. There was a mood about that we were on the up – but we were kidding ourselves to think that. The truth was that we just happened to have an ideal package for Hockenheim. This buoyant feeling was compounded by the next round, at Monza, a similar sort of circuit. And it rained, which suited me even more, especially since at the time Michelin wets were clearly superior to Dunlops.

In the first race I had a sixth – a fighting sixth, in a typical Monza slipstream battle, less than three seconds behind John Kocinski's winning time. The second race brought another third place, behind Pier-Francesco Chili and Kocinski, and just a second ahead of Foggy. This was actually an easier race, since the fifth finisher, Aaron Slight, was over half a minute back. Everyone in the team was peaking, convinced we'd turned the corner, were on a roll. But it was an illusion. From there on it was back to normal – eighths, ninths and tenths at the next three rounds. An isolated sixth and seventh was the best we managed for the rest of the year.

But, for the moment, we celebrated our Monza rostrum and let the future take care of itself, ending up in a bar along with Carl,

Scott Russell, Slight, and most of the other Superbike crowd. The bar didn't seem to have any normal lager, the sort of stuff you normally drink on the Continent, just some strange ruddy-brown stuff. Everyone was on this mystery red potion, but whatever it was, it didn't agree with me.

I had turned bumptious on beer before, and that night I got a major case of the strops for no reason. I picked a fight with Slighty, actually threatened to beat him up – as if I could. When that didn't work, I picked another one with all my mechanics, then Carl. Afterwards, me, Andrea, Carl and Michaela Fogarty and a couple of mechanics all piled into a hire car. Andrea was driving and couldn't find the way back to the track, so everyone was chipping in their two penn'orth, even though most of us were drunk and didn't have a clue. Eventually Andrea had enough of this, pulled the car over, got out and climbed into the back. 'If you're all so bloody clever,' she yelled, 'you find the bloody way back.'

Most of us had a go, with no better results but with even more yelling and screaming from the back seat. Carl, who at the best of times isn't the most patient man in the world, eventually decided he'd had enough, stamped out of the car and slammed the door. Half an hour later we're still lost and who do we pass but the multiple World Champion, stood at the side of the road looking forlorn? So he climbed back in.

When you're the rider in a team, people tend to look up to you, and unless it's someone you've got to know as a mate many of the crew hesitate before talking to you. Andrew, the team's computer boffin, hadn't even had a drink. Mostly he sat in the back trying to pretend he was somewhere else, but eventually plucked up the courage to tell us supposed hot-shots where we needed to go. At breakfast the next morning, Martin Bennett, the other mechanic we'd inflicted ourselves on, asked me if I could possibly arrange not to score any more rostrums. He liked the results but couldn't handle the pain and embarrassment.

Later, I bumped into Scott Russell, packing up his motorhome in the paddock, obviously hung-over and sporting a huge black eye.

'What's up, Scott?'

Apparently there was some sort of fracas at a nightclub. I think a woman was involved – there usually was with Scott – and some well-aimed Italian shoes. So we weren't the only ones to misbehave at Monza.

After Monza we came back to earth with a bump. Even at Assen, a circuit I've always enjoyed and gone well at, I came away with only a seventh and an 11th, which seemed mediocre rewards. The seventh place wasn't too bad, only 13 seconds off Kocinski's winning time after a terrific dice to beat Yanagawa's Kawasaki by about a wheel. But the 11th was nowhere, 50 seconds behind the winner after a lonely ride. I was riding hard and, I thought, riding well, but too many bikes were going better.

Mind you, some folk were surprised we rode at Assen at all. At about 7:30 on race day morning there's a loud rapping at the motorhome door. I thought it'd be Michaela looking for a bit of peace after a barny with Carl, or some pre-race panic or something. I swung the door open wearing just my underpants and T-shirt, and there's this little Dutch journalist. 'Good Morning,' he says. 'Have you heard about Princess Diana?'

'No.'

'She's been killed in a car crash.'

'Really. That's a shame.'

'You English riders will be pulling out of the meeting now?'

'Yeah, yeah, course we will.'

'You will?'

'Sod off. Don't be a prat.'

I'd qualified sixth or something, a real result on the Suzuki. The death of only one person could keep me off that grid, and that'd be me. I still can't understand all that fuss.

I don't want this to sound disrespectful – she was a very nice lady, I'm sure – but I couldn't believe the outpouring of grief when Princess Diana died. Yes, I was sad at her passing. But she was just one person and I didn't even know her…let me get on with my life.

At least I wasn't crashing much and, when I did, it was usually a high-side, which wasn't normally my style, but did show how hard I was trying. Chucking the bike away is always a bit embarrassing, but never so much as powering out of a left-hander in practice at Sugo in the penultimate round of the season. It wasn't a particularly fast crash, but I went quite high and landed heavily. I was stunned, perhaps momentarily, but got up and wobbled off the track before being carted off for my usual goodwill visit to the medical centre.

I'd banged my hand hard on the track, which had squashed a ring onto my finger, causing it to go blue. Maybe the doctor thought it was some sort of precious heirloom or ancestor-worship symbol, but he didn't have a clue what to do about it. There was a lot of yakking in Japanese and not much action. At this point my mechanic, Nigel Everett, wandered in to check whether he still had a functional racer for his bikes. He took one look at all the confusion before strolling back to the garage for a pair of side-cutters. Snip, snip and the ring was off. 'Ah, so,' cooed the medics, as though he'd just performed open-heart surgery.

That turned out to be the easy bit. Next they started tugging away to get me out of my leathers, which I was beginning to realise could have really cringe-making consequences.

'Nige,' I said, 'can't you do anything to stop 'em? I've crapped myself.'

Maybe he thought I expected him to set about them with the side-cutters. 'What the fuck do you expect me to do about it?'

'I don't know. What can you do?'

He pondered for a minute, then shook his head with one of those 'be brave' expressions your mum used to give you when you were having stitches in a gashed knee. 'They must deal with this stuff all the time,' he said, beating a retreat back to the pits. By then I'd realised that my underpants were fairly full, so the situation was becoming critical. I explained that I needed to go to the toilet. Like, *urgently.*

'No, doctor say X-ray.'

'No, toilet first.'

'No, X-ray.'

This could have gone on all day, so I just had to submit and keep a stiff upper lip – as opposed to my slightly flaccid sphincter. This wasn't the first time I'd had such a problem. Most motorcyclists are prevented from going fast by their brain. I'm different. With me it's my bowels. I suppose I wasn't the only one. Sometimes when you knock yourself out you can have all sorts of involuntary incidents – but that doesn't make it any less embarrassing when you come round.

Toilet mishaps aside, it was a hard year physically, with a lot of testing, a lot of racing, and seemingly not much time to regroup. But most of all it was tough mentally, because of all the expectations from the factory. That's why they pay you factory money, I suppose. It was also why I half-expected not to have a job for '98. The saving grace was that if I wasn't putting the GSX-R on the rostrum every weekend, at least I was always quicker than my team-mate, which is rule one in any race team. Much to my surprise Suzuki did renew my contract, although Mike Hale, who'd had a disastrous season, was let go. He was replaced by Peter Goddard, a veteran Australian with a reputation for being a good development rider. Goddard had been World Endurance Champion with Doug Polen the previous year.

Peter was very technical, in my view excessively so. Sometimes he seemed to think the job almost to a standstill. As a technical member of a team, which is what he's doing now, I think he'd be a major asset. But as a rider as well, he spent so much time pondering over the job, poring over telemetry readouts, that I honestly believe it became counter-productive.

At that time data acquisition was in its infancy but had already become an integral part of Superbike racing. We were gathering data from all the engine parameters, as well as chassis information like front and rear wheel movement, suspension travel, brake pressure... If it could be physically measured, we measured it. After each session you'd have a debrief with your crew – first with the tyre people, then the chassis people, then you'd look through your data, see where you were quick, and see how the numbers related to what you'd experienced on the track. Typically I'd spend an hour or 90 minutes sat in my leathers in front of a laptop computer going through this process. Then I'd go for a shower and eat. More often than not, hours later on my way back to the motorhome, Goddard's face would still be in his laptop, poring over every last digit of the telemetry. His mechanics, who couldn't set the bike up for the next day until Peter had analysed the last, were up until all hours working on his bikes.

For all that attention to the smallest detail, I never felt that he had a better bike than me. I always tried hard to set the bike up, but was much more reliant on feel. At some stage in the weekend, usually Saturday afternoon, you've got to forget about changing settings and trying different stuff. If it's not perfect by then, it's not going to be. Get used to it. There comes a point where you just have to get on and ride the bike, whatever shape it's in. By Sunday morning the last thing on my mind was different fork yokes or whatever, but rather, 'How can we get this thing round quicker – as it is?'

If it was still a struggle on the track, off it we were having a ball. Since '94 me and Andrea hadn't had a motorhome, preferring to stay in hotels instead when away racing. I'm not sure why the idea popped into my head, but one day in '97 I suggested we go for a camping trip. To me this meant a primus stove and a scrap of canvas surrounded by gnats. But not to her.

'Oh, yes, that sounds good,' she said, thinking of £150,000-worth of Yank motorhome into which she could plug her hairdryer and satellite TV. As usual, her version won out, so we got a motorhome.

Motorhomes are big, greedy, expensive things, but compared to fiddling about getting to airports and flying home after every weekend they transform your way of life. I loved the driving and travelling. One weekend you might be at Mugello and two weeks later you're due to race at Albacete. You're not going to spend three days and a ton of diesel driving home for six days, just to spend another three days driving south again. No, obviously you go direct and take a holiday.

We'd spend time on the road with Peter and Kim Goddard, sometimes Troy Corser, Colin Edwards, and occasionally Carl – although by then he'd got two kids and was a bit fed up with the travelling, so usually paid someone else to shuttle his motorhome to meetings. We had lots of time to kill so actually did the things you always wished you'd done when you're travelling, but never seemed to have the time. So I made Andrea pay for her bloody hairdryer, dragging her around World War Two battlefields, Hitler's Eagles' Lair, Mad King Ludwig's castle, museums, and any other anorak attraction that grabbed my fancy – anything to keep her away from the shops. Sometimes I'd be stood in an empty field breathing in the atmosphere of thousands of people having hacked each other to death at this precise muddy spot a thousand years before, and she'd think I was off my trolley. But even she enjoyed Colditz Castle. Not that you could park up just anywhere. The trouble with these big Yank buses is that two of them would totally jam up a normal campsite. Luckily the American Motorhome Club of Great Britain publish details of sites that could handle us, at least if we behaved.

Some time in mid-'98 the usual convoy was driving from Spain to somewhere else, and we found ourselves in Frèjus on the French Riviera with the Goddards, Slights, Edwards and Scott Russell's driver. The Goddard and Edwards motorhomes actually had cars lashed behind, so one Saturday Alicia Edwards and Andrea drove off to Cannes for the film festival and a spot of shopping while the guys went off to play golf. I wasn't bothered about golf anyway, and was suffering with insect bites, so I stayed in on my own to watch the FA Cup final on telly.

By half-time I was in a bad way with some form of allergic reaction to the damn bugs. I was feverish, my arms and legs were swollen, and I thought I had malaria. So I got on my moped and wobbled off into town. I'd been told just to go to a chemist, which will sell you more or less anything in Europe. Trouble was, I could just about order a beer in French and that was it. Somehow I managed to mime the mosquito attack from hell, and the chemist got the picture. Whatever it was that he gave me seemed to work. At least, I didn't die.

Otherwise, touring around without a care in the world was a great sort of life...no kids, doing what you wanted and a fair bit of money in your pocket. On the other hand, motorhomes might look swanky but actually owning one is anything but idyllic. They're so complicated, so many systems for this and that, that sooner or later everything seems to go wrong. Older ones have usually been sorted by previous owners, but ours was new, from a place in Wolverhampton. It was the first one I'd had which had an automatic levelling system, which was really neat – when it worked. You just pressed a button and a bunch of rams came down and there you were – parked, solid and level.

During the season we'd become friendly with Jurgen Zern, the manager of Udo Mark's World Superbike team. Rather than bring the motorhome back to England between trips, he suggested I park it in their compound in Munich. He even had a pal who could get us cheap Lufthansa tickets to and from the UK.

On our way to Munich for the first time, we pulled over into a picnic area for something to eat. We'd only be there for 40 minutes so there was no need, but I was feeling dead smug with my new toy and with a load of truckers looking on, I pressed the button to jack up the levelling system. There was the usual whirr of compressors and hydraulics, and there we were, sound as a pound. We had a tasty little snack, tidied up and were ready to go. But when I pressed the un-jack button there was a loud *bang*, then nothing. So the motorhome was up in the air and there was nothing we could do about it. I had a ferret around. No fuses were blown, and banging the legs with a big hammer had no effect.

This is where having a dad like mine comes in handy. What would he have done? I had a think, and worked out that if I took the weight off each leg with the wheel-change jack, I could probably move them out of the way one at a time. Well, maybe.

It took two hours. Trouble was, although the legs pivoted out of the way when you took the weight off them, they didn't shorten. They just sat there flapping about. So by the time we left each one was tied up to the chassis with trouser belts, string, bits of luggage strap and blind Yorkshire faith. The truckies, who'd been stood watching this pantomime for the entire evening, could hardly stand for laughing. And all that for a Cornish pastie and cup of tea.

The bike, though, was getting better. It certainly should have been. We were still doing a lot of testing, and a lot of money and effort was going into the job. Some of it seemed counter-productive. Either through politeness or secrecy, head office wouldn't really tell you what was going on. New parts would arrive for testing, so you'd try them and some would work and some clearly wouldn't. We'd send the duff ones back to Japan, yet they'd keep reappearing on the bike regardless, as though they had their own agenda. It was frustrating – and typically Japanese. Half the time your hands were tied.

Despite that, pre-season testing went fairly well, other than a big get-off at Eastern Creek when the throttle jammed wide open. Even the choice of tracks was sometimes a puzzle, because we never raced at Eastern Creek. It was a brilliant circuit to thrash around, but of limited use as a pointer to the season ahead. It also hurt.

At the time we were playing about with all sorts of new kit. Suzuki even toyed with button gearshifts, like F1 cars, although this was never used for racing. Fuel injection was the main thing, one different system after another, often tried back-to-back with the old carburettor set-up. The mechanics could swap between a complete set of carbs and an injection system in about 20 minutes. Both set-ups used the same carbon fibre airbox, although if the carbs were used a couple of redundant electrical block-connectors had to be zip-tied inside the box out of the way. For this particular session I was running carbs.

Eastern Creek has a fast back straight leading into a big fifth-gear right-hander, followed by a third-gear left-hander back onto the start/finish straight. You turn into the right-hander on a closed throttle then grab a load of brake as it goes into the left. At least, that's what you do if your throttle hasn't stuck wide open.

Throttle sticking happens, especially on the old two-strokes. But in the days before slick shifters you had plenty of chances to find out, because you closed the throttle at every gear-change. Now you just keep it pinned until you need to slow down. So there I was doing about 150mph down the back straight, shut the throttle at the end, and...nothing.... All I could do was get off the thing, so I grabbed a fistful of front brake and hit the floor. All the crew knew at the time was that I'd gone tits-up in fairly spectacular fashion. I didn't have a mark on me, but the bike had thrashed itself to bits.

'Throttle stuck wide open,' I said when I got back.

At this point mechanics always – even if you've known them for years and they really trust you – absolutely *always* check whatever you've blamed. You get used to it, but never in my career have I fabricated a reason for crashing – although plenty of times I've said I didn't have a clue why I fell off. Some other riders aren't always so honest. 'It jumped out of gear,' used to be favourite, because before telemetry it couldn't be disproved. Now some geek with glasses will tell you it didn't, you lying prat.

So the mechanic, Martin Bennett, automatically grabs what's

left of the handlebar and twists the throttle – which turned, just like it was supposed to. So even I'm wondering if I've been hallucinating. But no, it did jam, and eventually the telemetry proved it – stuck at 81.5 per cent wide open. Now, it's good to know what causes things like this, because they're not all that healthy. So Martin scratched his head a bit, fiddled inside the airbox and – lo and behold – got a reading of 81.5 per cent on the computer. It turned out that one of the fuel injection's connector blocks had come adrift and stuck in one of the carb slides. The bike was doing precisely 142mph at the time.

Falling off at 142mph never feels good, but it's always comforting to be proved right. After all, what's the point of lying to your mechanic? Even in my days racing a 125, if something happened that was my fault I'd always gone back and held my hand up – sometimes from the comfort of a stretcher – and said so. It isn't even a matter of me being more honest than some other riders and aren't I great? More importantly, how can a team make progress – which is at least as much in my interest as theirs – if part of their feedback is a lie? I've made mistakes and I've had mechanics who've made mistakes. It happens.

Mechanics have a tough job. The pay's often lousy yet the responsibilities couldn't be bigger. Seven years earlier, at Brands Hatch, the Suzuki 'Ironing Board' had seized up and pitched me off coming out of Clearways. At least, that's what my instincts told me at about the same moment Brian Morrison ran over my leg and bust my cruciate ligament. It turned out that the battery had fallen out and jammed between the swing-arm and the rear tyre, locking the wheel.

My mechanic at the time was Butch Cartwright. Working with him was Neil, a keen young kid who was infatuated with the race scene and came along as a team gofer. Normally he was very conscientious, but he'd forgotten to install the battery strap, and owned up right away. I spent the next eight months hobbling about, a right ball-ache.

But even experienced professionals make cock-ups. Years later Ambro, my Belgarda Yamaha mechanic, once forgot to Loctite a primary gear bolt, which unscrewed itself and ground through the casing, spilling oil everywhere and bringing me off. If a mechanic regularly made such mistakes he'd have to go. Clearly the consequences of such errors can be fatal, although at the time the focus is more on the effect on results. But Ambro was sound. And Neil didn't forget that battery strap on purpose. The bottom line for me was that over the years no mechanic messed up as often as I did, so who was I to complain?

It's not something you analyse at the time, but I suppose that much of this integrity, if that's what it is, comes from dad. He may have been daft as a brush – most of my mates thought so, although he seemed normal enough to me – but he had a very linear sense of what was right. It was an article of faith with him that you got the fruit of your labours, and if you didn't labour, you got nowt. That was what you deserved, and that was that. He was by no means the stereotypical ideal father, but I owe him a debt of thanks for that. Or perhaps I was just a crap liar.

For whatever reason, I was never one for coming into the garage and kicking spanners about in a tantrum. My mechanics always seemed to appreciate my being straight with them, and with the bike. Inevitably – although, again, this wasn't part of any plan – they were usually prepared to go the extra mile in their efforts. They'd work all night it they had to, and happily, for the common cause. You just can't buy that sort of dedication.

As well as changing to fuel injection, for the '98 season we also changed to Dunlop tyres. This handicapped us slightly in the wet compared to Michelins, but gave me more feel and confidence to push hard, especially on the front wheel. The other major change was the departure of Nigel Everett. He was a hugely experienced guy – by then he had over 20 years at the top level – but he tended to do his own thing in his own way. Worst of all he didn't get on with Simon Buckmaster, who by then was team co-ordinator. Martin Bennett, who I'd worked with for Hoss Elm in '94 and was an ace bloke very much in the Everett mould, became my chief mechanic.

I look back at the 1998 season as a whole as probably being me at my peak, with just the right balance between youthful exuberance and experience. I was still able to push as hard as ever, but prepared to ride with a little more reserve when the bike was telling me something was going to go wrong. Before, I'd probably have continued to push it until I ended up on my backside. Overall we did all right. I'd never been a hot-shot qualifier, but in Super-pole we usually managed to get on the second row, and once made the front. I enjoyed working with the Harris brothers and the team in general, so in that respect it was a fairly satisfying season.

There was no doubt at all that we were closing the gap to the front teams. From mid-season onwards we were running with guys of the calibre of Slight and Neil Hodgson most of the time. Sometimes, when things ran our way, we'd even be within spitting distance of Foggy, who regained the world title that year. All the work seemed to be paying off. We were running strongly, always there or thereabouts, and the results proved it: from Misano until the last round at Sugo we were never out of the top six. Austria was typical. Fifth place was a good enough result in itself, but it was only seven seconds off the win. We were *there*, within a gnat's chuff of where we wanted to be. Everyone was playing their part and it was solid stuff all round. We had only four non-finishes all season, two due to machine troubles, a crash at Misano and another on oil when I was lying third at Kyalami. And I was generally following rule one and beating my team-mate, Peter Goddard.

The pressure, though, was immense. As a rider you expect that. You're at the sharp end of a multi-million dollar project, the only guy who can do anything when the race starts. But the high expectations for results ran right through the team as a whole. Yes, everything was definitely getting better, but there was a crunch time ahead. Harris's three-year contract was due to end the following winter. All of us were aware that if results weren't to Suzuki's satisfaction, everyone could be out of a job, which only added to the stress.

Our best result in the latter part of the season was third in the second race at Brands Hatch, a truly epic race. When the lights changed, Troy Corser did his usual disappearing act, while I settled into a battle with Foggy. By two-thirds distance I realised – bloody hell! – we were catching Corser. Both of us piled it on. I broke the lap record a couple of times, Carl once, and by the end of the race we were pulling a second a lap on Troy, but he hung on to win by about four seconds.

I was the equal of Carl everywhere, but couldn't get past the feisty little sod, despite a couple of goes to dive inside him. Every time I got close he upped his pace a bit, so I had to up mine. I kept having little pushes so he'd hear my engine and keep on his toes. Some riders you can push like that and expect them to make a mistake, but Carl definitely wasn't one of them. For the last three or four laps I knew I had more side grip than Carl, but he had better traction, so although he was normally big on corner speed where I was more point and squirt, this was the opposite. Eventually I settled for thinking third would be a good result in front of a massive crowd. Maybe If I'd a had a rostrum in the first race, instead of a fifth, I might have had a bigger go at him. But third, in front of that huge home crowd – it was a good solid result, good for the team.

Even so, towards the end of the season the writing was on the wall. Rumours started to circulate on the paddock grapevine that Suzuki were fed up with Harris and that Alstare were going to take over the factory superbike effort. By Sugo, the last meeting of the year, literally in Suzuki's own backyard, I was absolutely convinced that even if someone else was going to be running the team in '99, I must have done enough to keep the ride. Sugo itself is always a difficult place to go, mainly because the grid's packed with local hotshots on full factory kit. On paper, my eleventh and ninth places look rubbish until you consider that this was ahead of Slight and Hodgson. Overall I felt as though I was riding as well as ever I had – and without crashing, too.

In two seasons, I reckoned, I was the only one who'd ridden the GSX-R properly. I'd had the odd rostrum and had definitely helped put us on an upward curve. Yes, I'd feel sorry for Harris if they did lose the contract, because I didn't believe most of the earlier problems had been their fault. But no one on earth knew that bike better than I did.

Whatever they decided I assumed that the factory would be in touch, either way, if only to say 'Thanks, Whitham-san, it's been nice working with you.' But there was nothing: no letter, no phone call, not even a text message. Just no job for '99. The Japanese can be odd people. They're honourable, I've no doubt of that, with an exaggerated sense of politeness. But often, rather than say 'No' they prefer to say nothing at all. So all autumn I heard nowt and didn't know what was going on. But when they signed Katsuaki

Fujiwara as team-mate to Pier-Francesco Chili it gave me a pretty solid clue I was out of work.

Looking back, my reaction surprises me. Maybe I should have been spitting feathers, but I was actually quite philosophical. After all, what else could I have done – hold a gun to team boss Francis Batta's head? And I had no complaints about their choice of riders. Chili was a good, hard, experienced rider who could win races, someone who must have seemed to Suzuki precisely what they needed. Yet early the following season, after finding out for himself what the bike was like, even he was quoted as saying that I'd ridden it better and harder than people gave me credit for.

Fujiwara I didn't know so well, although he was already on the factory's books in Japan and when we'd encountered him during testing he'd looked quick. Suzuki's other pet rider, Akira Ryo, was even faster – unbelievably quick. Me and Hale would turn up for testing and he'd spank us all day long around Sugo. I can only assume he didn't want to come to Europe or they'd have drafted him into the superbike team. So, as well as being brassed off about being out of work, I sometimes wondered why they'd been paying me a small fortune to ride their bike when this bloke would go faster for a few yen a day.

CHAPTER 20

'HAVE WE HAD ENOUGH, THEN?'

After being dumped by Suzuki I did nothing through the winter of 1998–9. There were plenty of offers of rides, but mostly back in Britain, and I felt I was at an age where I could race at home and do reasonably well, but too old to get back on the world stage again if I abandoned it. More than that, I thought that at 32, and with only two years of decent money behind me, I needed to get some cash in the bank. There wasn't much time left to repent on a bad career decision.

Once again, I turned to Rob McElnea for advice. 'Don't take anything you think is less than you're worth,' he said. 'Sit it out and ambulance chase.' It's an awful thing. You don't hope anyone will get hurt, but you want to be there to grab their ride if they do. Rob calls them vultures, smacking their chops when something falls down in the desert.

Whatever might turn up, I already had at least an occasional job. The Bol d'Or fiasco two years earlier didn't seem to have done me any harm and I'd been approached with offers of rides by two or three World endurance teams. Suzuki came up with a reasonable deal on a race-by-race basis, which allowed me to duck out if I got a really good offer elsewhere. So, if only to tide me over financially and keep Andrea in shoes, I was happy to accept.

The first endurance outing was at Le Mans in mid-April. I was the third rider in a team with Terry Rymer and Jéhan d'Orgeix, who'd both be doing the whole series whilst I'd join them just for the 24-hour events. I was the new boy and hadn't ridden at Le Mans before, but managed to qualify second behind the Kawasaki of Chris Walker, Steve Hislop and Bertrand Sebileau. I loved the bike, which was almost exactly the same as the GSX-R750 I'd ridden the previous year, and for once felt really useful in setting it up.

The trouble with endurance is that the bike doesn't just have to fit you, it has to suit two other blokes, as well. I'm not all that fussy about how I like the handlebars and footrests, whilst other riders are like the princess and the pea, needing everything millimetre-perfect. Too-Tall-Tel, of course, needed loads of leg-room, so if it fitted me and d'Orgeix, Terry had his head over the screen, and if it fitted him we could barely reach the clip-ons. Worse still, the other two used upside-down gearshifts, but I used a normal up-for-up road shift. While I was imagining pinging myself into the Armco after changing down instead of up, the team produced a clever reverse linkage which literally took a few seconds to change.

So far so good. From then on it was a cluster fuck from the word go. As fastest qualifier, I was asked to do the first stint, much like the '96 Bol d'Or. This time it didn't just *seem* like slow-motion. It *was* slow-motion. I ran across the track, no bother, and hit the starter button....*drrrr*...the engine turned over all right but just would not start. *Drrr....drrr*...nothing, except lots of noise and turbulence as the other 50-odd bikes cleared off. Every bike I'd ever ridden was wired so that if the kill button was off, the starter button wasn't live. But not this one. Meantime half of France is roaring past me down the straight. Eventually the penny dropped, I flicked the kill switch and set off like a dingbat, passing what seemed like hundreds of other bikes and getting more ruthless and frenzied with every one. I was so keen to hand over to the next rider somewhere near the front.

A few laps later, into the first chicane over the hill, I dived inside someone, clipped them and...oh bollocks...went down. The bike was OK, so I got going again, passed half the field again and handed over to Rymer. Then it was d'Orgeix, then me again. After my second stint we'd settled into a rhythm and were up to where we started – second place. So far so good.

Then, during d'Orgeix's second stint, it started spitting with rain. In no time conditions were horrible – part wet, part dry – the trickiest to get to grips with, because you've never any real idea how much grip you've got. In no time bikes started skating off. The pit

243

lane was chaotic, with riders changing tyres and others limping in with battered bikes. But at least our man didn't dump it miles from the pits. As d'Orgeix fired the Suzuki out of the last right-hander onto the start/finish straight – *bang!* – it spat sideways and chucked him off. Since we were one of the front-runners the TV director was concentrating on our bike and we saw the whole thing live on screen. For me and Terry it was almost as bad as crashing yourself, because although it's not you getting battered, it's your bike and you have a vested interest.

When d'Orgeix stopped sliding he can't have been more than a couple of hundred yards from the pit. The routine was that when conditions are as tricky as they'd become, the next rider due out on the bike – me – gets ready early, because a crash and an early pit stop is always a possibility. So there I was, pimping around with my leathers on, helmet handy, ready to go.

You could see right away that d'Orgeix wasn't badly damaged, nor was the bike, so all I was thinking was, 'Come on, come on, push it back to the pits, you berk.' But he made no attempt to pick the bike up, just wandered off holding his arm and sat on a straw bale. It was left to the marshals to pick up the bike, by which time we were all stood on the pit lane imploring the useless sod to bring it back. Eventually – it felt like 20 minutes but was probably only 30 seconds later – he decided he was going to bring it back after all. He heaved it away from the barrier where the marshals had parked it, fired it up, and drove it more or less straight across the track to the pit lane.

While he was lifted off the bike and wobbled to the back of the pit for treatment, the crew tore into the bike. It wasn't badly damaged, just a broken footrest and a lever. Meanwhile d'Orgeix is supposedly in worse shape, on his way to hospital with a suspected broken arm.

No time to worry about that now. It's my turn. Off I go, put in a decent session and hand over to Terry at the end of my stint. When he pits 45 minutes later, d'Orgeix still hasn't come back so it's my go again, by which time it's dark. The two of us carried on like this all night. Because we'd lost a bit of time due to the crash, and it was now dry, we were hammering it...posting back-to-back lap records all night long. Then it rained again, and this time it was

Terry's turn to slide off. There was never any doubt that he'd get the bike back, sharpish. He'd have carried the damn thing if he'd had to. He wasn't injured, just mad, saying, 'Sorry, mate,' between kicking stuff up and down the garage. He's a big, strong lad, very fit, very determined, and by this time he had a lot of endurance experience and knew the score – unlike me. Although he obviously knew I could ride a bike, there's a lot more than that to this 24-hour stuff. He was generous with his advice and helped me through the race.

By now I'm like a zombie...all I know is push, push, push, chasing my headlight beam through the darkness to make up even more lost time. I'd no idea how many sessions I'd done, what time it was. My head was scrambled and conditions were still treacherous. Then, hammering through the fast right-hander after the start, I got a foot or so off-line, touched the white line and went down like a sack of spuds. The bike smacked the tarmac with its titanium exhaust, and the whole of Le Mans lit up with the sparks. As I slid along the track I could actually see people's faces illuminated in the grandstand.

When the fireworks finished I was sat in the gravel trap next to the remains of the Suzuki. Its fairing was hanging off, the exhaust was torn out of the collector box, and the back tyre was flat from whacking the kerb. 'What a bloody mess,' I thought as I scrambled to my feet. The bike was even worse than it looked, with the right handlebar – the important one – snapped clean off. I was just wondering how I was going to get this heap back to the pits when a marshal trotted onto the scene. I'd been told not to accept any outside help or we'd be disqualified, although I'd only got half the story since marshals are allowed to help you move bikes out of the firing line onto a safer part of the track. Obviously the marshal knew this, if I didn't, so as he was trying to pick up the bike I'm yelling 'No, no, no,' with a rising degree of desperation and red mist. The third time he tried to help I just hit him, knocked him flat on his arse. He left me alone after that.

I grabbed the twist grip, which was just hanging on its cable, and actually managed to fire up the bike. What a din! Without the silencer, the engine's pouring flames and noise into the French night. Somehow I managed to wedge the handlebar against my knee and wobble back to the pits on the flat back tyre. This was more like trials than an endurance race.

By then I'm a bit flustered. I've trashed the bike, assaulted a marshal and deafened half of Normandy – and I'm knackered. The mechanics fired into the job instantly, throwing lumps away and bolting on new bits. Amazingly, within four or five minutes, it was ready to go. Meanwhile Terry's getting himself ready. As I'm lying on the floor hyperventilating into my helmet, he leaned down, flipped up my visor and said, totally deadpan, 'Have we had enough, then?'

'I don't know, man,' I gasped. 'I'm in bits. But I'll bat on. Go out and see how it feels.' And off he went.

By then we'd had four crashes, but the team were great. They never actually said they thought we were a bunch of retarded numpties, even as the back of the garage was filling up with expensive factory scrap. By daylight the track had dried out, we'd had no more dramas, and were clawing our way through the field. The team figured that if we maintained the same pace, we had a good chance of finishing in the top five. Other leading teams were having their own problems, and eventually we found ourselves in a safe third place. Then, bugger me if d'Orgeix didn't turn up. His arm, the team boss told us, was only bruised. Then he added a bunch of horseshit about it being very important for a French rider to ride the last session and take the flag – a matter of national honour.

I was too knackered to care either way and would have gone along with it. I was new to this game, anyway, and usually prefer a quiet life. But not Terry. He didn't seem at all impressed by the concept of Gallic pride. 'Fuck 'im', he screamed. 'Me and 'im's doing it,' he growled, nodding at me. 'That's it – d'Orgeix is not getting back on that bike!'

Over the years a lot's been said about 'Too-Tall-Tel' being too big to be a really successful racer. But not then. Terry just towered over the whole team with this crazy look on his face. Nobody dared mention French honour again. Since I'd done more damage to the bike than anyone else, I told Terry to take the last stint. Walker, Sebileau and Hizzy won by seven laps from the other Suzuki works team, with us a further 20 laps adrift in third. Terry didn't even want to let d'Orgeix on the rostrum, said he'd kick him down the steps if he tried, although he relented in the end.

As a team we'd been capable of winning the race. But with all the mishaps, third was a bloody miracle. Terry was a revelation. I'd always respected him as a racer, and we got on fairly well, although we were never close. But Le Mans gave me a new respect for just how good he was at endurance – and how tough, in a typically understated British way. Even under severe adversity he was always droll and upbeat.

Le Mans may have been an experience, but at least I got there. A few weeks before the race my mate Zac McMillan asked me if I could get some free passes for his next-door neighbour. 'He's a nice bloke,' Zac explained, 'but his wife's left him and he's been hitting the bottle, cracking up a bit. He could do with a nice break.'

No worries. Passes arranged. But the neighbour never arrived at Le Mans. 'Thanks, mate,' Zac told me later. 'Sorry, it was all for nothing. The bloke fell off leaving his drive, pissed as a parrot, and broke his leg.'

I can't imagine Suzuki made much except scrap from our Le Mans escapade, but third place gave me a decent bonus. If nothing else came up, I thought maybe I could scratch a living out of 24-hour racing. For pin money I was also doing a spot of test-riding for Rob McElnea's Virgin Yamaha team, by way of a second opinion. Two weeks after Le Mans Rob got another call from Belgarda Yamaha. Apparently Massimo Meregalli, then team-mate to Piergiorgio Bontempi in their World Supersports team, had broken his arm in South Africa. They needed a last-minute replacement for the Donington Park round, only days away. Rob had suggested me.

Rob thought it was actually a bit of a no-win situation, but it was worth a few quid so I accepted. Less than 24 hours later, on the Wednesday before the race, I met Belgarda at Mallory for testing, then on to Donington. I didn't qualify well – ninth – but felt fairly comfortable on the bike, although I was still struggling for feedback from the Michelin tyres it wore. Nonetheless, I was confident that in the race I could push harder and do a lot better than ninth and for once I was right. Everything went perfectly. I romped round Donington, cleared off and won fairly easily from the front. It couldn't really have worked any better. The team promptly said they'd put out a third race bike, and offered me a wage for the rest of the season.

Of all the adjectives thrown at me over the years, 'enigmatic' is probably the least used, but I declined. Effectively, I'd made my point and was hanging back for a good deal for the following year. At least, that's how Rob Mac read the score.

Donington also showed me that Supersports riders had problems of a sort I'd not encountered for some years. For instance, the front-end chatter – where the wheel develops a high frequency vibration into turns – was terrible. The team crew, many of whom I knew already, accepted that chatter was always a problem around Donington and there was nothing they could do about it. A session later I'd be complaining about the brakes or something – same story: live with it. It's a road bike. It's bound to have faults.

After riding Superbikes that could be tuned almost infinitely, it came as a bit of an eye-opener that supposed race bikes could be like this. Today's Supersports bikes are much better. They're actually designed to be raced. But back then the forks were fairly primitive, there was no such thing as adjustable rear ride-height, and you just had put up with a degree of handling problems. Soon the penny dropped and I realised that everyone else was stuck with the same issues. In fact part of me soon came to relish the idea that at some point you had to stop faffing and fretting about the last half-turn of preload and just race the damn thing.

There would always be someone whose bike, tyres or whatever, suited a particular circuit fractionally better than the rest. But generally there wasn't much to choose between any of the Supersport machines. Now it's very much more technical. The rules haven't changed, but in some ways it's more finicky than Superbikes, in that you have to fix the problems within those narrow parameters – and if you don't, at least one of your rivals definitely will. Nine years ago there didn't seem to be the same emphasis. It was just accepted that everyone would be out of shape to some degree.

But the thought uppermost in my mind as Andrea and me drove up the M1 from Donington was nothing to do with the niceties of handling. I was too smug about my increased marketability. 'I pissed that,' I thought to myself. I thought I was back on the map. So I went home, sat on my arse, and waited for teams to get in touch. Actually, I didn't have much choice because at Donington I'd heard that Suzuki weren't best pleased with me riding a Yamaha, let alone winning on it. But they couldn't expect me to do three races for them and nothing else throughout the year, and there was nothing in any contract forbidding me from riding anything else. Quite the opposite: I was on a race-by-race deal with them which specifically allowed me to take other rides which didn't conflict with the endurance calendar.

When I'd been offered the Belgarda ride, Rob Mac had informed Suzuki France as a courtesy. They'd faxed back to the effect that they weren't happy with my Donington excursion with Yamaha so I shouldn't bother turning up for their next 24-hour race at Spa. Maybe they were just looking for a convenient way out after all the crashing and trashing I'd done at Le Mans. Still, after their silence the previous autumn it made a change for Suzuki to actually tell me I'd been sacked. Rymer and d'Orgeix must have kissed and made up after Terry's Le Mans tantrum, because they went on to wrap up the 1999 endurance world title with a win at the Bol d'Or, with Christian Lavielle as the third rider in place of me. My only souvenir was a 500 Swiss Franc fine for thumping the marshal at Le Mans.

So I'd lost my job with Suzuki. I was unemployed and needed something else – fast. Maybe if I'd gone back cap-in-hand to Belgarda, their door may still have been open. But shortly later I got yet another call from Rob Mac. Apparently Team Roberts' rider, Jean-Michel Bayle, was injured, and they hoped I might ride for them at the Jerez grand prix in ten days' time. Rob thought it was a good idea, not least for what I might learn from working alongside Kenny Roberts. Little did we know.

CHAPTER 21

AT THE COURT OF
KING KENNY

Just days after the Donington win, off I went to Andalusia and a debut ride on the Modenas KR3 Proton, a mouthful no one ever seemed to use. Everyone just called it the KR. It was an easier experience to sum up than make work: great team, hard bike to ride fast. The 500cc two-stroke triple pumped out 165bhp yet weighed only 130kg. I've got mates heavier than that. The power delivery was also fairly peaky, probably more so than the big-bang four-cylinder 500s, so with almost nothing pinning it to the ground it wasn't the easiest thing to ride. Its one advantage compared to the fours was that it was lighter and a touch nimbler, so a tight circuit like Jerez ought to suit it well. I no sooner arrived at Jerez than I was right into the action and soon got into my usual routine: try hard, fall off, get up, try hard again. Two days of that put me 22nd on the grid – but at least that was two places ahead of my team-mate, the same Mike Hale I'd been with at Suzuki in '97.

The race went much better – for a while. I found myself pegging around in ninth or tenth place, which would have been a brilliant result if it had lasted. Kenny Roberts Jr, who was dicing for the title that year on a Suzuki, had been running at the front until he was punted off the track, rejoining in about 15th before charging back through the field. When he came past me I upped my game a little. It was all a bit out of control at times, and I had the sense it might end in tears, but I managed to cling onto the back of him for three or four laps, having a few moments, but enjoying myself. It probably pissed him off no end, but I actually got under him into corners a couple of times. The third overtaking move, into the first corner, was also the last. I lost the front and ended up in the gravel trap.

I didn't find out until later, but after the race Kenny Jr spoke with his father, my boss. I'm not sure Junior knew quite what to make of me. He said I was dangerous and a bit loose, and some of the time I looked like I didn't have a clue what I was up to, but that some of the stuff I was doing was immense. All in all, that was pretty high praise from a future World Champion. So Kenny Sr decided that if his regular riders couldn't make it, he'd like to keep me on the bike. It must have helped, too, that I'd posted the fastest first split of anyone all weekend.

It was a good feeling. I'd joined a team run by a man who's every biker's hero, a proper legend, and had no idea how we'd relate. In the event it was strange. You'd find yourself coming into the garage during a practice session and nothing was more important at that moment to Kenny Roberts – who is practically a god, after all – than listening to what I had to say. That felt very, very weird.

I got the sense early on that because of his status some of the people around KR tended to suck up to him a bit too much. From the beginning I was determined not to. There wasn't any point saying something was fine if it wasn't. And I rode hard, which not all his riders had. He could see that. So, legend though he was, I fired back at him. We took the piss out of him and he took the piss out of us. We got on famously. I think he fancied Andrea, too, which probably helped.

Despite the crash, Jerez was as competitive as the bike had been for ages, so there was a good feeling around the team. Afterwards we went out for a meal – me and Andrea, team manager Chuck Aksland, Mike Hale, Randy Mamola and Kenny. We hadn't even got to the restaurant before Andrea admonished me not to say anything embarrassing if I got drunk in front of my new team-mates. Don't worry, lass, I reassured her, just have a quiet word in my ear if I get going. And anyway, I told her loftily, I'll not get drunk. Naturally the wine flowed and two hours later I'm spannered. To be fair, everyone was pretty trolleyed. Kenny, who doesn't give a shit, weighed into Mike Hale, telling him he was so slow he needed a flashing yellow light on the back of his bike – this to a guy he's paying to ride his bike who'd just finished 16th. And, since it was coming from Kenny, Mike just had to grin and bear it.

251

Then I stood on my chair. Andrea could see what was about to happen and was tugging on my trouser leg telling me to sit down. 'Shush, woman,' I said, firing into a speech that began something like 'When I was a boy, if someone had told me that I would be eating food and getting drunk with Kenny Roberts and Randy Mamola, my heroes…' I nearly died the next morning when I sobered up enough to remember it, and still cringe about it now. Naturally, I bollocked Andrea for letting me make such a prat of myself.

Despite the obvious fact that I was a pillock, they seemed happy to put up with me. From the outset I gelled well with the team – particularly Chuck, part of the Aksland motorcycling dynasty which also included Skip and Bud; and with Kenny himself, who is simply one of the sport's most impressive thinkers. If I'm perfectly honest, I don't think I ever rode the bike to its full potential. I came in mid-season and never seemed to have time to take a breath, let alone do any testing. I was always coming to terms with new circuits, not to mention a bike which however you set it up was always a bit scary and loose at the back.

Compared to superbikes, GP two-strokes were a different breed of animal in that it's much harder to ride around their problems, because they'll bite you on the arse. They demanded near-perfect set-up rather than to have you fighting against them, because they'd always have the last word. Yes, it was easy to go fairly quick on them, but *really* quick was a different matter – and that last half second per lap was the one that really hurt. One of the things that separated the fast men from the rest was a talent for getting the bike working with them. Set-up was absolutely everything, far more than it was in World Superbikes at the time. Now superbikes have moved on. With 200bhp you just can't ride round problems any more. You'd either be slow or on your arse, and we've seen plenty of the best do both after being up there with the leaders the previous week. It's become that technical.

Although I reckoned I was pretty good at setting up a bike, at this level I was still learning. But I believe the team appreciated me because I always put in 100 per cent and was prepared to push hard, which not all of their riders were. Yes, I did fall off and knock myself about a fair bit but, far from them complaining, that showed them I was trying as hard as they were.

That particular habit didn't take long to get into. In practice at Jerez, just two corners and a couple of minutes before Michael Doohan's career-ending crash, I binned the KR. The speed with which it went from everything being in control to horribly wrong was staggering. I remember coming out of the corner, feeding in the power – no traction control, no naff-all, and a power curve like a gable end – then...*raaa!*...and I'm flying through the air. I didn't actually feel anything, just saw the rev-counter needle hurtle clockwise before I was thrown through my own screen at 100mph.

They dragged me off to the medical centre and were peering into my eyes with a torch to see if anyone was at home when there was a big commotion and Doohan was wheeled in. It was one of the pivotal moments in GP history, for he never raced again. In contrast I wasn't damaged, just winded and missing a bit of skin. But if a man like Doohan could get bitten so badly it was pretty graphic evidence that these two-strokes could turn nasty. They never gave any warning. You had to be like a gunslinger with 'em: sharp.

It doesn't happen in grands prix now, because there's so much more of a comfort zone with the four-strokes, with traction control and far less vicious power bands. But with the two-strokes, it wasn't just nuggets like me who got into bother. Everyone crashed – Schwantz, Doohan, even Rainey. And, because of the nature of the bikes, the crashes were usually big ones – you were usually thrown over the high-side. For most of the season the entire 500 grid was hobbling about like walking wounded.

Bayle was back for the next round, Paul Ricard, but two weeks later I was on my way to Mugello, this time in place of Hale who'd broken a hand and ankle at the French GP. I qualified 16th, an OK showing at such a fast track, finishing 14th for two championship points. Bayle retired after about six laps.

The next three rounds, Catalunya, Assen and Donington, all brought retirements. In Spain I lost the front end and fell off, in Holland the bike seized, and at Donington I ran into the back of Nobuatsu Aoki on the brakes into Melbourne Hairpin on lap two. The poor sod must have wondered what hit him. I came rattling up his inside without much hope of stopping, and we both ended up where I belonged, if he didn't – on the floor. It was a good job it wasn't someone like Jim Moodie I'd run into. In practice I'd

253

high-sided out of Coppice, bruised both my ankles, so could barely walk, let alone run away.

Although we were dogged by seizures throughout the meeting, Assen was one of the high points of my brief time on the KR. The bike worked really well there, partly because the corners are mostly fast and flowing, so there's less chance of being spat over the high-side. In the race I passed Norick Abe quite early on before seizing yet again. He went on to finish fifth, so we were obviously competitive.

Assen was also the scene of probably the best compliment I've ever been paid in racing. Kenny had a habit of sneaking out onto the track during practice, and spent much of one session watching at turn one. As luck would have it, Assen was one of the few grand prix tracks I already knew and I'd always liked turn one. It's banked and allows you to chuck the bike in hard and power slide coming out without being too worried it's going to come round and spit you off. I'd passed quite a few quick guys at that very spot.

After the session KR walked up to me and said, 'Fucking hell, turn one, you're the fastest man through there.' Coming from him, that's a pretty major compliment. After the race he made a point of apologising for not putting a bike under me that would last.

Kenny must have been in a good mood all round at Assen, since even Andrea got a compliment of sorts. Just as I was leaving for another practice session, he trotted over and yelled in my ear. 'If the garage door's shut when you get back', he said, 'just keep going round 'cos I'm going to drag your wife back in there.'

By this time Team KR was like a game of musical chairs. Sometimes they had one bike running, sometimes two, sometimes three. The team's big problem was that they never really knew whether Bayle was going to turn up and ride or not. Sometimes he'd even turn up and then not ride. So as well as their contracted riders, Bayle and Hale, they had me and sometimes an Australian lad, Mark Willis, hopping in and out of the squad. They must have used half their budget buying leathers.

Perhaps the best run I had on the KR was at the Sachsenring in Germany. Bayle pitched up for practice, so everyone assumed he'd recovered from being injured at Catalunya. His bike was ready to go, tyre warmers on, but he just didn't ride it. By then the former motocross superstar had already made his money, unlike me, so probably didn't think he needed to endure more pain just for a few extra dollars, but I thought it was an odd attitude.

Like Jerez, Sachsenring's a tight circuit, so our power disadvantage wasn't such an issue. On the other hand powering out of so many slowish corners was always a lottery. I was running well in ninth and making ground when the front end washed out at the last corner on lap eight.

The real-life aftermath to Sachsenring was worse than anything that could happen on the track. When Barbara, Andrea's mother, had died we'd all been concerned how her husband, Roy, would cope. He was already well into his seventies and a typical working man of his time. He'd earned the bread as a panel-beater and welder, and his wife baked it and did all the other household stuff. But to our surprise he became a competent housekeeper, even taking over from Barbara the task of cooking our traditional 'Sunday' lunches – usually on the Monday after race meetings.

In some ways he was chipped from the same block as my dad. He was about as idiosyncratic, and at least as tight. Although he could look dapper in a couple of fine bespoke suits handmade by a tailor he knew in Heckmondwyke, he thought nothing of wearing cast-off clothes. He once turned up in a pair of wellies he'd found at the tip. They were five sizes too large, but apparently didn't slop about too much after he lined them with carpet. He'd still come to watch me race whenever he could, once accosting Kenny Roberts in the team hospitality suite whilst looking like a tramp.

Shortly before Sachsenring Roy had fallen off a tractor and knocked himself about enough to visit his doctor, a rare event. He'd seemed generally off-colour, but no one seemed too bothered, so we'd flown to Germany without giving it much thought. But when Andrea returned, she'd found the dog going mad downstairs and her father upstairs, dead in bed. He'd had a massive heart attack a couple of days before. It hit all of us, especially Andrea, hard – but at least she was spared the pain of watching him wither away as her mum had done.

In late August we went to Brno for the Czech Grand Prix. Although I'd raced on the old road circuit, this was another new track for me and in practice I struggled, especially with all the downhill-entry corners, which put a lot of load on the front tyre. By then Hale was back from injury. He'd damaged his foot badly crashing a superbike at Brno some time before and warned me that this was the one place on the GP calendar it wasn't wise to get hurt.

'The hospital's like stepping back into the Third World,' he cautioned.

'It's no bother,' I replied with my usual gift for getting it wrong. 'If I do crash I'll only lose the front. It'll be a harmless low-side.'

My harmless low-side occurred on the second lap. I hadn't made a good start and found myself in the middle of the pack entering a sequence of downhill bends. The last of these, a right-hander, leads onto a straight, so it's vital to get a good drive. Mine was too good. The KR slid, gripped and high-sided, flipping me high in the air. I remember formation flying along with the tank, which had flown off before the rest of the bike even hit the ground, then landing hard in a perfect sitting position with a resounding bony crunch, almost like a tree branch snapping. But there was no pain, partly because I was pumped up with adrenaline, partly because I knew there were lots of race bikes around me and I was focussed more on not being run over.

But I knew something was wrong. As I tumbled into the gravel the thought that maybe I'd broken a femur or two crossed my mind, but in the usual weird, detached way – almost as though it's happening to someone else. By this time the tank had split, spilling out fuel and lighting up like fireworks, while the bike had tumbled into the barrier and set it merrily ablaze. I could already feel the heat, and since I didn't want to burn I tried to crawl to safety. That's when I felt it – not a sharp pain, but an ominous grating feeling that told me crawling wasn't a good idea. So I lay back down, got as comfortable as I could and started taking inventory. First my feet: they moved, which was good, but it hurt like hell, which wasn't. From my knees to my chest was just an intense, dull pain. That was when it occurred to me that I'd broken my pelvis, which I knew was serious because of all the internal organs that the bits of bone can puncture. A broken pelvis had nearly killed Dave Leach. Mike Hale's words came ringing back to my ears.

The marshals went first to Luis Cardoso, who'd also come off in the mêlée and was unconscious but otherwise not in bad shape. A few minutes later there was a ring-a-ding-ding and a Keystone Cops fire brigade arrived in a beat-up 1936 Zastovar fire tender with a bloke ringing a brass bell for all he was worth. My recollection's probably tainted, but it's mainly of fat blokes in fireman suits getting in each others' way and tripping over hoses. Eventually I'm carted away to the circuit medical centre, where I'm X-rayed. Dr Costa, the grand prix doctor, was very matter of fact. 'You've broken the pelvis,' he said, pointing at the film, 'here, here, here and here.' I wasn't keeping count but there seemed to be quite a lot of 'heres'.

All I really knew was that I'd never experienced pain like it. I was screaming in agony even before they carried me to a helicopter. Despite Mike Hale's words of caution, the last thing on my mind now was the quality of local medical facilities. The chopper landed outside a typical Eastern Bloc hospital, utilitarian and shabby. Medics lifted me and the medical scoop onto what I can only describe as a wooden sack-cart, and off we creaked to intensive care which, to be fair, looked clean and modern, although Andrea, having taken three hours to find me, later described some of the rest of the place as fairly primitive.

The risk from major pelvic injury is collateral damage from shattered bones to blood vessels, nerves and internal organs. Luckily I had none of that, except for a punctured bladder, but major surgery was required. By this time I'm blacking out now and again, and at one time became convinced that if I passed out again they'd nick my kidneys. At the very least, this was perhaps not the most sensible place for someone who pays £10K a year for medical insurance to go under the knife. 'Get me out of here,' I implored Andrea, 'get me out.'

Between Andrea, Rob Mac and the team, they did it. By nine o'clock the next morning a British doctor and nurse had arrived on a Lear jet, booked an ambulance, and we were on our way to the airport and a flight to Leeds. In no time we'd checked into hospital in Huddersfield, where Andrea had arranged for Mr Milling, the orthopaedic surgeon who'd put me back together before, to be waiting.

He studied the X-rays with a frown on his face. 'Not really my field,' he said. 'But I know a man who can do it and you're in luck

– he works out of Leeds. His name's Tony Smith and he's the premier pelvis man in the country.' So off we went to Jimmie's Hospital in Leeds.

Dr Smith ummed and aahed over the X-rays. Apparently the bones weren't badly displaced. The old method of treatment would have been to stick me in a pair of pelvic pants for three months, which I didn't much fancy. Instead, he told me I'd wake up tomorrow with either internal bracing and fixation, or with an external scaffold. He wouldn't know which until he'd had a poke around inside.

I woke up with the scaffolding option, called a 'fixator,' but with a few screws inside as well. Apparently I'd been lucky. None of the nerves and arteries passing through the pelvis had been damaged, nor the femur sockets. I could expect to make a full recovery. A week later I was told I could go home. But first there was a test. I had to prove I could use the loo.

'But I don't want a poo,' I protested.

'You will in a minute,' smirked the occupational therapist, producing a monster suppository.

I made it to the loo – just – but it still wasn't over. Next the catheter had to come out of my bladder. 'Routine,' I consoled myself. 'They do this all the time.'

The therapist started yanking on the tube, but it didn't want to budge. It wasn't so much painful as weirdly uncomfortable. After a bit more puffing and puzzling nothing had happened and she went to get someone else. Then there were two women alternately contemplating and heaving on my willie. Ah, it's a glamorous life being a grand prix racer.

Throughout all this I wasn't even aware of all the carnage and drama I'd left behind in Brno. I vaguely knew that the fire had still been raging as they carted me away. It was breezy and the wind had blown the bike blaze onto the straw bales and tyres lining the track. I was conscious that it was all a bit of a mess, but at the time I had other things on my plate.

A couple of days after I got home from hospital, Dave Leach dropped by.

'That was a big 'un,' he said.

'Oh, you watched it on telly?'

'I was there, about 100 yards away. Saw the whole thing.'

Then he went on to describe the entire trackside being consumed in flames, spectators being evacuated and what little fire-fighting equipment the circuit possessed being totally overwhelmed. On top of that the track was so damaged that some riders were threatening not to race in the restart, and global TV schedules were thrown totally haywire.

'We apologise for the interruption to services. This was caused by Whithams beyond our control.'

'Oops,' I thought. 'Did little me do all that?'

I was visiting Dr Smith for regular check-ups and the pelvis seemed to be healing well. After about three months, by which time the pin sites were weeping and a bit infected, he decided it was time to remove the fixator. I'd assumed this would entail at least a local anaesthetic and booking in for an operation, so I asked, 'When?'

'Now if you want,' he said, nipping out of his office and reappearing with a pair of Mole grips. He set to unscrewing the scaffolding part, leaving the steel pegs sticking out of my pelvis. The pegs stuck out about an inch, and I'd assumed there was a similar amount inside me. But no – he just kept unscrewing and unscrewing until – plonk! – about 4 inches of titanium fell to the floor. They were just self-tappers, but otherwise it was proper engineering. I didn't feel a thing and didn't even need stitches. Apart from a couple of X-rays to make sure the pelvis had healed properly, it was job done.

Even so, I still wasn't as mobile as I'd hoped to be. Before I broke the pelvis, I'd been stopped for speeding on a 1200 Bandit. At the time I had nine points on my licence. Since another three would probably have meant a three-month ban, I decided to appear in person – by which time I was on crutches with a scaffold round my hips. If I thought I'd get the sympathy vote, I couldn't have been more wrong. The beak took one look at me and decided I needed protecting from myself – with a six-month ban. I'd have been better just pleading guilty by letter.

There was an even more bittersweet postscript when I returned to hospital 12 months later for a final X-ray check-up. Tony Smith wasn't there. I was told he'd moved to practice in Boston.

'Oh, Lincolnshire?' I asked.

'Massachusetts.'

Apparently he'd been turned down for a research grant in the UK, and the only way he could continue his work was in the States, which is certainly a loss to us. 'You were very lucky to see him,' explained the doctor. 'You probably wouldn't have been walking straight for the rest of your life if you hadn't had Tony.' The bloke's a genius.

We're brought up in the UK to assume we've got a safety net in the Health Service, and that anyone can get the treatment they need, which just isn't the case. I admire the National Health Service, but for most of my career I've had private medical insurance. This wasn't, initially at least, because I thought it was better, but because if I wasn't to spend half my racing career on waiting lists I needed the treatment I wanted when I wanted it. Through most of that time I've been fortunate to have met the right people and ask the right questions, and to be in a financial position to afford what they recommended.

It's still shocking to find out that someone else with the same injuries might have received a totally different standard of treatment. To some extent it's pot luck. When I broke my ankle in Ireland, I came back with my X-rays and showed them to Mr Milling at Huddersfield Royal Infirmary, asking if everything was OK. By this time he'd already put me back together so often we were on first name terms.

'It's fine,' he said. 'Where was it done?'

'Belfast Royal Victoria,' I replied, thinking this probably wasn't the hub of medical science.

'You couldn't have picked better. They're used to putting bits of broken bone together. They do more knee-caps there than anywhere in the world.'

With the pelvis healed I had a racing career to get back to. But where? Team Roberts were happy to keep me on, and Kenny even paid me the huge compliment of saying I was the only guy to race his bikes: the rest just rode them. But the more I thought about it – and I had a lot of time to think – the less it seemed like a good idea for my career. It wasn't that I was scared of the bike (although I was, a bit): I wanted to get onto something

I felt could be competitive. Although just being in the premier class had its attractions, I so much wanted to sit on a grid on a bike I thought I had a chance of winning on and, with all due respect, the KR wasn't it. They were a fantastic team, and it was a tremendous feat for them to build a bike at that level, but it just wasn't a front-runner.

CHAPTER 22

An honorary
Italian

The new millennium began on a tragic personal note when Andrea's brother Allen died on New Year's night, aged just 49. At his best Allen was a lovely, generous man, as well as being a talented mechanic, but he'd been wrestling with alcoholism for years. Sometimes he'd manage a few months off the bottle and for a while after Barbara's death had even moved back in with his father. But Roy's death the previous July was more than Allen could take and he'd totally lost it. He took to sleeping on a tatty mattress at the garage where he worked. His only heating was from a gas bottle. When the gas ran out he died from cold in a drunken sleep. This left Andrea without a single close relative, which hit her very hard.

On the racing front prospects were more promising. I'd been dabbling with Belgarda Yamaha, one way or another, since 1994. Around the time Dr Smith was unbolting my pelvis, Julio Bardi, Belgarda's World Supersports manager, asked if I'd be prepared to do a full season in World Supersports for them the following year. It was a team I already knew well, I liked the crew and the atmosphere and I was confident of their ability to put out a competitive bike. My only reservation was that stepping down to a 600 seemed a slightly backward step. But by then I was 33 years old. Whichever way I looked at it – and I think this was more realistic than negative – I had a maximum of maybe five or six years left. Ideally I'd like to spend that time earning a bit of money and not chasing a hopeless dream. So I signed for the Italian team.

That's not to say I wasn't still hungry and ambitious. If the Donington ride the previous May was anything to go by, we should regularly be running near the front. A world title wasn't out of the question. If there was a downside it was that we were going to be running Michelin tyres – which, as usual, didn't fill me with confidence. Belgarda seemed to have no such reservations.

If I had any doubts, they didn't survive the opening round, Phillip Island, although to be perfectly honest it was a pretty jammy result. The Australian track had never been my favourite place on the Superbikes, and as usual I didn't really gel with it even on the 600 Yamaha. In fact my qualifying was pathetic – way down in 21st place. The only saving grace was that in World Supersports the whole grid was usually very tight. One weekend I qualified just 0.7 seconds off pole but in 15th place.

Although I was used to making hot starts and knew I could beat a lot of the guys ahead of me, charging through from the fifth row was a big ask. Any sort of decent result was going to be hard work. After qualifying I suggested to Andrea that the only way we'd have any chance would be if it rained. I woke up the next morning to hear the beautiful sound of rain. It was pouring.

It simply couldn't have gone any better. By the time they red-flagged the race I was leading. The restart was even easier, since I knew how I stood against my main rivals. The only guy I had to watch for was fruit-bat Ruben Xaus, who was going like a train on a Ducati, but he'd lost time in the pits in the first leg so I had at least 20 seconds in hand on him. He kept pulling away, but there was no need to chase him. I just rode to my signals and won on aggregate time. The result was particularly sweet because it had been so unexpected – and because it was my first race after Brno's crash and burn.

At Phillip Island the traditional place to celebrate or drown your sorrows is the Island of Capri Italian restaurant, and all the Yamaha boys, Nori Haga included, plus the Kawasaki gang were doing one or the other. Basically, it was the paddock out for dinner and a beer. As usual we had a few drinks and it got a bit silly. People were standing up, making speeches and generally dicking about, the usual post-race giddiness.

Andrea, who never seemed able to make up her mind whether I should behave or make a prat of myself at times like this, thought my Sambuca trick would keep the party buzzing. This involves sticking glasses to your skin after the heat from the flames of the burning spirit has dragged out the air. 'Watch this, lads,' I thought as I stood on the table, ripped off my shirt, downed a Sambuca and stuck the glass over my right nipple. 'So far, so good,' I thought as they cheered for more. Never one to quit while I was ahead, I grabbed another glass for the left one. At first it wouldn't light, but I'd made the rim damn-near white-hot trying. So when I finally put it onto my chest it made a sickening sort of sizzling noise and smelled like someone shoeing a horse. It hurt like hell. Not that I got any sympathy – the Belgarda lot always thought I was mad anyway.

At the next round, Sugo a week later, I was going well with leaders, Teuchert and Kellner, when the tyres went off, big-time, although I managed to cling on to fourth ahead of Iain MacPherson. Next came my home round at Donington. After practice I was confident of repeating my win of the year before but lost out, finishing second to Stéphane Chambon. Although the little Frenchman was the reigning World Champion and a brave, aggressive rider, I'd thought I had the beating of him.

So by the time we'd gone from my home round to Belgarda's backyard, Monza, the championship was looking good. I had a canny ride to finish second to Paolo Casoli's Ducati 748 in a typical Monza slipstreaming war, getting a wheel ahead of him into the last corner but running a fraction wide and losing drive. My team-mate Massimo Meregalli placed fourth, his best result of what would turn out to be his last season as a rider.

By the time I came away with a sixth place from Hockenheim I'd had a first, two seconds, a fourth and a sixth, was leading the championship and was even beginning to nurse thoughts of a world title. That's when it started to go to pot with the first in a whole series of front-end crashes, and five consecutive DNFs. Maybe there's something about years ending in zero, because it was shades of 1990 all over again – I didn't understand quite why it was happening. Most of the time I wasn't doing a lot wrong: running at the front in every race, not riding ragged and trying to set up the bike so I could get away with pushing the front end, which has always been my style. It was immensely frustrating. Unlike Dunlops, the Michelins just didn't tell me when to stop pushing. And once you've landed on your butt three or four times you're half-expecting it every time you go out.

Sandwiched between the Misano and Valencia rounds in mid-June, Andrea and me had our own meeting at South Crosland Church of the Holy Trinity. We got wed. A few months earlier in a fit of romantic nonsense I'd taken her to dinner in a local restaurant in a chauffer-driven Roller, got down on one knee and popped the question. What could she possibly say but 'Yes'? The reception was up the road at the local Hilton. Parents beamed, the Po' Boys played, world racing stars rubbed shoulders with uncles and aunts and mates from schooldays, and pretty well everyone got totally wrecked.

Looking back, that was the year's high-point. On the track, a season which began so well turned into a major disappointment. Some of the fault was mine, some not. If it wasn't binning the bike it was something else. At Assen we were disqualified because the bike wouldn't start in post-race scrutineering. In all there were five races on the trot in which I didn't score a single finish, and only one round left. The championship had gone. Brands Hatch, the final round of the season, was too little, too late, but an absolutely brilliant race to be part of. I finished third, two thousandths of a second behind the winner, Karl Muggeridge. But that was no consolation for eventually placing sixth in a series I'd thought I could win. Even so, it was a particularly tight season. My 104 points was only 32 behind the winner, Jörg Teuchert – also on a Yamaha R6 – and only three points covered the top three.

Overall it was almost as devastating a season as I'd had. No, there wasn't the anguish of 1990, but for the first time in my career I ended the year feeling that I'd let a team down. The bike was good enough to win the title, no question. I even felt that the tyres were, too – but not with me on it – although, to be fair, nobody that year went really well on Michelins, except in the wet. Casoli and Xaus were riding Michelin-shod factory 748 Ducatis, and they often struggled too. The tyres to have that year were definitely Dunlops or Pirellis. You could go quick on the Michelins, definitely, but not for long or you'd end up chucking it away.

One thing I had no complaints about was the team. They were typical Italians, so passionate and committed. You'd do one fast lap and they're doing back-flips. Then half an hour later they could be suicidal, but every single one of them wanted to win so badly.

My mechanic was Fabio, a brilliant bloke whose emotions were never under wraps. It got so I pretty well knew my practice lap times even before he told me: just the expression on his face gave the game away to within a tenth of a second.

If I wasn't always flying on the track, at least I was in real life: 2000 was the year I finally qualified for my pilot's licence. Being brought up on an airfield I was always interested in planes and flying. Dad had a pilot's licence for most of his adult life, and some of my earliest memories are of flying with him when I can't have been more than five years old. But for many years I was too busy with other things – mainly bikes – to take much active interest.

In the mid-'90s I'd got a microlight licence, which was fairly easy to get. It was flying, I suppose, but mainly just short hops, looking down at the scenery. Shoey, my partner in 'Speed Freak' track days, also had an interest in flying, so we decided we'd both go for proper pilots' licences. He happened to live next door to Woodford Aviation flying school, which had once been Avro's main base, where the World War Two Lancaster bomber first took to the air. I began lessons in the winter of '98/'99 and was going well until I broke my pelvis at Brno. I eventually qualified in 2000.

By then 'Speed Freak' was doing well, so we decided to buy an aeroplane between us. We found a thing called a Zenair that looked the part, at an airfield near Cambridge. We drove down there and prodded and poked as though we knew what we were doing, when we really didn't have much of a clue. It must have been a pretty impressive bluff, at least as far as the owner was concerned, so we bought it. So far so good.

At the time my pilot's licence was only days old and the thought of being up there in charge of an aircraft terrified me as much as it probably did the people below. So I arranged for an experienced flying friend, Stewart, to sit in with me on the flight back to Huddersfield. Unfortunately something cropped up at the last minute and he couldn't join us, nor could we find anyone else. The only sensible option was to postpone the flight back, but having just become owners of our very own flying machine, we weren't feeling very sensible. I called another mate, Barry, who'd once had a licence – about 30 years before. And off we went again to Cambridge.

The Zenair's owner did the proper thing and took Barry for a circuit round the airfield, which he managed quite well considering the Spitfire was state-of-the-art when he'd last had the controls. Barry and me waved goodbye to Shoey, who'd be driving north with a car-full of spares, and took off. We didn't have a clue between us – but what was worse was that neither did we have a map. No worries: the Zenair had a satellite navigation system. Barry pushed and prodded at this box of tricks but couldn't make sense of it.

Plan 'B' having failed, we moved seamlessly to Plan 'C'. Use the compass. 'Just fly west,' said Barry, 'until you get to the A1. Then follow it north until the M62, then west to Huddersfield. We can't miss.'

With my luck, we ought to have ended up somewhere near Dover but it was, it turned out, a good plan. The other benefit of not having a map was that we'd only the vaguest idea when we were in restricted airspace, so we just did our best to keep out of the way and droned along as though we were entitled to be up there. Luckily, although the weather was overcast, visibility was good. Somewhere near Newark we glimpsed Emley Moor TV transmitter, an enormous concrete tower just a few miles from Crosland Moor, and made a bee-line for it. We were home in no time.

Flying has become the other love of my life after motorcycles – and the family, of course. The two pursuits have a lot in common, the freedom thing most obviously. But you can't be good on a bike unless you have some feel for it. The essence of riding's about what you feel through your backside rather than what you're doing with your hands, which becomes instinctive. Flying a light aircraft is similar, so it's probably no surprise that a lot of ex-racers also fly. It's about empathy with the machine.

But there's one big difference. Cock-up on a bike, and you're probably going to lose a bit of skin but walk away from the accident. Planes are different. I'm naturally a confident type of person, at ease with most machines...tractors, tools, whatever. Most machines I can look at, listen to, and have a reasonable chance of making them work without killing someone – quite apart from the healthy disregard for doing things the conventional way that I learned from dad. With flying, you just can't do that. Your first mistake might well be your last, and even dad understood that.

I've had friends who wouldn't come up in the Zenair because they assumed they were going to get the regular Whitham – the dangerous dickhead they'd always known. When they've finally been persuaded, they've been surprised to be sharing the cockpit with this other Whitham who actually takes something really seriously. That's how it has to be.

Back on the ground, Belgarda Yamaha were more than happy to keep me for 2001, so that's where I stayed. This year, though, I'd have a hotshot team-mate to keep me on my toes. Meregalli was hanging up his leathers to take over the team's management; Casoli, who'd narrowly finished second in the 2000 championship, would be taking his place. The little Italian was definitely quick, probably the fastest team-mate I've had with the exception of Niall McKenzie – very competitive, very hot-wired, although I always thought I had the beating of him. On paper it looked a strong pairing.

You hear a lot about team-mates not getting on, but I could never understand it unless you were stuck with a real oddball like John Kocinski. Throw any two blokes together at random and the odds are they won't become mates. But that's not to say there'll be daggers drawn all the time either. After all, you see each other for around 25 days a year, including testing, and sometimes get to share a room with them. Surely it's not that hard to tolerate someone for so little time? Mind you, what they made of me may have been different. Paolo was a nice enough lad and we were OK together. I didn't spend a lot of time with him, partly because he had his family, I had Andrea. And he wasn't my type of guy. He was very stylish, smooth, articulate – all the things I'm not. Sometimes I'd take the piss out of his typical Italian preening, but we got on fine. And like any sort of relationship, stress can get to it – say if the team's doing very badly. That's usually the way it is: after all, you're just team-mates, not betrothed. If you read anything else in the bike press it's usually tosh. If I had a bosom buddy in the team it was the manager, Massimo, with whom I've always got on famously.

I also made a point of getting on with the team's young chef, Carole, who'd been classically trained in London. Even apart from the money, this was a definite step up from the burgers we'd once subsisted on at racetracks. The food was beautiful – but always, *always*, Italian. They're a strangely unadventurous lot when it comes to eating. Brits seem to take easily to any sort of food – curries, Chinese, Italian, French, even Mongolian. In the hospitality area, in restaurants, hotels, wherever we were – it had to be Italian. When the team went out on the evening after a race, if there was an Italian restaurant within a thousand miles that's where we'd go. Then all they'd do is complain about the food, because it was never as good as momma or Carole made. My usual contribution was to order an Hawaiian pizza, which is about as Italian as bangers and mash, just to piss them off. Sacrilege. Carole would climb on his cordon bleu high horse and announce that there were only 12 classic pizzas, and there was pineapple in none of them, so I'd always make a special show of enjoying it.

The season started well – briefly. At Valencia for the opening round I was running strongly but pushed too hard trying to stay with Pere Riba and lost the front into Turn One. It was an exact replica of the same race the previous year – except this time I couldn't blame Michelin since we were now running Dunlops. Phillip Island, unbelievably, also looked like going the same way as 2000. Yet again the race was held in a beautiful downpour but this time I aquaplaned and slid off coming out of MG Corner whilst in the leading bunch. Next, at Sugo, I was leading when the wiring loom went wonky and the bike just stopped.

So three rounds gone and there wasn't a point on the board, although I'd been competitive at every round and riding well. Casoli hadn't begun well either, until his season kick-started with a win at Sugo. At Monza it was my turn.

As usual it developed into a draughting dice, with MacPherson, Andrew Pitt, Casoli, Teuchert and Muggeridge. This always looks good on the telly, and it's even better to be part of. At any circuit where there's lots of slipstreaming the approach is less about trying hard than being patient and having a strategy. Pushing and pushing just knackers you and your tyres. It's a bit like being in the peloton in a bicycle race, working together and saving your resources for the final sprint. If someone pulls 100 yards on you, you'll have a go to catch back up. But normally you're almost cruising in a group, but fast.

It's always a bit of a lottery, but I played it right, taking the lead at just the right time. There was no point going too early because there wasn't much likelihood of getting away from the group, so with one lap to go I made sure I got a good tow past the pits before diving in front into the first chicane. From there, I knew that the rest had two chances to get back at me: into the Ascari chicane or on the back straight into Parabolica. Even if someone did me at Ascari, I'd have a fighting chance of getting them back at the end of the straight.

Once in front, I just put my head down and went...manic, but just under control. I didn't know it – I never look back – but Muggeridge had made a right cock-up of the first chicane, messing everyone else up, and only Casoli had got a clean run through. Ascari...no front wheels alongside, no engine noise from another bike...still in front.

I've never had a defensive frame of mind even in situations like that, reasoning that if you're bang on it you're going to be hard to get past, whatever the other bloke does. On tighter circuits, with lots of slow corners where you can just park it and get in everyone's way, it's different. But at somewhere like Monza riding defensively means riding slower, which is the opposite of what you need on a last-lap sprint. But this meant there was room inside me and as I braked into the long last corner, Parabolica, Casoli seemed to come from nowhere and dive under me. In situations like that you can only think 'Fair enough' – if he holds it. He didn't, just as I hadn't in a mirror-image move the previous year. He was just too hot and ran a few feet wide. I put my bike where he wanted his to be and held him off to the line for a Belgarda Yamaha one–two.

This was really special for the team, since Monza is their local track, and much more than in the sense of being in the same country. If you high-sided at Lesmo Two, you'd practically end up in their yard. Inevitably, the result was followed by the biggest party of the year. We backed that up with a good showing at Donington, this time with Casoli winning and fourth place for me. Then normal service resumed: Lausitzring, retired, electrical problems again.

The final run-in for the championship was so-so: the bottom

step of three podiums, a fifth and a seventh had left me fourth in the series on 106 points. Pitt's 149 points took the title through sheer consistency, for he never won a race all year but scored in every round. Casoli was just two points behind in the standings, meaning he'd missed out on consecutive World Championships by just five points all-told. At the time I was more concerned about being beaten by a team-mate for only the second time in over a decade.

Unlike the previous season I didn't have the sense that I'd let anyone down, but still ended the year with mixed feelings. And 2001 should have been my strongest season. I knew the bike, knew the riders I was up against and was on the tyres I wanted. I felt I was still riding well and the Dunlops definitely helped – but whilst I didn't fall off that often, I always seemed to do so at crucial times. It was a frustrating year.

And even to achieve that much I had help from an unexpected source: Andrea. In the first practice session at Assen, the day after my 35th birthday, the bike wasn't working badly. But without really noticing, over the next couple of days we somehow slowly walled ourselves into a corner chasing settings that went nowhere. As usual, I shrugged it off thinking it'd be all right come the race. I was very wrong. From the start I plummeted backwards through the field. I was struggling into corners, struggling to change direction, struggling to be accurate. I guess you could say I was struggling.

Then the gods intervened. It began to drizzle and after two or three laps the race was stopped after a monster pile-up. We had about 15 minutes before the restart to make an unrideable bike work. When I got back to the garage it was less like a de-brief, more like a whinge: 'Just can't ride it…it's awful…don't know what's wrong…no corner speed…no confidence in the front end…' While I'm grinding on feeling sorry for myself, the crew are thrashing about checking tyres, forks, everything. Nothing seems to be wrong. No one has a clue. Team Belgarda has become Team Baffled.

Like all racing wives, Andrea knows better than to stick her oar in. Shoes and shopping, she's an expert. Racing she leaves to us pros. So it was a bit of a surprise when she piped up: 'You know, the only time this weekend you haven't complained about that damn bike was your first session on Friday, and the times were pretty good. Ever since then you've been disappearing up your own arse trying to find something better.'

Obviously, your first reaction's something like, 'Don't be daft, lass. What the hell do you know?' I mean, Belgarda was a pretty slick team with some very bright blokes. Then I got to thinking, and she was bloody right. The bike had started off OK and we spent two days making a donkey out of it. So I told the lads to put Friday's settings on the spare bike. We'd nothing to lose after the pig's ear we'd made of it so far. And as soon as the flag dropped I knew I could ride it. From running ninth in the first part I ended up second on the road, and third on aggregate behind Casoli and Pitt.

We never did find out what was wrong with the handling. We'd just spent two days making a perfectly good bike – a potential winner – bad. We had good people in the team who, at every other circuit, made the bike better than it arrived, but not this time. There was absolutely no doubt: if I'd been on the same bike for both parts of the race I'd have been challenging for the win. It was a classic example of chasing your tail with your head up your arse, and not seeing the wood for the trees, which is itself a classic example of mixed metaphors. Only someone as divorced from the details as Andrea could have spotted it. This was the first time in racing she ever told me to get a grip. Maybe she should have done it sooner and more often.

We went out that night – obviously, after two rostrum finishes – to – obviously – an Italian restaurant in Groningen. On the way back to the hotel, whizzing along in the hire car, we came a cropper. Unbeknown to me, the Dutch had a cunning way of stopping you cutting corners when you're trying to straight-line roundabouts: a series of four or five huge concrete lumps, like dragons' teeth. They're painted white, so there's no excuse for not seeing them. But I didn't and hit the bloody things with both right-hand wheels. There was a huge bang, and I was immediately aware we might not be going much further in this particular hire car, seeing as it was tottering along like a drunk with one shoe missing. Somehow we made it the two kilometres back to the hotel, but by then both wheels were totally pretzled, both tyres just shreds of smelly rubber.

Now it's times like these that you can tell if you've got a really good team manager. I got to the room, called Massimo and got him out of bed. We had an early flight out in the morning, so whatever he came up with, it had to be fast. He didn't even tell me I was stupid, which was pretty obvious, just asked whether it could be fixed.

'Yes, probably. But we need at least two Ford Focus wheels. With tyres.'

'Right. Meet me in the car park in five minutes.'

This was going to be interesting.

Five minutes later, there we were in the middle of the night like a couple of burglars, him with the jack from his car, me with the jack from mine. We skulked around the car park until we found another Focus. Trouble was, all the Belgarda crew had Fords from the same rental mob, so we had to be careful we didn't rob ourselves. Eventually we found one with fluffy toys in the back window, so that definitely wasn't ours. Job done.

I did feel bad about it – leaving some poor blameless bloke with two knackered wheels when he'd probably been doing nothing worse than getting a night's kip – but not as bad as I'd have felt explaining myself to the car rental folk. Besides, the bloke did get an extra jack out of the deal, holding up one corner of his car. Naturally Andrea gave me the usual grief about the business, but shut up when she saw the donor car in the morning. Her jaw didn't half drop.

For what would turn out to be my last season, 2002, Casoli was again my team-mate. Pre-season testing had gone well. The series began with the usual jaunt to Valencia and – for a change – a finish: sixth. Next stop, Phillip Island. Again, practice produced the strangest thing. I'd qualified well, but with the worry that we might suffer tyre problems towards the end of the race. In order to give me a feel for how worn rubber worked, for the Sunday morning warm-up session we stuck on a knackered back tyre. I expected a right slithery time but – heaven knows how – lapped a second quicker than I'd qualified and 1.5 seconds quicker than anyone else in the session. It was unbelievable. Nothing like that had happened before. I thought it was my day. I'd never felt so strong.

In the race I was strong, but not for long enough. I led after a lap, pulled out over a second on the field in the first half of the second lap, then dumped it at Lukey Heights as Jack Burnicle groaned in despair on the Eurosport commentary. I was pushing, obviously, to try to open a gap, but didn't feel as though I was taking liberties. But to all appearances it was a novice mistake in a race that seemed to be there for the taking. I was sickened, but only had myself to blame.

Matters picked up briefly with a good second place at Kyalami, then the gremlins took control again. Sugo: sidelined by a broken pick-up wire. Monza: clutch. Neither were my fault, yet although I ran reasonably strongly most of the season I sometimes had the nagging feeling that my best riding was behind me. The British round at Silverstone, though, was one I seemed destined to win. We had a few handling problems, mainly the usual front end chatter, which on a fast, open circuit like Silverstone costs you more time than at a scratchy place where you can compensate with sheer aggression. So, as usual, my qualifying was ordinary, back on the fifth row. But on race day it rained, and I thought maybe we were in for a result after all. Normally any handling problems – especially chatter – don't show themselves in the wet, because the reduced grip means you simply can't work the chassis so hard. Even so, a win looked a long shot.

It was one of those races where so much is happening you wouldn't have a clue what was going on without your signals. I started reasonably well and just kept plugging away as a lot of the leading riders slid off. You enjoy a bit of light reading in a race like that, especially when it's your signal board saying 'fifth', 'fourth', 'third', as the laps tick off. By the time it said 'second' I could see Casoli, my team-mate, a fair way ahead. By then I had a few things to ponder over. Other riders were still sliding off regularly, so there seemed a fair chance of the race being stopped. Did I push hard, hoping for a win but risking crashing and looking a prat, or settle for a safe second? I seemed to be in a comfortable groove so decided to keep pushing as I was, which is sometimes easier than riding cautiously.

Without seeming to try very hard, my signals were telling me I was lapping 1.5 seconds quicker than Casoli, who seemed to be slowing. When I passed him, he immediately pulled the pin and came back at me, scuttling up the inside into the second left-hander on the infield. 'Brave move,' I thought to myself, 'if he wants it that bad,' but before the thought was finished his front wheel folded on him and down he went. That'll do me.

Even then it wasn't over. By now it was getting so slippery that even the 600s were spinning up and kicking sideways in a straight line. Three went down in one heap. Then I went down at Club Corner, but by then there was so much carnage that the race was red-flagged. I won on count-back from Casoli and Muggeridge. Muggers must have been spitting. He was still on his wheels whilst both the bikes that beat him were battered and covered with mud.

It was jammy, true, but it was a win. The luck didn't last for long, though. In Germany I was disqualified, yet again, after the bike failed to start in post-race scrutineering. The next round, Misano, produced a hard-earned third place in searing heat. Then, in late July, came the 'European' round at Brands Hatch.

Throughout most of my Supersports years I'd been crap in timed practice. Early in my career I seemed to be as good at qualifying as at racing, and it's a bit of a mystery why I seemed to lose the knack. But I did find it increasingly hard to stick my neck out when there wasn't an actual result at stake, and hard to risk doing something that might not work out. True, there's more to being quick in qualifying than simply getting a good grid position. If you go a second quicker in the race than in practice you don't really know how your bike's going to behave, because you've never pushed it to those sorts of limits. Yet I usually seemed to be able to go as fast in a race on a knackered race tyre as I could in practice on a qualifier.

Later in the season I grabbed a rare pole position at Brands Hatch, and had a few other front row starts, but more often than not qualified relatively badly. You might imagine that my team boss would want to get to the bottom of this, but mainly Massimo just trusted me to get on with it. It was similar in pre-season testing. If we went to, say, Valencia, we knew which teams had been there before and what times they'd done. Casoli seemed to view this as a personal challenge. Whatever it took, he had to go faster. I wasn't bothered. So long as I got my bike feeling good, working the way I wanted it, and doing reasonable times, I was content.

Normally through practice I'd be somewhere near the front, but towards the end of the session when people were throwing in lots of qualifying tyres and going mad, I'd slip down the standings. People who I knew with certainty I could beat come race day would out-qualify me. They'd often get under my feet for a lap or two in the race, but I was always confident of getting past. So normally a so-so grid position didn't hurt me. Even from the third row I could usually get through and be mixing it with the front row after a lap. I rode mainly on aggression and instinct anyway, and could usually raise my game if I needed. Race day, not practice, was what rattled my cage. I'd always go flat-out on the warm-up lap, so that I'd know how fast I could take the first corner and in what gear, which would usually be different from every other lap of the race. Usually it worked, and I'd pass a load of riders into the same turn on the first racing lap.

My preference was usually to take the first corner on the outside. You ran the risk of being shoved onto the grass or caught up in someone else's accident, but usually got a run around the rest of the field. At the likes of Monza, where it's a long run to the slow first chicane, it didn't matter so much. But at Brands, where it's surprisingly steeply uphill from the inside grid positions, the outside is definitely the best line. I always had some sort of a plan for the race as a whole, but you can never have a definite one, because the situation's so fluid. Mainly you have to make it up as you go along. Once or twice I've actually drawn a chalk arrow on the grid to indicate where I'm going to blitz through the field. It may have psyched a few people out, but it was really no more than a joke. There are so many bikes moving at different speeds and directions that you just can't tell in advance and have to play it all by ear.

After setting pole at Brands, I found myself in one of those elevated states of confidence that sometimes have a reason, but as often don't. Either way, I woke up on race-day morning convinced I was going to win. When the race began I was in the groove, riding well on a bike that was doing what I wanted. It was all too easy...until it wasn't.

The race turned into a two-parter when Fabien Foret, who'd finish the season as champion, crashed at Bottom Bend. In the restart I was running second, taking stock and working out a strategy when the R6 hit the bumps at Clark Curve. The back wheel stepped out, I shut the throttle, the bike unloaded and spit me off in a big high-side – but not quite. Instead of finding myself flying through the air, I was sat on the top yoke with my feet flapping somewhere around the front mudguard. This is not best position from which to control a bike.

It was horrible – far worse than being flung off. There was nothing at all I could do, but plenty of time to imagine how much it was going to hurt. I couldn't steer, couldn't slow, couldn't get off it – all at 100-plus mph. Luckily, the back of my right thigh somehow jammed on the front brake and the bike flipped end-over-end with me on top. It sounds alarming, but if the bike hadn't flipped I'd have smacked head-on into the barrier, but fast. Compared to that a dislocated left elbow, broken left wrist and torn knee ligaments was a result.

At the time I didn't think I'd been knocked out, but watching the videos later I must have been unconscious for a couple of minutes. The medics shovelled me into an aluminium scoop, stressing that I shouldn't move anything and obviously concerned I might have broken my neck, although I was fairly confident I'd only broken an arm. It was such a horrific crash that the race was stopped almost instantly, and for a few moments a dead quiet descended on the huge Brands crowd.

Whilst this was going on, Andrea – how much of this have I put the poor lass through over the years? – had sprinted down the pit lane to the ambulance. As I saw her face poking over the barrier, I nodded to her that I was all right. One down, 100,000 to go…so as they were loading me into the ambulance, I stuck my thumb up to the crowd, which got a big roar. That was a good feeling.

In no time at all the medical centre had reset the elbow under local anaesthetic, braced the other bits, and sent me off to hobble back to the paddock. Now the only problem was going to be driving home – until Foggy, in a moment of mad generosity, offered me and the missus his chartered chopper while he drove North in my Vito van. Thanks, mate.

By early September I was just about fit enough to ride at Assen, having missed only the German round. Considering the state I was in, seventh seemed a good result. Luckily the Italian round at Imola – best remembered for Colin Edwards' double to take the Superbike title – was another three weeks away, giving me more time to recover.

It was, although I didn't know it at the time, the last race of my professional career – and a good one, especially considering I still wasn't 100 per cent fit. But even as I crossed the line I knew that my fourth place might not last. During the last few laps the bike had lost bottom end power, which I'd experienced before. The total-loss ignition the Supersport bikes run is odd in that with a low battery, they'd run fine at high revs, but splutter and cough and hardly run at all low down. It was like riding with a switch rather than a throttle. Sure enough, the battery was on its last legs and failed post-race scrutineering. This was the third time in two years and the second in 2002 that this had happened, which just wasn't good enough. Other teams didn't seem to have the same problem. That's my only criticism of the team.

Nonetheless, I'd had three thoroughly enjoyable years with Belgarda Yamaha, a terrific bunch of blokes with whom I'd always got on well, and still do. In each season I managed at least one win and plenty of rostrum finishes. The team, I have to say, was brilliant. They were always behind me, never blamed me for anything, were always there for me. But overall the results were slightly disappointing. I always felt I was good enough to win the World Supersport Championship, but never even came close enough to be contending for the title over the last few rounds. I'm not sure why, because I applied myself as well as I knew how, but never achieved the consistency to deserve the championship. And I was now 36 years old – still competitive but definitely not getting any better. I never gave up in a race or a championship, and I never would, but I felt at the back of my mind that my best chance of winning was behind me with the disasters of 2001.

CHAPTER 23

THE STRANGEST WINTER

After the chemotherapy I didn't know if I could still have kids, but Andrea became pregnant soon after we began trying, although she miscarried first time around. When she conceived again in the Spring of 2002, she didn't behave any differently from the previous time. She was careful about what she ate and drank, but otherwise carried on as normal, even riding her horses until the eighth month. In fact she really bloomed, and seemed much healthier when pregnant. Even so, only a stupid person would move house under such circumstances, so that's what we did – leaving Healy House for a half-restored old farmhouse a mile from the airfield. I promised her that by the time the baby was due in November she'd have at least heating, hot water and a kitchen. We made it by the skin of our teeth.

Dad had been blooming in his own way too. He'd always said he'd retire to the Isle of Man, a place he loved, and in '96 bought a house and moved to Andreas in the north of the Island. He reckoned it was like living in England 40 years before, which, being a bit of a throwback himself, suited him down to the ground. When he'd had his first heart attack he'd lost his pilot's licence, but in 2000 became eligible to fly again with a new, less strict kind of licence. He had his Jodel aeroplane in yet another hangar he'd built, an airstrip next to the house, a new lady friend, Maria, and had two pretty blissful years flying back and forth between Andreas and Huddersfield.

Then, two days before Andrea was due to go into hospital to have the baby, the phone rang. It was Maria, sobbing her heart out, and even before she said anything I knew why she was calling. Dad had been out flying around the Island with a mate,

Ken. They'd landed and as they were pushing the Jodel back into the hangar dad had a massive heart attack. Ken reckoned he was dead before he even hit the ground.

Two days later, on 25 November 2002, the 5lb 13oz bundle we'd later name Ruby arrived. So as one life ended, another began. It was the strangest emotional turmoil. I didn't know what to think. The elation at becoming a father, mixed with the grief at losing dad, was bittersweet. To make matters worse, three days after coming home Andrea developed a raging temperature and was readmitted to hospital, out of her head and hallucinating that Ruby had died. Mum, as ever, came to the rescue, caring for Ruby whilst I shuttled back and forth to hospital.

When the dust settled, we consoled ourselves that dad hadn't suffered and there was a naturalness about his going. Although 72 isn't exactly old, he'd had a full life – fuller than most, without a doubt. He'd died doing what he loved and with none of those important things left unsaid between us, the sort of things that can gnaw at your grief. I missed him, of course, and still do. But not, as time passes, in sadness – more likely with a giggle about the daft things he used to get up to.

In his place was something precious. Since Andrea has arthritis in her hips, the delivery was by Caesarean. We already knew from the scan she was a girl, had four or five names in mind, but decided to see which one most suited. A day or so later I was looking at her and thought she looked like a Ruby. Andrea agreed, so Ruby it was. She's now five and has hardly given us a moment's concern, other than through our own stumbling attempts to get the hang of this parenting lark. She's bright, lively, good fun – a right little character, which I suppose most kids are, but she's the first one I've really got to know.

Dad and Ruby were to me the most important events of the winter of 2002–3. But in the parallel universe of bike racing, events were about to change too. I knew retirement was going to come eventually but, like most racers, tried to put it to the back of my mind. All I hoped…all I ever hoped…was that I'd know when the time was right and not keep going too long. The last thing I wanted was people thinking 'There goes that sad old git Whitham. I can remember when he was good.'

At the end of 2002 a few people at Yamaha were keen to give me the bullet, and you couldn't really blame them since I hadn't really delivered consistently. On the other hand I couldn't see who they could draft in who would definitely do better than me. But although Belgarda are to some extent directed by Yamaha Motor Europe, they were very much behind me and wanted me to stay, so I signed a contract for 2003.

As usual, we tested in Valencia, in January. I went as quick as I'd ever gone. The team seemed happy. But something wasn't quite the same, and even now I can't explain it accurately. Over each winter you'd usually have a month or so off when it seemed like you were living a different life – a normal one, for most people – and the thought of actually racing seemed a million miles away. Then you'd get to your first pre-season test, put on your leathers, see your new bike with your name on the screen, and within a few laps it'd be like you'd never been away.

But this year seemed different. Somehow I didn't feel at home. Sitting in the garage waiting for the forks to be changed, I felt almost like an observer rather than the guy who's supposed to be the main man. It didn't help that at the same test Casoli high-sided and cabbaged his head, although he eventually made a full recovery.

On the plane coming home, I realised what it was all about. I'd had enough. I already knew I would need a couple of eye operations which, unless timed perfectly, would involve missing at least one meeting or test. I'd first noticed a problem the previous season. Occasionally, invariably when I was very tired, a cloudiness would develop in the vision of my left eye. At first I thought nothing of it, but over a few months it became more frequent and persistent, so at the end of 2002 I'd visited my optician. A pressure test – the one where they blow a puff of compressed air at your eyeball – indicated glaucoma in both eyes, although only the left showed any damage. I eventually had a couple of operations at Moorfield's Eye Hospital, the first in 2002, to insert a valve to bleed off the pressure. Glaucoma damages the optic nerve, and I've some loss of sight in the left eye – basically, I can't see my own nose with it – although it's never a practical problem. It's possible that the damage was caused by one of the chemotherapy drugs, although there's no way of knowing for sure.

Although it would have been convenient to hang the retirement decision on the glaucoma, and sometimes I even said as much, in all honesty I don't think even that had a lot to do with it. Nor even the fact that Ruby had been born the previous November, and at almost the same time my dad had died. Major events like that inevitably change your view of the way racing fits into your life, but I'm not even sure if they were the main issue.

At the heart of it was an awareness that I wasn't getting younger, or quicker. And the last thing I wanted was to sit on the bike just for the wages, just to make up the numbers. I like to think I've always been an honest racer in terms of the effort I gave to teams, but after Valencia I didn't believe I was going to be able to do what Belgarda were paying me to do. But there were no absolutes, no flashing neon lights saying, 'James Whitham, it's time to pack in.' To begin with, it was just a nagging feeling.

What always scared me was that even though I was getting older, if the invitation presented itself I seemed just as prepared to take the same risks as I had when I was younger and supposedly dafter. Earlier in my career I'd imagined that as the years passed I'd get smarter, more experienced, and that would make up for what I expected to lose in sheer do-or-die balls. But it never seemed to happen that way. I may have lost a bit of speed, but I seemed just as prepared to take a big last-lap chance and risk hurting myself.

Mulling over this now, it sounds like a rational process of risk assessment. But at the time, in the heat of a race, it's anything but. To take that chance, or not, is more like an instinct than a decision. You either take it or you don't – and, usually, I did. Sooner or later, I reckoned, it's going to end badly. Above all I didn't want to be getting slower and still be taking the same chances – just as dangerous, but past it too.

Once these doubts started to take root, I couldn't see any way back. Once they entered my head they wouldn't go away. For the life of me, I couldn't see how I could legitimately go racing with this sort of stuff in the back of my mind. As usual, I turned to Rob McElnea, telling him I was thinking of packing in. 'Thank fuck,' he said which, with hindsight, is much what I'd have expected him to say.

The thoughts behind it aren't ones we usually say out loud, but it was sort of racers' code for 'Chalk up another survivor: Racers 1, Grim Reaper 0.' Maybe anyone currently racing would struggle to understand it, and I'm not sure I did at the time, but for we has-beens, leaving racing in more or less one piece is one the biggest wins of your career. There were probably times when you'd have got long odds on it, but James Whitham the person had outlived James Whitham the racer. Although it was never an issue during my career, calling a halt to it allowed me to be thankful I hadn't done more permanent damage to myself. Much to my surprise, pretty well everyone said the same as Rob. Andrea asked if it was truly what I wanted, and when I said it was, that was it: 'Well, pack it in, then,' she said. It was as simple as that.

That's not to say you welcome retirement. I'm sure anyone who packs in voluntarily, as I did, has mixed feelings about it. I felt relieved, and also sad. I missed it. I still miss it, and think I always will. But I think I did the right thing at the right time, for me. All riders are different. For my money Frankie Chili went on a bit too long, but if you love your racing and still want to do it, why should anyone else complain?

Belgarda seemed disappointed I wouldn't be riding for them but respected my judgement. Simone Sanna and Jurgen van de Goorbergh took the places of Casoli and myself. As it turned out neither won a round, although van de Goorbergh finished third in the championship that Chris Vermeulen ran away with, with Sanna way down in 17th.

So the big question now was what was I going to do with all this spare time? Or, rather, with my life? Obviously, a big lump was going to be missing, but as a racer you always know that sooner or later that's going to be the case. You can't carry on racing until you're 70. Nothing else is likely to give me the same satisfaction as racing, but everyone who's raced at the top level must experience that feeling. Few of us are ever likely to be as good at anything else, but you have to be sufficiently mature and at ease with yourself to deal with that. To Foggy, it seems important to be seen as the racer he used to be, but that doesn't bother me one bit. Someone put it well the other month: when you retire you pass the baton on to the next generation and move on. That sums it up for me. It's their game now, not mine. You're a has-been, Whitham, get used to it.

Another thing that toned down was the Po' Boys. As happens with bands, the members changed over the years. Carl left and was replaced by Mick McGowan. Then Dud fell ill, later dying of a brain tumour. His place on guitar was taken by yet another of Jep's contacts, Raving Bob Harris. Tony Marchant, a well-hard ex-Castleford rugby league player, would often join us as roadie and minder.

In the late '90s the band had gone from strength to strength. It was never more than a hobby, although when we were all keen we might do as many as two gigs a week, if more typically just a couple per month. Initially it was mainly local stuff, showbiz hotspots like Swillington Miners' Welfare Club, near Castleford. As we were setting up for our first Swillington gig the hall was full of old boys playing dominoes, who didn't exactly look like our sort of audience. We'd usually get the set rolling with the Sex Pistols' *Anarchy in the UK*. 'You know what's going to happen, don't you?' muttered Raving Bob. 'We'll fire into *Anarchy* and 100 sets of false teeth are going to drop into pint glasses.' Luckily, before we went on a few younger folk arrived and by the time we tuned up the place was packed. In the gents between our two sets, two old boys were overheard chatting.

'Who are they, this lot?' said one.

'I dunno, but they put arses on seats,' replied the other.

We weren't at all bad, but I definitely wasn't the strongest member. I was once asked why I never seemed to smile whilst drumming. The answer was simple: since I wasn't very talented I had to think about every bash of the skins. The frown was just concentration. It didn't help that I didn't practice much. If I'd been keener, maybe I would've done. But I loved gigging in front of an audience much more than jamming away on my own. So I was at best a very average drummer who never got any better – quite the opposite of James Toseland, who's seriously talented on the piano.

What I did bring to the Po' Boys was contacts with the racing world. By '97 we'd somehow become the unofficial backing band to World Superbikes, regularly playing at Donington and Brands

Superbikes, as well as at *MCN* 's bikers' weekends at Skegness. Skeggie was good. We backed bands like Bad Manners, Suzie Quattro and Toyah Wilcox, who was brilliant. Buster Bloodvessel from Bad Manners was a lovely bloke. From there it snowballed, until we were also gigging at Assen every year, then at Imola, for the last round of the World Superbike Series, with Honda picking up the tab.

Honda also asked us to play at their end-of-season party at Birmingham's Sports Bar, after Colin Edwards won the world title in 2000. After our first set Honda's 'Kipper' Herring got up to interview Edwards on the stage, alongside the championship trophy, an enormous pewter motorbike on a plinth. When they'd finished, the trophy just got put down and abandoned. We only noticed it after everyone had gone and wedged it in the back of the van with our kit. Fully three months went by before Kipper rang and asked, 'Have you by any chance seen our trophy?' It must have looked grand on Jep's sideboard.

We had some unbelievably good experiences with the band, plus a few slightly hairy ones. Playing to 15,000 people on a lovely summer evening at the *Performance Bikes* Frenzy at Cadwell Park was brilliant – for a time. We were headlining, with Uncle Pete doing a stand-up comedy routine, plus a guy stapling cards to his head and lifting things up with various pierced parts of his body, which was pretty grotesque. Unfortunately the organisers had totally underestimated how many people would turn up and – more crucially – how much they'd drink. On the whole bike audiences are a fairly easygoing bunch, except when they run out of beer. When they did, long before our set, it turned a bit ugly. Empty bottles were ricocheting off the stage, the beer-less beer tent was ripped down and set ablaze and all the three old security blokes could do was keep their heads down.

When Mark Forsyth, who was running the show for *Performance Bikes*, appealed for calm, he may as well have been still asleep in that bus at Hockenheim. No one took a blind bit of notice. So he turned to the biggest coward in the place – me.

'You're going to have to go out and calm them down,' he said. I tried, and the mob settled down a little, but there was still the odd can flying at us during our set. Luckily none of them hit me. That's the best part of being a drummer: you feel relatively safe behind a nine-piece drum kit and some heavy cymbals.

Our gigging tailed off a couple of years ago, so now the Po' Boys only do the occasional bash. Most of the band have other commitments, but to some extent we were the victims of our own success. Unless it was a big gig, the guys found it hard to get excited. Playing in front of 10,000 race fans outdoors at Brands Hatch for good money is one thing. An audience of 200 at the Pig and Whistle in Pontefract is harder to get excited about.

If I have an audience now, it's more likely to be as a TV race commentator – or, now and again, as a has-been celeb at some sort of parade. One of the biggest in the UK is the Goodwood 'Festival of Speed', which I'd always wanted to do. Three years ago a letter arrived inviting me to take part. The organisers would find me a bike. I'd find Andrea a new dress. Great.

It turned out that the bike I'd be riding up Goodwood Hill would be Bruce Anstey's 2003 TT-winning 600 Triumph Daytona. Historically, the bike's special – the first Triumph to win a TT for almost 30 years. But to ride, it was boring. The motor felt stock and probably was. So instead of gracefully parading this chunk of British heritage, I ended up pulling a pile of wheelies up the hill to amuse myself, and maybe the crowd.

At the top of the hill, after a big inflatable arch marking the finish line, you arrive in a holding area through a pair of gates. I got it into my head that it'd be good to do a big stand-up wheelie under the arch – and did, up to about fourth gear. I was just telling myself how impressive this must look when I realised I'd made three small mistakes.

Firstly, I'd underestimated how quick I was going, probably somewhere over 80mph. Secondly, I realised just how much slowing down room I'd already used poncing about on the back wheel. And the straight wasn't a straight anyway, 'cos there was a right-hand bend into the holding area.

Oh, and it had been raining.

Now, none of this should deflect you from the view that I behaved like an absolute cock.

I realised as the front wheel touched the road that it was going to be touch and go. I jammed on a load of front brake, realised I wasn't going to stop, so locked the front wheel and baled off the bike, rather than hit a solid-looking gatepost.

Unfortunately I was the last man up the hill, so the holding area was full of legends with about a million world titles between them…Spencer, Doohan, Schwantz, Agostini, Taveri, plus lots of others like Granty, most of whom had been my heroes.

Into this gathering of the great and the good cartwheeled the TT-winning Triumph, now in three pieces after taking out the gate post, shortly followed by me, after my own glancing excursion against the same post. I looked up, and all I could see was legends and heroes, and all I wanted to do was die. Ago's face was a picture. Whatever the Italian is for 'Who the hell is this idiot?', his expression just about summed it up.

I'd done a rib, broken my nose and pushed some teeth through my lip, so there was a fair bit of claret about the place, although what hurt most was my pride. All things considered, the most diplomatic thing to do seemed to be to stay on the ground, feign concussion and hope for a spot of sympathy. I didn't get much, but at least they didn't lynch me.

Andrea never did get to wear that new frock. After they checked me out of Winchester hospital we packed up and high-tailed back to Huddersfield as fast as we could. I was already making arrangements for the rebuild as we were driving north and later paid for the Daytona to be rebuilt. Triumph actually stamped a new frame with the original numbers since the original was utterly mangled. It's one thing to trash a bike you've been lent to race, but dicking about destroying a museum piece – possibly the last British bike ever to win a TT – is a different matter. It wasn't my finest hour.

A year earlier it had been someone else's turn to make a scene – as this individual often does. The event was the 2003 Barry Sheene Memorial Meeting at Scarborough. A group of ex-racers were due to put in a few parade laps around the Oliver's Mount circuit, where Sheeney had ridden the year before, just a few months before he died. Several were on bikes Sheene had actually raced. Amongst the guests riders were Mick Grant, Kent Andersson, Phil Read, Tommy Robb and Steve Parrish. The guest of honour was Prince Philip.

With 'Stavros' Parrish around, you never quite know what's going to happen. On this occasion he'd turned up with a remote-controlled fart machine, which he hid under the tank of Read's MV Agusta – right under the noses of lots of big burly chaps with wires in their ears and ominous bulges in their jackets. Granty actually watched him doing it, squeaking 'You can't, you can't, it's not right,' which is how I came to know it was there.

So there we were lined up in front of our machines like a bunch of debutantes, ready for inspection by His Royal Highness, the mayor of Scarborough and assorted heavies and brass. We'd all been briefed to speak to the Prince only if spoken to, although no-one had mentioned fart machines. It was unbearable. As the Prince approached the MV, I'm telling myself not to look at anyone, in case I piss myself. Mick's face was already scarlet with embarrassment. Peter Hillaby, the organiser of the meeting, introduced the first in line to His Highness.

'Sir, this is Phil Read, eight times world cham…'

PARP!

It was loud. They could probably hear it in the stands.

The strange thing was, Parrish didn't laugh at all. Mick was holding his breath and going even redder, but no-one said a thing. Stavros made the thing parp three times altogether, but it just didn't register. Maybe royals are programmed to tune out such vulgarity. Maybe they never fart. But we didn't half crack up about it afterwards.

Most parades aren't quite so juvenile, but usually they're not very serious. Yet one of the fiercest rivalries I ever experienced was after I'd finished competitive racing, at the Goodwood Revival meeting, also in 2003. Amongst the guests was former 500cc World Champion Wayne Gardner. As a rider I'd had immense respect for him, mainly because he was so determined, hard as nails. Ironically it was Gardner who gave us the pre-race briefing: steady for six laps then anything goes for the last two.

OK, I thought, it's a laugh, no one's taking it all that seriously. It's mainly just us old farts putting on a show for the fans. But in the race I got hooked up with Gardner himself. Over the last three laps the two of us pulled away from the rest, and I was flabbergasted at just how much he wanted to win. He'd been retired for about a decade by then, of course, whilst I'd only just packed in. It turned into a pretty big shitfight. He won the first race by about half a bike's length, I won the second by a wheel, both of us riding on the ragged edge.

The funny thing is – and this probably sums up racers, 'cos when all's said and done we're all only comparing testicles – if he hadn't been so damn keen to win, I wouldn't have been so keen to beat him. So at Goodwood the next year we both knew what the job was even before we started. Same result, a win apiece, with Gardner again minutely ahead on aggregate. Yet he didn't say anything. There wasn't even a smile. I can imagine him in his heyday being a not very endearing bloke.

Obviously Carl Fogarty had a similar reputation. As an opponent I rated him highly, because he just would not be beaten. And he could ride his way round problems better than anyone else I knew. He really had no right to win a lot of the races he won. Everyone seemed to recognise that except Carl himself.

But for all his wins and championships, you could watch him and know exactly how he was doing what he did. There was no mystery about it. The very top riders just did it maybe a little better or more consistently than you, but were basically doing exactly the same. Only a couple of times have I seen riders doing things I simply couldn't comprehend. One's Valentino Rossi, who's simply a magician, even if his wizard's hat has slipped a bit lately. The other's Giancarlo Falappa, especially on that day at Brands for the 1993 'Irish' World Superbike round.

That said, to me they were all mates, wrapped up in the same crazy business. I wanted to beat them bad, but I can't remember holding any grudges, can't remember anyone I wanted to beat more than anyone else. Which I suppose is just another way of saying I wanted to beat every one of them.

To do that, race-craft's involved, obviously, and mind games. You'd quickly learn that some riders were easy to psyche. All you had to do was laugh at their shoes or haircut and they'd fall to bits. Others seemed utterly impermeable to anything. On the track during a race you try to work out where you're stronger, where your opponent is weaker, and where you might make a move that wouldn't allow them to come back at you right away. But if it came to a last corner lunge, planned or unplanned, I was usually up for it.

A case in point was the incident with Jim Moodie at Mallory Park in '93 when, hard as he was, he came off second best. Now, Jim's tough but also a very bright rider. At Mallory he did everything right but ran a tiny bit wide at the Hairpin. Maybe there wasn't room for a pass, but it was certainly an invitation, and I was in there and won. I did the same with Rob McElnea at the same place. He ran right up the inside to deny me room, but I managed to get half a wheel inside him, and that was that. I can still hear his cry of 'Bastard' as I scuttled underneath his Yamaha, barely in control. And once other riders actually expect you to have a go, which I think they usually did with me, that's half the battle. That's your psychological edge.

There were some riders I really rated, some I didn't – and in both cases it wouldn't necessarily be what the public thought, what the individual's reputation suggested. Some guys seemed to have things on a plate, whilst others struggled and maybe didn't get great results but always rode well, rode hard. Mark Phillips springs to mind. He was just plain quick – quick into corners, and quick out. He was never an easy man to pass, let alone beat.

Other people I rated less highly compared to their popular reputation. Remember Juan Garriga's arrival in World Superbikes? Good bike, good team, lots of pomp and ceremony, and he was going to kick everyone's arse. That didn't last long. He packed in after about four meetings.

I got on well with most people in the paddock, and certainly never had fisticuffs with any of them. Apart from anything else, I'm far too chicken. When fists are flying, I'm always careful to be somewhere else, even if it means running. But just because you got on OK and shared an occasional beer with your rivals didn't mean you wouldn't stitch them up on the track given half a chance. There, the gloves were off.

Foggy's approach was totally different. Every year he seemed to need a designated Public Enemy Number One to make him tick. Scott Russell, the first enemy, I think he now likes and respects. But obviously they have a lot in common: both World Champions and both quite mad.

I also made a special point of trying to get on with team-mates, because the better you got on the more work got done, which had to be better for both of you. Some riders take a completely opposite view, which I think is pretty immature and stupid – although that might sound more convincing coming from someone less immature and stupid than me. Some of my team-mates were oddballs, sure enough, but I dare say they'd say the same about me. I was never in the Kocinski league, although I used to enjoy watching the weird goings-on at his motorhome. Fast and very, very talented, for sure. But that lad had a few issues.

Perhaps we all did. Yet even so, simply because someone rides a race bike quicker than most people on the planet doesn't necessarily mean they're any different from the blokes you know at work or down at the pub. For every racer who's lively and funny, like Russell or Colin Edwards, there's another who's stupid, or dull, or strange, or simply unpleasant. If there is a common theme it's that most of them have some component missing that most people in normal life possess. The lift, as they say, doesn't go all the way to the top floor. After all, you have to be a bit weird to race motorbikes for a living.

CHAPTER 24

TRUST ME,
I'M A PUNDIT

The work I'm probably best known for now is being a talking head on TV – World Superbikes and Supersports for Eurosport, and British meetings for ITV and now Eurosport. The commentary thing – I still don't regard it as a proper job, not that I'm much of an expert on those – started back in my Belgarda years when Jack Burnicle had Niall McKenzie as his tame pundit. We were friends around the paddock anyway, and Niall had been a good mate since the Cadbury's Boost days, so they'd often get me in as the third mike for the second Superbike race, because by then my racing was over for the day – unless I'd had a nightmare and was spitting out my dummy somewhere.

It never occurred to me for a moment that these fleeting appearances might lead to anything, but in '03 Niall had to miss three or four rounds because of commitments elsewhere, so Jack invited me to take the second mike. Even then, I regarded it more as a bit of a laugh, something positive to do around racing, never imagining it would become a regular thing. When Niall was again too busy to commentate the following year, Eurosport asked me to do the whole season with Jack. That year all our broadcasts were from the Eurosport studios, but in '05 we went to a few rounds and have been on-site for all the WSB events since. Being on site is obviously so much easier and makes for better broadcasting. You get the gossip, a true sense of the atmosphere and conditions, see riders' body language – the stuff you'd never get from a sound booth in Slough. And some of the locations are special. At places like Monza, it's almost a religious thing to walk under that tunnel. It still gives me goose bumps.

Like everyone who's reading this book, I've ranted at TV

commentators – 'Can't you see so-and-so fell off two laps ago, you dozy pillock...no, he's not taking it easy, his friggin' tyres have gone off...' But it's not an easy job. Some races almost commentate themselves. If it's an exciting race with lots of action, all you have to do is fill in who's doing what, explain anything you might spot, but mainly let the racing speak for itself. Steady races are harder because you've got to try to keep the show moving, keep up some sort of tempo, keep it boiling. But even then it's quite enjoyable if you have something pertinent to talk about, because in that sort of spread-out race you have time to explain things you can't in an all-action race.

As the ex-racer, my job isn't 'Welcome to sunny Phillip Island' or whatever. It's knowing the riders, knowing the bikes, spotting things that maybe Jack wouldn't see. I didn't know Jack at all until he first arrived at World Superbikes to do Eurosport commentary, first with Steve Parrish, then Rob Orme, but we now spend a lot of time in each other's pockets, sharing hire cars, flights, hotel rooms. We get on all right. We're completely different in character and age, but I like to think that works quite well... you don't want to be agreeing with each other all the time. It's better for a bit of banter, a bit of spark.

I enjoy being around the paddock as much as ever, because I'm still hugely interested in the bikes and the racing – plus I get to see some of my old mates. Sometimes it's difficult to be on the periphery rather than at the cutting edge of things. It's not that, as the media, you've no right to be there. Without the media there'd be no publicity, no sponsors, and no racing. But we are peripheral to the action, even getting in the way of the main business now and again.

As media you're allowed a lot of access, because all the teams are now media-savvy and recognise the importance of what we do. Jack will get in someone's face at times that I never would, because he's never raced and doesn't truly understand what riders and crew are going through at pressure moments. Obviously, I see it because I've been there and recognise the body language, so I'm more reticent, more aware of what's going on. Jack, although he's quite thoughtful and sensitive, never seems to feel like that. He's always ready to ask a question, because he sees that as the reason he's there – and, of course, he's right. Teams generally suffer the intrusion, even when he gets under their feet, so he's never actually been told to shove off yet, but one day it might come to that.

So sometimes I feel like a spare part. Because of my background, I see tyre men, riders, mechanics as having more of a legitimate role than I do as a pundit. That's something I've got to get over, because now my primary duty is to the viewers, not to the teams. You've got to be prepared to be a bit of a pest if you're going to get any in-depth information. And you certainly find that if you have a camera following you around you can pretty much do what you want. That's the power of television. People just accept it.

Of course, as the heat builds up prior to a race you get to know which riders are talkers, which are the opposite. If one of them's babbling ten to the dozen, just to keep his head straight, he may as well babble to me – which means, to you too.

A commentator should enhance whatever's happening on track, supplement the action with information. Getting across who the riders are, their age, history and the rest, that's largely Jack's job. Mine's to get across the subtleties of what's happening, what it's actually like to be doing what those guys do, what strategies they might be evolving, what's going on with their tyres, and so on. Jack's brilliant at the factual background, because he's genuinely interested and gets ridiculously excited about the most trivial bits of stuff. For me it's more about what the riders are thinking and feeling: a participant's-eye view rather than Jack's giddy spectator.

That's the theory, at any rate. Of course, we've had our share of cock-ups. When TV works, it looks seamless, simple. But there's always so much going on that the viewer has no idea about. There have been times when the ISDN line's gone down and we've had to commentate on our mobile phones. If you see an on-screen apology for 'poor sound quality' that's probably the reason.

You might be in a sound booth in Czecho, being directed either from Paris or Slough, and sometimes it's hard to tell whether you're on air or not. Lots of times we've sat there mouthing to each other, 'Are we on?' and not really having a clue. At Donington in 2007 the live feed from Feltham went down, so we couldn't hear the British director, just a Frenchman saying he was coming to us in two minutes forty seconds. What we didn't know was that we were already live for British viewers, so Jack, me and Neil Hodgson sat there completely oblivious, just prattling on. If I have one rule, it's that if you've got a mike next to you someone, somewhere is listening, so I don't swear or slag people off. Jack's not so careful. He's let rip a few naughties.

There are two things you, as viewers, might have a problem understanding. First, you might be watching the action on a 42-inch plasma screen and see every little detail, whilst we're watching on a tiny monitor like a fishbowl. So we miss stuff that seems obvious, like a crash just starting in the top corner of the screen just as the director cuts to the next shot. And second we're trying to look at about two other things at the same time...the timing screen, our notes, whatever. It's not as easy as it looks. And there's no point looking out of the commentary box window. All you can usually see is the start straight anyway, and talking about that just seems daft, because it's probably not what you're seeing on your TV.

As a former racer there's a bit of poacher turned gamekeeper about the whole business. Inevitably I have mixed feelings about the media. Like any other field, there's good and bad. Some other commentators I respect and like, others I can barely stand listening to. The type of audience makes a big difference too. When I first began working for ITV in 2006 I thought I could carry on doing exactly what I'd been doing for Eurosport. But terrestrial TV has a completely different audience. Not only is it three times bigger – maybe 800,000 watching British Superbikes of a Sunday – but, unlike the bike enthusiasts who are Eurosport's main audience, most of them have never even been near a bike. So we can't assume they know who's who, are interested in the technical details, or know a high-side from a high-five. Consequently your commentary is much more to do with what's actually happening on screen, explained in a way that's understandable to the layman. Barry Nutley, ITV's main commentator in 2006, has his own style – very excitable, very loud. He's possibly not to everyone's taste, but as a bloke I have a lot of time and respect for him. Compared to Eurosport, the ITV format definitely detracts from the spontaneity and is probably a bit basic for a bike race fan. For sure there's no room for the sort of chit-chat I enjoy with Jack. But if you want to see racing on terrestrial TV, that's the price you have to pay.

Commentary is something I love doing, and I'd like to keep at it. Trouble is, I suspect my role – the rider's perspective – has a shelf life, although Parrish is still at it long after he retired and is still brilliant. I don't think I have the accent to be a front man. I'm probably only ever going to be a quirky sidekick to someone like Jack.

That said, I love doing stuff to camera. It's the Fred Dibnah syndrome, I suppose. If you'd told Fred after that first programme about bringing down chimneys that in 15 years he'd be a TV star, he'd have laughed into his pint of Thwaites. I talk the way I talk, and if I try to be different it doesn't work, even though it sometimes lumbers me with having to explain to a viewer what a nugget is.

Being on the other side of the media fence sometimes feels odd, but as a rider I never hated the press, and can't remember a time when I was ever shafted by them. Carl went through a few hard times with them, but unlike him I didn't always say the first thing that came into my head. It helped, too, that during my career we had some good correspondents at world level, like Kipper Herring and Andy Downes. But mainly I suspect I wasn't as famous, and therefore as interesting to the media, as guys like Foggy.

As well as TV work, I do the odd bit of scribbling for bike magazines like *Two Wheels Only*. When I raced I used to laugh at magazine test riders. Some seemed to have egos far bigger than their ability. Since doing tests with them, I've found that some ride well whilst others struggle. You wonder how they can write 3,000 words about the new GSX-R1000, say, when they were going slower than any reasonable rider would go round on a CG125.

But I do like new model launches. Say you're at a Yamaha R6 world press launch, the preening of some of the press can be funny, especially since most of 'em aren't that quick. Naturally I still think I am, although you get a few surprises. At Almeria in 2004, me and Niall McKenzie were on track and having a bit of a do. After a few laps I noticed a headlight about 200 yards behind. 'Bloody hell,' I thought, 'that's getting closer. If that's a journo, he's in the wrong job.' I also thought that if he got past me, I'd never live it down. So I nipped past Niall and pushed on. Still the headlight kept getting closer....closer...until, 'Bloody hell, it's Randy Mamola. My reputation's safe.' He hadn't raced for the best part of 20 years, whilst I'd only been retired for two. He's still bloody quick, still something else on a bike. Good to watch.

CHAPTER 25

WHAT AM I DOING HERE?

I never won a world title. Four British championships is four more than most racers manage, but maybe you're asking yourself why I didn't do better. Sometimes, especially when thinking of the Belgarda years, I do myself.

A lot of riders might genuinely claim that they never had the right bike, and it's a matter of speculation whether they would have made the step up to the next level if they'd had better kit. You'd watch some up-and-coming riders who you'd be convinced could really go places if they had the right equipment, but when they get it they don't deliver. Tim Bourne was a case in point. He did really well on his own bikes, got a Kawasaki deal – a better team, better bike, better tyres – but went slower. Until it happens, you just don't know.

I had seasons when I was riding well on crap bikes. And I had years when I had the same bike everyone else was winning on, but I didn't ride it so well and didn't win as often as I should. And I had pretty much everything in between.

One of the good things about bike racing is that even at the top level it's still really about who dares to, who can, lean a bike over the furthest, open the throttle earliest, and brake hardest, without crashing. It's not about going mad, although that's probably often the case at club level. At higher levels it's about getting the bike going well, getting a good set-up, making the bike into something you can ride hard and fast. But whether it's the Racing 100 Club at Carnaby or the last bend at Monza, that last lap move is still often about who's prepared to take the biggest risk. It's not even about psyching yourself up, it just comes naturally.

A racer can't really cheat – whatever the bike is, it's still got to be ridden – and he can't hide. But any nutter, and there have been a few, can fall off trying too hard. Most riders have a trip-switch which won't allow them to knowingly hurt themselves. It's partly a fear of crashing, but also more than that. All the top guys know what they need to do to put in a faster lap. The tricky part is having the balls to do it and still stay right-way-up. You need aggression and adrenalin, but not too much because otherwise you'd just crash your brains out. And you need to think rationally about what you're doing, but not so much that you lose your instincts. It's a tantalising balance. Car racing seems to be much more predictable, more precise: if you have the right set-up, the optimum fuel load, you'll go so quick. Not with bike racing, which is a lot more variable, more individual.

Is natural talent the most important element, or is racing an acquired ability? One thing's for sure: being a champion is about so much more than technical talent, machine handling, ability at setting up a bike, and even bravery, although all those elements are important. Lots of riders have all those skills in abundance, yet never become champions. So natural talent isn't enough, but really wanting to win isn't either – it just makes you fall off a lot. Some riders really understand their bikes, think about it, and are quick. Some just try their nuts off – like me, I suppose.

Even the fitness element is overstated. Some of the kids now seem to think you need to be some sort of word-class athlete. I trained as hard as anyone, and only once was I ever physically wasted in a race. That was 30 laps into a Daytona 200 race when the bike blew up and I was almost glad it did. But so long as you can manage long races in hot conditions, that's all you need. More can be counterproductive. Neil Hodgson is obsessive about training, whilst Carl Fogarty just seemed to think he was better than everyone else anyway, so why go through the pain?

Foggy is an obvious yardstick for anyone to compare me against, because he's a contemporary as well as being one of my closest mates. The reason I didn't do as well as him is simple: I wasn't as good as him. You can worry about it, wonder about lucky breaks, about being in the right place at the right time, and so on, and you can go on pondering about that for the rest of your life, but it doesn't answer the question – not honestly, at least.

For Foggy, winning was always the most important thing, yet it irritates me when pundits suggest that was all that made him a winner. It can't possibly be just that, because any idiot can have that sort of focus. Look at the sad cases on TV talent shows. Every one of them says they know they're going to make it big one day, yet just one in a million will. And whilst determination is admirable, without talent you're going nowhere. Yes, Foggy was determined, as focussed as any person I've ever met, and with an absolutely unfailing belief in his ability. But without talent, the only thing that sort of determination gets you is a hospital bed.

Foggy behaved – and, it must be said, usually performed – as though winning was his destiny; I sometimes had to pinch myself to believe people were actually paying me for racing at all. I always thought I was all right...pretty damn good, usually...but always figured that I'd rather under-promise and over-deliver. Rather than shooting my mouth off about how good I was and how well I'd do, I'd rather say less and do better. It wasn't so much a preconceived strategy as an extension of my personality. Whenever I had a real good result, instead of telling myself I knew I could do it I'd tend to regard it as a bit of a one-off. It was easier to live that way, figuring I'm not going to win every weekend, than deal with a sense of underachievement.

For those sort of reasons one of my most satisfying seasons was 1991, riding a five-year-old Formula One Suzuki which a lot of people thought was an old shed. Actually, it wasn't that bad. It wasn't slow, it did what I wanted and I liked riding it – and loved it even more when other riders would ask how the hell I was going so fast on such an old nail. Needless to say I'd tell them nothing to dissuade them from thinking I must be some sort of superman. I suppose it mattered to me what people, especially other racers, thought. Foggy wouldn't have given a stuff. In fact he seemed to make a conscious effort to be abrasive – because he was good enough to get away with it, and he thought people expected it of him as a manifestation of his legendary determination. Even since stopping racing, he's carried on much the same.

I guess the bottom line is that I set myself lower standards than Foggy. Some people might criticise that sort of attitude, yet I firmly believe that even if I had possessed his degree of self-belief I wouldn't have been as quick as him, because you've got to deliver it on the track and – bloody hell! – I crashed enough trying. If I'd thought like Foggy I'm sure I'd have crashed even more often, going even faster, and been hurt even more often.

Throughout my career, two questions often ran through my mind as I sat on the grid waiting for a race to start: 'What am I doing here?' and 'When are they going to find out I'm no good?' I thought that all the time. I always had a sense that one day it'd suddenly finish, and it could be next week or in ten years' time. Yet as the years went by, it didn't. I really enjoyed what I did – how could I not? – but it always seemed slightly unreal, like a bit of a fantasy. Carl always thought he wasn't paid enough, whilst I could scarcely believe they were paying me at all to do something I loved. Lots of very good racers are like that, at least some of the time. You might watch us on TV, lined up on the grid, and think we exude self-believe by the skip-load, but that's usually not how we feel inside.

But when you're actually racing, as opposed to just thinking about racing, your personality changes. When the flag drops there simply isn't time for self-doubt. If there were, your career would have ended long before. I don't believe that anyone on track could have tried harder than me. Not having Carl's manic degree of self-belief didn't mean I wasn't committed. I was just as hard a rider as anyone else and harder than many. I was never frightened of anyone either: on a last lap set-to, I'd have a go at absolutely anyone. If someone cleared off into the lead, fine, except you're obviously disappointed you're not going to win. But I always thought that if it came to stick or lift, any sort of last lap, last corner situation, I'd definitely have my money on me.

Even so, during some of the worst racing times I had definite self-belief problems. I even went to see sports psychologists, thinking I only had one chance at this career and it was worth trying anything to make the most of it. That's not to say I was any sort of racing wallflower. You need self-belief in any sport, and I did have it. I knew I wasn't a numpty, not by any means. But Foggy always seemed to have more, yet I don't buy the notion that's all that made him what he was.

It's more to do with the totality of what's inside you. Carl *had* to think the way he did. It wasn't a matter of him thinking like he did, therefore he was, but more that that's what he needed to do to win. He had the talent to do it, certainly. But to harness that talent he had to think the way he did, just as he had to have a hate complex about certain rivals like Aaron Slight and Colin Edwards. That wasn't so true in his early days, when he was as uncertain as the rest of us, but as he developed he became more self-contained, more focussed. Above all he seemed instinctively to know what brought the best out of him, made him work best, whether it was demonising other riders, thinking the world was against him, or even deluding himself that whatever went wrong wasn't his fault – which is an obvious corollary of setting yourself up as the best in the world. No rider wins every single race, yet they have to maintain their personal delusion that no one is better, even when all the evidence says otherwise. Carl seemed able to sustain that position. I never could.

For Carl, winning seemed to be self-validation. I always liked winning – what racer wouldn't? – but perhaps it was at least as important to do justice to myself and to my team. There were times when I'd get off a bike not having won but knowing that I couldn't have gone any quicker; nor, I was often convinced, could anyone else. At other times not winning was deeply disappointing, because I felt I'd not done as much as I should. I don't think that sort of notion ever entered Carl's head.

Although I can sort of understand it now, for a long time it just seemed unreal, illogical. If a rider with absolute mountains of self-belief didn't win, there had to be a logical reason – obviously, because it couldn't possibly be their fault. I was never like that, although Foggy is to some degree and plenty of Yanks seem to be riders who need to exist in their own bubble of perfection, even if it's complete bollocks most of the time.

The problem with too much self-belief, not that I'm an expert, is that you have to lie to yourself a lot. Logically, if you don't win a particular race but you're Mr Perfect, then the problem must be the tyres, suspension, or whatever; and there are riders who truly think that way. I spend quite a bit of time with Foggy and even though he looks back on his career as a whole and thinks he was the best man ever to ride a motorcycle, now even he's able to look at individual events in a more balanced way.

Take Mike Hale, who I rode with for Suzuki in '97. A lovely,

lovely lad, in many ways not a typical in-your-face Yank. But his self-belief and confidence was amazing, far above what his performances that year justified. He didn't have a single rostrum finish all season, but was absolutely convinced that was just because of the bikes, and that on the right tackle he could win the championship.

Another rider I can think of, who we've met before but I won't name in case he beats me up, has similar heaps of self-belief. Even now he honestly thinks that with the right team he could be British champion, when he's got as much chance of winning Pop Idol. But if that's what he needs, that's what makes him happy, makes him faster, then that's fine. All of us find our own means to make us what we want to be. Racing's always going to be a highly delusional business.

I'm from somewhere else altogether. Maybe that's because I started racing not to rule the world, but mainly because I had friends who raced, I admired what they did, and it looked fun. I generally thought it was a pretty cool thing to do, even though it's given me some very un-cool moments since – crapping myself and having a catheter removed spring to mind. When I started racing I never once thought I'd be better than average. But as you improve, one day the notion dawns that 'Bloody 'ell, maybe I can win a club race.' Then when you do, next thing your mates are egging you on to do a British championship round, and you're thinking 'What, me, do you really think so?', half flattered and half quivering at the thought.

And on it goes, sort of incrementally, almost unnoticed, and before you know it you're sat on a World Championship grid, wondering, 'What the fuck am I doing here?'

I was once interviewed on the grid by Suzi Perry before a big race at Donington. She asked whether I was looking forward to the race.

'No.'

'Oh', she goes, a bit startled and speechless. This is live on camera.

'But it's too late to get out of it now.'

It probably came across as quite funny, but that wasn't why I said it. It was the honest truth.

Obviously you chat about all aspects of racing with other riders. Most of them, at least some of the time, feel the same: why do I put myself through this every single weekend? When I stopped racing I thought shitting myself on the grid would be the last thing I'd miss, but in fact it's what you miss as much as anything...the dry mouth, the racing pulse, heaving guts. It's weird. Even now, when I watch a grid forming up I actually feel nervous for the riders.

It took me a long time after packing in to work out which bits of racing I'd liked and which I hadn't. I thought no longer riding fast round a track would be the hardest, but I can always do that on track days and press launches. It may sound bonkers but I do miss the grid, and obviously the Sunday night feeling after a good result. You're not going to believe this, but the feeling of simply walking away in one piece from a big crash is up there too. When it didn't hurt too much, that 'cheating death' feeling, the racing gladiator bit – that was immense.

People are conscious of fame, but that's bollocks too. Take some of the talentless prats on 'reality' TV. They're famous for...what? – being ugly and loud-mouthed. In what sort of country can that happen?

But even world-class bike racers are good at only one thing, and that's riding bikes. The rest of the time they're as useless, boring, tongue-tied and plain fallible as anyone else. And funny sometimes, and good company – but aren't most people? I happen to be in a position to write this book. That's not because I necessarily have anything to say that you couldn't say just as well. It simply means a publisher thinks he can sell it.

Because of what I did, people knew who I was, whether locally or in bike circles. I'd walk into a shop, say, order something and give my name, and even though they knew nothing about bikes, they'd recognise it, say something like, 'You're nuts,' which I took as a massive compliment, 'cos I'm not. Well, mostly not.

CHAPTER 26

WHAT A GOOD DO

So that's it – so far, at least. But there's plenty of life in the old dog yet.

Being a professional sportsman is a weird take on life – as, I suppose, is anything that brings most of its rewards when you're young. Being at your peak before you're 30, especially if it attracts a degree of fame, just doesn't fit easily into the natural order of things. I'm pretty sure that however long I live I'm not going to be good enough at anything else to get the same sort of feelings, the same satisfaction, as racing gave me. I didn't win a World Championship, but I was – modesty aside – a world-class rider. Most people don't get to be a world-class anything, so I can be thankful for that. I just happened to be good at something a lot of people thought was important, although in many ways it wasn't really. Bringing up Ruby with Andrea is the most important thing I've ever done. I'm not world-class at that, any more than you are with your kids; I'm just giving it my very best shot. But that's as important to me as it is to you.

I'm probably looking at what's gone before, and what lies ahead, through the opposite end of the telescope from you. To most race fans I was, first and foremost, James Whitham, racer. That's what defined me to most people who took any interest in what I did on the track. Yet, although there were obviously times when racing totally preoccupied me, that was never how I saw myself. There was always more to me – family, friends and interests, private hopes and ambitions – than that. I'm sure that's true of most professional sportspeople.

It probably helped that being part of a large, close family, none of whom were ever afraid to call a spade a shovel, ensured that my feet never got far from the ground. They still do.

Susan still lives at the airfield with husband Paul and daughter Anna. He's into tractors, welding, anything practical, while she can barely make a cup of tea without scalding herself. Instead, she's into horses – a talented eventer – and runs a livery stable. Their house is what you might call lived in, much as ours was when we were growing up. The last thing on their minds is keeping up with the Joneses or anyone else.

Mary's now Susan's neighbour, having split up from husband Matt. A free spirit who ploughs her own furrow, she's bright as a button and just as potty as Andrea or me. Her three kids are just as crackers, running around the airfield like feral things.

In some ways Jane, the youngest, was the most adventurous of us, leaving her first job to go to the Australian Outback with Operation Raleigh and living out there for five years. She now lives about five miles away with baby Daisy and husband Phil, who has a flourishing specialist foam supply business. Mum now lives just down the road from them, and still brings her own brand of common sense to everything.

I did well out of racing although it'll be a long time before I'm in a position to stop earning. That's not what I want anyway. Other than the odd brainstorm flash car, I rarely did anything lavish when I raced. The house is paid for, and there's enough money coming in from bits and pieces for us to live comfortably. Life clearly doesn't stop when you quit racing, and I'm probably busier now than I've ever been. There's the airfield to be run, although Sue and Paul deal with most of that day-to-day. I've a couple of houses I rent out. There's bike testing, commentating, the odd parade and celebrity appearance. I still trail-ride now and again on a KTM 300, still keep fit on the mountain bike, and keep accumulating sentimental old bikes. In the workshop I always dreamed of there's a pair of Yamaha twins, an RD250 and an RD350LC, a couple of TZ250 racers, a Suzuki X7 and – how sad is this? – a mint Yamaha FS1E moped like the one I used to shiver my way to Blackpool on.

Keep it quiet, but Whitham's also made the odd racing comeback. Nothing flash, just a couple of outings a year in the

'Forgotten Era' class with the Classic Racing Motorcycle Club. I turn up, Jeremy Lodge brings along his MT125, Steve Bevington a TZ350G, and off I go. It's really a throwback to the old club racing days – mostly about the being there, having a laugh and enjoying the craic. No pressure, no ambition. Instead of riding for a team, I'm riding just for me. It's mint.

When I look back on my racing career now, I think I possibly could have done better and would maybe have done a few things differently. But I did better than a lot of people would have in my position; and I firmly believe that some riders better than me either fell off and got hurt, ran out of money or simply didn't get the breaks. So yes, there are small regrets, but overall I can count my blessings.

Most important of all, I'm still in the clear with the Hodgkin's, the glaucoma's under control, there aren't too many creaks from old racing injuries, Andrea's a star and Ruby's a peach.

So, all round, what more could I ask for?

What a good do.

RESULTS

1983*

	125cc
Carnaby	7, 7
Elvington	5,6
Cadwell Park	6, 5, 5
Carnaby	7, 9
Cadwell Park	4, 5, 4, 5, 4, 4

1984*

	125cc
Cadwell Park	3
Mallory Park	1, 1
Mallory Park	2, 2
Cadwell Park	1, 1, 1
Cadwell Park	1, 1
Carnaby (ACU Star)	2, 1, 2
Mallory Park (ACU Star)	5
Silverstone	3
Oulton Park	1
Mallory Park	4
Carnaby	1, 1 , 1

* some results from these years have been lost in the mists of time

1985

	80cc	125cc
Snetterton (ACU Star)	2	
Cadwell Park	1	
Thruxton (ACU Star)	1	
Brands Hatch (ACU Star)	1	
Carnaby	1	
Cadwell Park (ACU Star)		
Scarborough	1	
Donington Park	2	1
Donington Park (ACU Star)	2, 1	
Mallory Park	3	
Cadwell Park	2	
Carnaby (ACU Star)	1	
Cadwell Park	2	3
Mallory Park (ACU Star)	1	
MGP	DNF	
Mallory Park	1	
Scarborough Int	2	1
Silverstone (ACU Star)		DNF
Carnaby	2	1

Championship positions:

ACU 80cc: 4. J Whitham

ACU 125cc: 1. Robin Milton 2. J Whitham

Marlboro Clubmans: 1. Gary Buckle 2. J Whitham

1986

	80cc	125cc	Superstock
Vallelunga Euro	13	4	
Zolder Euro	DNF		
Mallory Park Int	5	1	
Hockenheim Euro	DNF		
IoM TT	10 (400cc Production)		
Mallory Park	1		
Assen Euro	DNF		
Scarborough	2	1	
Scarborough	1		
Mallory Park	1		
British GP, Silverstone	17	DNF	
Cadwell Park	1	1	
Carnaby	1	1	
Cadwell Park	1	4	
Silverstone	1	1	
Brands Hatch Int			8

Championship positions:

ACU 80cc: 1. J Whitham

ACU 125cc: 1. Dave Lowe 5. J Whitham

Motoprix UK Championship: 1. Steve Mason 4. J Whitham

1987

	1300	Superstock	Other
Brands Hatch (Eurolantic)		19, 15, 12	
Donington Park (Eurolantic)		13, 10, 12	
Brands Hatch	1		
IoM TT	Snr: 13	F1: 17	
Donington Park	13	7 (Heat 3rd)	
Cadwell Park	7		
Scarborough	3		
Mallory Park	9 (Heat 8th)		
Cadwell Park		2	
Cadwell Park	8	7	
Mallory Park	3	1	
Scarborough	2, 4	1	Gold Cup: 4, 4
Silverstone (abandoned)	7		
Donington Park	2	3	World F1: 11
Cadwell Park	6 (heat 1st)		King: 4th
Kirkistown			N. Robinson: 5, 8
Darley			Stars: 2, 1
Carnaby		DNF	
Brands Hatch Int[1]	10	1	9

Championship positions:

Motoprix 1300cc: 1. Roger Marshall 3. J Whitham

MCN Superstock: 1. Keith Heuwen 7. J Whitham

ACU Superbike 1. Roger Marshall 8. J Whitham

1988

	Senior-stock	1300 prod	1300	F1	Other
Brands, Eurolantic					7, 11, 9
Donington, Eurolantic		6			8, 7, DNF
Kirkistown		1	1		
Scarborough	1				
Brands Hatch		9			
Mondello Park			3, 4		
IoM TT	Snr: DNF	F1: DNF	750 Prod: 4	600 Prod: 22	
Donington Park		4			
Carnaby	5	1		5	
Cadwell Park	2	2		4	
Knockhill	2	7		2	
Snetterton	3	2			
Mallory Park	2	1		DNF	
Cadwell Park	3				
Donington Park				4	
Thruxton	7	2		2	
Cadwell Park			1		
Mallory Park	2	2		2	
Scarborough	1	3		1	
Cadwell Park	3	DNF		2	6 (King of Cadwell)
Kirkistown					2, 1
Carnaby			1, 1		
Brands Hatch	2			4	3
Macau GP				DNF, DNF	

Championship positions:

Seniorstock: 1. Brian Morrison 3. J Whitham

ACU 1300 Production: 1. J Whitham

ACU F1: 1. Darren Dixon 2. J Whitham

1989

	600 Super-sport	1300 prod	1300	F1	Other
Brands, GB v Europe					8, 4
Donington, GB v Europe					DNF, 4
Scarborough	1		1 (Heat 1st)		
NW200		1	2		
Donington Park	10				
Mallory Park	4	1			
IoM TT	SS600: 3	Prod 1300: DNF		6	
Cadwell Park	4			2	
Donington Park	DNF	1		3	
Assen World F1				5	
Knockhill	3	1		2	
Snetterton	3	4		4	
Cadwell Park	2	3		2	
Donington Park			DNF, DNF		

Championship positions:

ACU 600 Supersport: 1. Paul Brookes 5. J Whitham

ACU 1300 Production: 1. Dean Ashton 3. J Whitham

ACU TT F1: 1. Steve Spray 4. J Whitham

1990

	Senior-stock	TT F1	1300	WSB	Other
Daytona					DNF
Jerez WSB				20, DNF	
Donington WSB				12, DNF	
Mallory Park		2			
Snetterton	DNF	DNF			
Donington Park	8	7			
Cadwell Park			4		
Pembrey		DNF			
Knockhill	1	5			
Snetterton		8			7 (Race of Aces)
Donington Park		6			
Thruxton		3			
Mallory Park	DNF	DNF			
Oulton Park		4, 3			
Donington Park	9	3			
Kirkistown			2, 3		4 (Sunflower)
Brands Hatch		11, 13			

Championship position:

ACU Supercup: 1. Terry Rymer 5. J Whitham

1991

	400 Super-sport	TT F1/SB	1300	OTHER
Donington Park		4		
Pembrey	1		1	
Castle Combe			3	
Thruxton	2		4	
Snetterton		DNF, 5		
Mallory, UK v USA				7, 4
Brands, UK v USA				11, 9, 6
Donington Park	1	7, 7		
Brands Hatch	DNF			
Cadwell Park	DNF		DNF	
Snetterton		3, 2		1 (Race of Aces)
Mallory Park		2, 1		2 (Race of Year)
Cadwell Park	1	1		
Donington Park		2, 2		
Oulton Park	2		8, 3	
Cadwell Park		2, 3		
Mallory Park	DNF		1, 1	
Hockenheim, Suzuki Cup				DNF
Oulton Park		3, 3		
Donington Park		1, 2		
Darley			1, 1	
Kirkistown		2, 2		
Knockhill		2, 2		
Brands Hatch		2, 1		5 (Powerbikes)

Championship positions:

ACU Supersport 400: 1. Steve Ives 7. J Whitham

TT Supercup: 1. Rob McElnea 5. J Whitham

TT Superbike: 1. J Whitham

1992

	750	WSB
Mallory Park	1	
Donington WSB		11, 14
Donington Park	2	
Brands Hatch	3	
Hockenheim WSB		DNS
Donington Park	DNF, 2	
Mallory Park	2, 4	
Snetterton	5, 5	
Knockhill	DNF	
Cadwell Park	DNF, 6	
Oulton Park	3, 7	
Scarborough	1, 1, 3	
Brands Hatch	5	
Macau GP	3, 2	

Championship position:

ACU Supercup: 1. John Reynolds 6. J Whitham

1993

	TT Superbike	WSB
Mallory Park	1, 1	
Brands WSB		DNF, DNF
Knockhill	1, 3	
Scarborough	1, 1	
Mallory Park	1, 1	
Snetterton	1, 1	
Oulton Park	1, 1	
Donington Park	2, 2	
Albacete WSB		11, 11
Donington Park	2, 2	
Brands Hatch	1, 1	
Snetterton	DNF, 1	
Cadwell Park	1, 1	
Anderstorp WSB		5
Cadwell	4	
Oulton Park	1, 1	
Brands Hatch	1, 1	
Assen WSB		5, 5
Monza WSB		DNF, DNF
Donington WSB		3
Kirkistown	5, 4	
Knockhill	3	
Brands Hatch	2, 3	

Championship position:

HEAT Supercup: 1. J Whitham

1994

	WSB	BSB
Donington Park		2, 2
San Marino, Misano	11, DNF	
Spain, Albacete	3, 3	
Thruxton		1, 1
Austria, Zeltweg	7, DNF	
Donington Park		1
Indonesia, Sentul	1, 4	
Japan, Sugo	DNF, 10	
Holland, Assen	5, 5	
San Marino, Misano	8, 4	
GB, Donington Park	DNF, DNF	
Australia, Phillip Island	DNF, DNF	

Championship position:

World Superbike: 1. Carl Fogarty 7. J Whitham

1995

	WSB	BSB
Donington Park		1, DNF
Mallory Park		1, 1
Oulton Park		1, DNF
Brands Hatch		1, 1
GB, Donington Park	3, 8	
Oulton Park		1, DNF
Snetterton		1, 2
KnockHill		2, 1

Championship position:

British Superbike: 1. Steve Hislop 3. J Whitham

1996

	WSB	BSB	Other
Donington Park		DNF, DNF	
Thruxton		2, 2	
GB, Donington Park	DNF, 10		
Oulton Park		1, 2	
Snetterton		1, 1	
Italy, Monza	7, 6		
Brands Hatch		1, 1	
Knockhill		2, 2	
Cadwell Park		1, 1	
Holland, Assen	6, 14		
Mallory Park		1, 1	
Bol d'Or			5
Brands Hatch		4, 5	
Bishopscourt			1, 1, 1 (Sunflower)
Donington Park		3, 1	

Championship position:

World Superbike: 1. Troy Corser 12. J Whitham

British Superbike: 1. Niall McKenzie 2. J Whitham

1997

	WSB
Australia, Phillip Island	DNF, 13
San Marino, Misano	
GB, Donington Park	8, 10
Germany, Hockenheim	14, 3
Italy, Monza	6, 3
USA, Laguna Seca	8, DNF
Europe, Brands Hatch	8, 9
Austria, A1 Ring	10, 6
Holland, Assen	7, 11
Spain, Albacete	DNF, 10
Japan, Sugo	DNS
Indonesia, Sentul	9, DNF

Championship position:

World Superbike: 1. John Kocinski 8. J Whitham

1998

	WSB
Australia, Phillip Island	DNF, 12
GB, Donington Park	8, 8
Italy, Monza	8, 5
Spain, Albacete	11, 10
Germany, Hockenheim	9, 10
San Marino, Misano	6, DNF
South Africa, Kyalami	4, DNF
USA, Laguna Seca	6, 5
Europe, Brands Hatch	5, 3
Austria, A1 Ring	5, 6
Holland, Assen	DNF, 5
Japan, Sugo	11, 9

Championship position:

World Superbike: 1. Carl Fogarty 8. J Whitham

1999

	GP500	World SS600	Other
Le Mans 24 Hours			3
GB, Donington Park		1	
Spain, Jerez	DNF		
Italy, Mugello	14		
Spain, Catalunya	DNF		
Dutch TT, Assen	DNF		
GB, Donington Park	DNF		
German GP, Sachsenring	DNF		
Czech GP, Brno	DNF		

Championship position:

World 500: 1. Alex Criville 32. J Whitham

2000

	World SS600
Australia, Phillip Island	1
Japan, Sugo	4
GB, Donington Park	2
Italy, Monza	2
Germany, Hockenheim	6
San Marino, Misano	DNF
Spain, Valencia	DNF
Europe, Brands Hatch	DNF
Holland, Assen	Disq from 3rd
Germany, Oschersleben	DNF
GB, Brands Hatch	3

Championship position:

World SS600: 1. Jörg Teuchert 6. J Whitham

2001

	World SS600
Spain, Valencia	DNF
Australia, Phillip Island	DNF
Japan, Sugo	DNF
Italy, Monza	1
GB, Donington Park	4
Germany, Lausitzring	DNF
San Marino, Misano	7
Europe, Brands Hatch	3
Germany, Oschersleben	5
Holland, Assen	3
Italy, Imola	3

Championship position:

World SS600: 1. Andrew Pitt 4. J Whitham

2002

	World SS600
Spain, Valencia	6
Australia, Phillip Island	DNF
South Africa, Kyalami	2
Italy, Monza	DNF
GB, Silverstone	1
Germany, Lausitzring	Disq from 7th
San Marino, Misano	3
Europe, Brands Hatch	DNF
Germany, Oschersleben	injured
Holland, Assen	7
Italy, Imola	Disq from 4th

Championship position:

World SS600: 1. Fabien Foret 6. J Whitham

INDEX

Bangers goes down
to the pond.
The duck is on the bank.

1

It quacks at Bangers.
"Quack ! Quack !" it goes.

2

What is it doing
on the bank?
Bangers sits down to see.

3

Oh yes!
The duck is sitting
on some eggs.

4

There is a crack.
A little duck pops out
of one of the eggs.

5

Bangers claps his hands.
"Quack! Quack!"
goes the duck.

Bangers runs back
to the house.

He gets some of Mum's eggs from a box.

He puts the eggs
in Dad's best chair.

Then he sits on them.
He thinks a little duck
will pop out.

"Crack!" go the eggs.

Bangers gets off
the eggs.
Is there a little duck?

No! There is a big mess.
But there is
no little duck.

Mum comes in.
What a mess in Dad's chair!

14

She picks up Bangers
and smacks him.

15

"Bed for you!" she says.
"And no eggs for tea!"

16